DARIO FO
People's Court Jester

Tony Mitchell was born in New Zealand. He received a PhD in Drama at Bristol University in 1976. He lived in Rome from 1978 to 1983 and was a Rome correspondent for *Plays and Players* and *Sight and Sound*, as well as having contributed to *Theatre Quarterly, Gambit, Theater, Film Criticism, Stills* and *The Literary Review*. His translations of Dario Fo's plays have been performed in Australia and New Zealand. He now teaches drama at the University of New South Wales in Sydney, Australia.

The photograph of Dario Fo on the front cover is reproduced courtesy of the Belt and Braces Roadshow Company.
Unless otherwise indicated, all other photographs are reproduced courtesy of La Comune.

DARIO FO
PEOPLE'S COURT JESTER

TONY MITCHELL

A Methuen Theatrefile
Methuen · London and New York

A METHUEN PAPERBACK
First published as a paperback original in 1984
by Methuen London Ltd, 11 New Fetter Lane, London EC4P 4EE
and Methuen Inc, 29 West 35th Street, New York, N.Y. 10001
Second, revised and extended edition 1986
Copyright © 1984, 1986 by Tony Mitchell

Typeset by Wyvern Typesetting Ltd
Printed in Great Britain by
Richard Clay (The Chaucer Press) Ltd,
Bungay, Suffolk

British Library Cataloguing in Publication Data

Mitchell, Tony
   Dario Fo.—(A Methuen theatrefile)
   1. Fo, Dario—Criticism interpretation
   I. Title
   852′.914   PQ4866.02Z/

   ISBN 0–413–602508

Acknowledgements

I would like to thank the following people who provided me with valuable assistance in preparing this book: Dario Fo and Franca Rame, Piero Sciotto, Walter Valeri, Michael Imison, Diana Hoskers, Nicholas Hern, Mary Remnant, Joel Schechter, Steve Grant, Catherine Itzin, Mary Fulton, Guy Gazzetta, Marian Farrugia, Tim Fitzpatrick

Parts of Chapter One, originally appeared in *Theatre Quarterly*, Vol. ix, No. 35, Autumn 1979.

CONTENTS

Introduction   7

1 'Mistero buffo' – popular culture, the giullari and the grotesque   10
Recovering 'illegitimate' forms of theatre – the *giullari*
Language as burlesque – *Grammelot*
Addressing the audience – prologues, interludes and asides
The texts in performance
The TV performances
Zanni's Grammelot
The Massacre of the Innocents
The Morality of the Blind Man and the Cripple
The Wedding Feast of Canaan
The Origin of the Giullare
The Origin of the Underling
The Resurrection of Lazarus
Boniface VIII
Texts from the Passion
Mao Tse-tung and a Chinese *Mistero buffo*
The 'other stories'
The *Obscene Fables*

2 Biography and output 1951–1967   34
Early influences
Radio origins
Revue and *avanspettacolo*
Musical activities and the cinema
The early farces
The 'bourgeois period'
The television fiasco
Historical drama in an epic context
Graveyard humour and witchcraft
Popular music, an adaptation and circus satire

3 Theatre in the service of class struggle 1968–1973   53
Nuova Scena: a new theatre for a new audience
La Comune and *Accidental Death of an Anarchist*
Political documentaries
The 'roadshows' and Fo's arrest

4 Political theatre on shifting ground 1974–1983   71
The Palazzina Liberty and *Can't Pay? Won't Pay!*
Political pamphlets
Return to TV and *Female Parts*
Confronting terrorism and *About Face*
Adapting Brecht

5 **Fo in the UK**   95
   Adapting Fo – *We Can't Pay? We Won't Pay!*
   Adapting Fo II – *Accidental Death of an Anarchist*
   The marketing of Fo in the UK
   Adapting Fo III – *Female Parts*
   Mistero buffo in London

6 **At home and abroad 1984–1985**   110
   Teaching praxis
   Accidental Death of an Anarchist on Broadway
   Adapting Fo IV – *Trumpets and Raspberries*
   Fo and Shakespeare, Rame and *Elisabetta*

Notes   128

Selected Bibliography   133

INTRODUCTION

After the success of *Can't Pay? Won't Pay!*, *Accidental Death of an Anarchist* (which by 1983 had been performed in 24 theatres throughout the world), and *Female Parts*, all of which ran for nearly two years in London, the work of Dario Fo and Franca Rame finally received some of the acclaim it deserved in the UK when the two Italian author-actors did performances of *Mistero buffo* and *Tutta casa, letto e chiesa* in London in 1983. But behind these five plays lie 30 years of theatrical activity which is largely unknown to English-speaking audiences. In chronicling the Fos' theatrical and political development from the revue sketches of the early 1950s through their commercial successes in Italy in the 1960s, and their subsequent formation of an alternative circuit of militant political theatre after 1968, I have had to rely mostly on secondary sources and the authors' own retrospective accounts of their work up to 1977. My own direct acquaintance with their work dates from that year, in which most of their major plays were transmitted in a retrospective cycle on Italian television.

There is little doubt that Dario Fo is one of the world's great modern actors, as well as being a prodigious mime. He himself has described the chief quality of great acting as *souplesse*: 'what distinguishes great actors from average actors is their *souplesse*. This means that they have a great understanding of the *technique* of acting, and they understand so deeply, and are involved in, what they are performing, that they don't 'splash about' . . . They don't show that they are exerting themselves. They make you forget that they are acting.'[1] This definition could have been tailor-made to fit Fo himself. However, as well as pinpointing one of the main difficulties a foreign actor has to encounter in performing the massive parts which Fo writes for himself in his plays, it also raises the question that often Fo's performances are acclaimed (as *Mistero buffo* was in London) as 'great acting' rather than as essentially political vehicles of an 'epic', 'popular' theatre in which a Marxist, but satirical critique of modern society and its institutions and injustices is put forward in no mean terms. Unlike Olivier, or Scofield, or most other actors who could fit Fo's definition, Fo is also an improviser, frequently performing topical sketches about current political events in an off-the-cuff way which enables audiences to witness a process of creation at work in which a political discourse becomes a piece of theatre. At the same time, he is a political worker, negating all the distinctions and role-divisions involved in conventional theatre set-ups. He will often step onto the stage (with the house-lights still up) from the audience, where he has been chatting to comrades, selling books and political pamphlets, or helping stage hands and front-of-house workers, and once on stage, directly address the audience as equals. In his work there is none of the paraphernalia of a star performance which is normally associated with 'great acting'. In his definition of the type of theatre he proposes as the 'destruction of the fourth wall', he intends not only a rejection of naturalism and the representation of a character for direct address, asides and presentational commentary, but also this rejection of the hierarchical form of the conventional theatre situation. As an actor and a playwright, Fo is essentially a political animal, who has exerted considerable influence on attempts to unify a fragmented and conflicting Italian left through the medium of political satire. His debunking of the follies of repression has become a rallying-point for audiences of several thousands at a time in football stadiums, converted cinemas, circus tents, public squares, occupied factories and even de-consecrated churches. A good proportion of these audiences are people who would feel too alienated ever to set foot inside a red-plush, establishment theatre. Fo and his wife have performed to workers, students, housewives and unemployed people in an environment of truly 'popular theatre' in which it was the normal theatregoer's turn to feel alienated. They have shared the stage with workers reading statements about sackings, occupied factories and other political struggles, and with the relatives of prisoners detained without trial on political charges, and then called for donations from the audience to numerous political causes. They have also catered for the neglected middle-class theatregoer by performing in traditional theatres, packing them out nightly. Audiences who managed to get into the relatively tiny Riverside Studios in London for Fo's and Rame's performances were thus seeing them very much out of context, as frequently their style of performance in Italy has to be modified, and they have to use microphones, in order to get across to audiences of up to 5,000.

The Fos' theatrical and political activities have often created a mistaken impression of them abroad as being ultra-left extremist propagandists calling for the total overthrow of the bourgeois state and sympathising with the philosophies of armed struggle propagated by the Red Brigades and other Italian terrorist groups. The fact that the Fos are considerably further to the left of the Italian Communist Party (PCI) does not automatically equate them with a terrorist position, and nor does the continued help they have given to political detainees held in prisons under laws which find them guilty until proven innocent. In fact, since Franca Rame left the PCI in the 1970s, the Fos have not been members of any political party or group, but became comic and satirical mouthpieces for a vast, post-1968 movement on the left of the PCI. This movement has in recent years been increasingly ostracised, victimised and depleted while the PCI has modified and revised its political stance until it has become little more than a reformist social democratic party. The depletion of the extra-parliamentary Italian left is a direct result of terrorism and the repressive laws it has led to, under which innocent people are likely to be branded as terrorist sympathisers if they take part in any politically militant activity. Many of these repressive laws came into effect due to direct pressure on the Italian state by the PCI. In 1983, the number of people held in Italian prisons on political charges has been estimated at 5,000. Franca Rame has described the current situation in the Italian left as 'a coma of consciousness . . . people are afraid to even start up a petition, because the State immediately criminalises you, and brands you as "aider and abetter" or a fellow traveller.'[2] So, far from being supporters of terrorism, the Fos are victims of it. This is not, however, tantamount to depicting them as moderates – on the contrary, in their continued involvement in situations of political struggle, they have shown an indomitable energy in applying theatrically the precepts of Marx, Brecht,

Gramsci, Mayakovsky and Mao Tse-tung in the teeth of state and institutional repression, and frequent censorship of their work from as far back as the 1950s. The Fos are exponents of a cultural revolution, in the sense of restoring the culture of the peasant and the working class to those from whom it has been expropriated by the middle class. One of the principal tools of this cultural revolution, and one of the most difficult for non-Italians to appreciate, is Fo's restoration of Italian regional dialects to prominence in the Italian theatre. A great part of the tradition of Italian comedy, as exemplified in modern form in the plays of Eduardo de Filippo, is based on the numerous and widely differing, idiosyncratic regional languages to be found throughout Italy and Sicily. But as has already happened in the UK, these dialects are beginning to die out as young people move to the cities and the regularised language of television becomes more and more widespread. In influencing a resurgence of dialect in modern Italian comedy by adapting the language of the Po Valley in the 16th century in *Mistero buffo* and its sequels, Fo went a step beyond a mere re-excavation of popular culture. He combined dialect with *Grammelot*, an invented language devised by mediaeval strolling players to avoid political censorship, to create what is virtually a new theatrical language, which, combined with mime and gesture, almost transcends linguistic boundaries. This language is yoked to the voice of the underdog railing against the machinations of politicians and authority figures of church and state. While *Mistero buffo* is largely dependent on an ecclesiastical background of corruption and repression, it is by no means exclusively so, and its political implications remain universal. His other plays, however, often rely on a more contemporary political background which I have tried to sketch in where necessary. But the most universal aspect of Fo's work is its most lively and communicative – its comedy. Not the reactionary comedy of the Whitehall farce or the TV comedian, but the irreverent, popular comedy and political satire of the militant opposed to all forms of social and political repression. As Fo once replied to a criticism by a member of one of his audiences in one of the many debates after a performance:

> As far as a preoccupation with ridicule, laughter, sarcasm, irony and the grotesque is concerned, I have to say – I'd be a liar if I said otherwise – it's my job. I've been teaching this lesson for years – the origins of the grotesque and Marxist and pre-Marxist culture and irony . . . Nothing gets down as deeply into the mind and intelligence as satire . . . The end of satire is the first alarm bell signalling the end of real democracy.[3]

1: MISTERO BUFFO

Popular culture, the giullari and the grotesque

Italian actor-playwright Dario Fo, who also combines the roles of director, stage designer, song-writer, and political campaigner, has in recent years become the most widely-performed dramatist in the European and world theatre. He has himself performed his solo *pièce celêbre, Mistero buffo*, throughout Europe, Eastern Europe, Scandinavia, and in Canada and Peru, and it has become one of the most controversial and popular spectacles of the post-war European theatre. When *Mistero buffo* was presented on Italian television in 1977, after Fo had performed it live more than 1,000 times to audiences in Italy of more than a million and a half, and throughout the world to an estimated 40 million, public outcry from sources as varied as the Vatican (who described it as 'the most blasphemous show in the history of television,')[1] and the Italian Communist Party, was as vociferous as the widespread public acclaim.

What Fo had done, virtually single-handedly, was to distil the popular, comic, irreverent elements of mediaeval mystery plays and religious cycles into a political and cultural onslaught against the repressions of the Catholic Church and the landowning classes throughout history, and express them in the language of the Italian peasantry (and, by extension, every class of oppressed people), fuelled by the epic-didactic concepts of Brecht and Mayakovsky, and the political precepts of Mao Tse-tung and Gramsci.

Recovering 'illegitimate' forms of theatre – the giullari

The title *Mistero buffo* (literally 'comical mystery') is borrowed from *Mystery-Bouffe*, an 'epic-satirical representation of our times' written by the Russian poet Mayakovsky in 1918, a hymn to socialist optimism and 'the road to revolution' which was performed under Meyerhold's direction with Mayakovsky playing the role of the Man of the Future. The play deals with seven couples representing the proletariat of different countries who are encouraged by the Man of the Future to steal Jove's thunderbolts for electricity, expel the devils from hell and the angels from heaven (including Rousseau and Tolstoy), and who finally create a promised land full of 'good things' such as machines, cars, trains, technology and food. Mayakovsky has been a constant influence in Fo's plays, one of which, *The Worker Knows 300 Words, the Boss Knows 1,000 – That's Why He's the Boss* (1969) has the Russian poet as one of the protagonists in a series of stories intended to convey a sense of the urgency of building a working-class culture. However, the origins of Fo's *Mistero buffo* reside in the surviving texts and descriptions of the *giullari*, the mediaeval strolling players who performed in the streets and piazzas of Europe:

Mistero (mystery) is the term used since the second and third centuries AD to describe a sacred spectacle or performance. Even today in the Mass we hear the priest announce 'In the first glorious mystery . . . In the second mystery . . .' and so on. So *Mistero* means a sacred performance, and *mistero buffo* means a grotesque spectacle.[2]

In extracting the grotesque elements of the mystery plays, Fo's intention is to bring to the foreground their popular origins, and mock the pomp and postures of the church hierarchy while popularising Christ and biblical legend, which is seen from the mediaeval peasant's point of view.

> The inventors of the *mistero buffo* were the people. From the first centuries after Christ the people entertained themselves – although it was not merely a form of entertainment – by putting on and performing in spectacles of an ironic and grotesque nature. As far as the people were concerned, the theatre, and particularly the theatre of the grotesque, had always been their chief means of expression and communication, as well as putting across ideas by means of provocation and agitation. The theatre was the people's spoken, dramatised newspaper.[3]

At the basis of almost all of Fo's 40 or so plays is the theatrical tradition of the *giullare* (the Italian equivalent of the French *jongleur* and the Spanish *juglare*), the mediaeval strolling player who busked and performed to the peasants of Europe, frequently on the run from persecution from the authorities, censorship, and co-option into the courts, from which arose the 'official' tradition of the commedia dell'arte. Fo's task in *Mistero buffo* is the retrieval and recovery of this unofficial, 'illegitimate' theatre contained in the original repertoire of the *giullari* before it was appropriated and transformed by court influence, a process described by one of Fo's foremost Italian commentators, Lanfranco Binni:

> The 'epic theatre' of the mediaeval *giullari*, in which the *giullare* became the choral, didactic expression of an entire community and the feelings, hopes and rebellion of exploited people to whom he performed in a piazza, projected their desire for liberation from the religious sphere set up by the authorities. Performances expressed an insistently human passion, with a human, exploited, peasant Christ who refutes the injustices of the hypocritical religion of the rich to such an extent that this 'epic theatre' of the *giullari* was either physically suppressed (by persecuting the *giullari* and cutting off their heads) or neutered and re-translated into an aristocratic vein. Thus the *giullare* who performed in the piazza, sharing a rapport with whoever recognised themselves and their own sufferings in his stories, became the 'court jester' who had the sole task of entertaining courtiers, so that his expressions of anger and hope through physical means and rapport with others was transformed into the recitation of verses of 'quality' whose chief value lay in the weaving of amorous rhymes, or even the dehumanised, objectified description of peasants 'at work', mocked for their 'vulgarity' or transferred into an aristocratic context and given an abstract, 'pastoral' dimension, accompanied by flutes and amorous sighs for gentle nymphs.[4]

A common misconception is that the theatrical traditions of farce and comedy in Fo's theatre stem from the commedia dell'arte, but the *giullari* are essentially pre-commedia, the popular, unofficial mouthpieces of the peasant population, while the performers of the commedia are regarded by Fo as the professional 'court jesters' officially recognised by the ruling classes. Although a number of his routines are culled from the repertoires of *comici dell'arte* like Ruzzante and Zanni who survived the transition from piazza to court, Fo sees these performers as essentially idiosyncratic and rebellious in terms of the canons of the commedia, and peasant rather than court figures. Fo himself in the context of the contemporary Italian theatre experienced the acclaim and stature of a 'bourgeois court jester' when he became a prominent figure in the established, mainstream Italian theatre during the mid-sixties, only to renounce this position of commercial success and seek an alternative, 'fringe' theatre network, performing in factories, piazzas, and *case del popolo* (Communist Party community centres) to a predominantly non-theatre-going audience.

Language as burlesque – Grammelot

One of the most notable features of *Mistero buffo* is its language, which Fo describes as 'fifteenth century Padano', a mixture of the various dialects of the Po valley, Lombardian, Venetian and Piedmontese, which are adapted, sometimes modernised, and frequently parts are completely invented, and even treated as an incomprehensible foreign language which relies on the actor's physical illustration and verbal explanation. Mime, action and gesture assume primary importance, and Fo has continually modified and stylised the language of the plays to such an extent that it functions more as a codified system of sounds similar to 'scat song' in jazz. Particularly when performing outside the Po valley, Fo developed an onomatopoeic language which served to complement his mimic gestures and express the physicality of situations rather than conveying information about the situations, which Fo frequently consigned to an explanatory prologue.

Alongside this emphasis on the physical sound-structure of the Padano dialect, Fo also elaborated a totally invented language called *Grammelot* – a phonic, abstract sound-system in which few recognisable words of any language occur, and which relies on suggestion. In his prologue to *Zanni's Grammelot*, with which he frequently opens performances of *Mistero buffo*, Fo explains the tradition of *Grammelot*:

> *Grammelot* is a form of theatre that was re-invented by the actors of the commedia dell'arte, but it goes back to even before the 1500s. It was developed as an onomatopoeic theatrical technique to put across concepts by way of sounds which were not established words in the conventional sense. *Grammelot* was invented by the *comici dell'arte* to escape censorship, and when they fled to other countries in the 1500s because of the enormous repression they suffered under the Council of Trent, which effectively denied them the possibility of performing in Italian towns and cities. The majority of them went to France, and we are told that, in order to make themselves understood, they used a form of language similar to French, although only a few words were actually French. Just as there is a foreign language *Grammelot*, so too there is an Italian one, particularly in its dialects. The most famous *Grammelot* was Zanni's. Zanni is the prototype of all the masks of the commedia dell'arte, or at least the father of the most important ones, such as Harlequin. But he's no invented character, he was real. The character

of Zanni is directly linked to a category of people, or at least a social class: the peasants of the Po valley and the mountains that extend down to the Po valley.[5]

In fact Fo, reviving the tradition of Zanni, first developed *Grammelot* when he performed *Mistero buffo* in France in 1973, and in the course of performances he has even built up an American *Grammelot* in a piece called *The American Technocrat*, which he has performed at anti-nuclear rallies: a grotesque parody of an American nuclear technician in which he mimes and makes the sounds of aeroplanes and space craft, producing perhaps one recognisable English word in ten (such as 'yeah' or 'OK' – Fo speaks fluent French but virtually no English), but with a deceptively exact inflexion and accent. He also uses this American *Grammelot* in his frequent topical burlesques on American politics, such as his famous impersonation of President Ford tripping while getting out of a helicopter and almost getting killed by the blades, and in one of his asides in the television version of *Mistero buffo*, he relates how *The American Technocrat* caused several Americans to walk out of a Paris performance precisely because they couldn't understand a word of what he was saying, but could detect he was satirising Americans.

Grammelot then, chiefly functions in *Mistero buffo* and some of Fo's other plays, such as the version of Stravinsky's *Soldier's Tale* which he rewrote and directed for La Scala in 1978, where it was used to embody the different dialect the soldier spoke, as a form of burlesque mimicry, and Fo has extended its onomatopoeic potentials to more modern contexts such as the Grandfather's simulated drug hallucinations in *Mother's Marijuana is the Best* (1976) and to a representation of the working of factory machinery and a production line in *Mistero buffo*, in a highly orchestrated gibberish of machine language. Perhaps the most apt description of the language of *Mistero buffo* was given by the critic Renzo Tian: 'Padano, which is reminiscent of Ruzzante but isn't the language of Ruzzante insofar as its concern is to provide an example of an imaginary Esperanto of the poor and disinherited.'[6] In *Knock Knock! Who's There? Police!* (1972), his sequel to *Accidental Death of an Anarchist*, Fo recounts another branch of *Grammelot* which places it in the tradition of Molière, through the mouthpiece of a Superintendent of Police whom Fo performs in the play:

> Scapino, Antonio Scapino, went to France in the 1500s and met Molière . . . and immediately Molière said 'Save me, you must save me, they've censored my latest play *Tartuffe*, and cut the entire ending. You must help me!' 'But I'm a bad actor, and I'm even worse in French.' 'Yes, but you act with gestures, with your face, your hands, you're an extraordinary mime – you come out and act with gestures, and add the odd word or two here and there for effect, or just snort or mutter or talk nonsense, it makes no difference – you put your message across with your hands, with gestures, with pantomime, and they can't censor that.' 'All right then, but who do I have to play, what do I have to say, what's my character?' 'A servant – you can call yourself Scapino, you're a servant in one of the richest households in France, whose eldest son goes into politics, and you teach this youth all the tricks of the trade, the art of hypocrisy, of *tartuffaggine*, the ultimate in Jesuitry . . . OK?' . . . Now for your information this marvellous talk is called *Grammelot*, it's all muttered and spat out in a continuous stream. It doesn't matter if you can't pick up the words, the gestures are what matter.[7]

In this extraordinary set-piece, Fo is using the character of the Police Superintendent to describe *Grammelot* as an example of the speechifying antics of the Italian Christian Democratic Party in the 1970s, which illustrates how Fo continually makes historical leaps to refer to present political reality, a technique which is continually present in *Mistero buffo*. His use of *Grammelot* and the techniques of the *giullari* is educational in serving to stress and illustrate the origins of popular culture, but no mere academic, intellectual exercise, since he continually roots his historical didacticism in contemporary political and social reality to score comic points and make gags at the expense of political authority figures. As the critic Jean Chesneaux has put it:

> Dario Fo is indifferent to both the elitist little world of the professional scholars and to that of theatre professionals. He has moved out of that world to find the workers and the common people. For Dario Fo history is an active relationship with the past, and a distant epoch like the Middle Ages – as *Mistero buffo* shows – can be just as fertile as a more recent period when it comes to fuelling the active social struggle of the present. What matters is the political quality of this link between the present and the past, not the distance of centuries.[8]

The language used in *Mistero buffo*, in both its inventiveness and its historic complexity, is a major factor in Fo's achievement in bringing to life the origins of an essentially popular, politically aware, peasant theatre, and prove it can be entertaining and enjoyable as well as culturally and politically relevant to popular audiences. In freeing this popular theatrical culture from the academic and bourgeois mystifications it has been subjected to over the centuries, he restores its wit, comedy and enjoyment value by taking imaginative liberties with it while illustrating to his audience a key concept which he extrapolates from Gramsci: 'If you don't know where you come from, you don't know where your potentialities lie.'[9]

Addressing the audience – prologues, interludes and asides

The diverse nature of the material in *Mistero buffo*, the complexity of Fo's verbal acrobatics, his continual paring, modification and stylisation of the texts, and the 'living newspaper' aspect of the spectacle, have obviated often lengthy explanatory prologues to the individual pieces Fo performs. These prologues have become concretised into *discorsi* or *interventi*, direct addresses in which Fo speaks to the audience to explain the situation of a particular piece, using satirical illustrations from topical political events, incorporating impersonations of popes and politicians as well as analyses of current events. These have in turn become an expected part of the performances, set pieces and sketches which exist alongside and complement the *canovacci* (improvisations to a theme) which comprise the source material of *Mistero buffo*. Fo traces these asides to Cherea, a contemporary of Ruzzante's:

> . . . sometimes when he was performing he'd pretend there was a wasp annoying him . . . Eventually the wasp was flying all over the place, off the stage and into the audience even. Cherea would follow it and involve the audience in the grotesque situation. Ruzzante also used direct address with his audiences, not for any aesthetic contrast, but to enable them to participate in the events on stage with a constant awareness of their fiction.[10]

A key concept in Fo's theatrical praxis is his adoption of the concept of 'breaking down the fourth wall', and these moments in which he addresses the audience directly are similar to Brecht's alienation effects, allowing the audience to detach itself from the historical frame of reference of the pieces and make contemporary analogies. Fo's topical sketches, such as Pope John-Paul II skiing, his impersonation of John-Paul I as a grinning simpleton whom he compares to Pinocchio, or Paul VI riding a brakeless bicycle down the hill in Castel Gandolfo, or a skit about *carabinieri* spotting UFOs, become performance vehicles in themselves, contextualising the religious and spiritual aspects of the biblical plays by producing a modern counterpoint. As a reviewer of a performance in Milan in March 1979 described it:

> The *discorsi*, analyses and polemics have their own separate place in the spectacle, introducing and motivating the individual pieces Fo performs or relates. The structure of *Mistero buffo* takes the form of a text, an explanation, and another text. The fact that the explanations are as entertaining and as well received as the pieces in the play doesn't change the situation. The opposition between language and dialects, between direct dialogue with the audience and fictional story-telling to an ideal audience, between mime and the display of vocal resources, distinguishes perfectly the two areas of the spectacle, which are integrated and complementary, both bringing laughter and applause.[11]

The form of the *discorsi* or asides is modified in the same way as the texts themselves – according to audience response, feedback and discussion. Fo frequently ends performances with what he refers to as the 'Third Act' – debates and discussion with the audience, who express criticisms and suggestions which often help shape the development of the play in terms of political content, style, language and entertainment value.

Fo regards his audiences as an essential element of the process in which he shapes his performances, and their reactions are a strong factor in his elaboration of the frequent improvisations he makes around the texts of *Mistero buffo* as well as in the prologues and *discorsi*. The rhythm of each performance of the play he sees as being the result of a spontaneous but guided (by the performer) collaboration between the comic and a participating audience who it is the comic's job to keep involved and participating by means of a technique he refers to as 'fishing for laughs':

> The comic fishes for laughs by virtually throwing out a comic line, or a hook, into the audience. He indicates where the audience's reaction has to be gathered in and also virtually where the hook is cast, because otherwise the tension built up between stage and audience would die down. Winding in the hook doesn't mean snuffing out the audience reaction, but correcting its flow with a flick of the rod. The comic's ability lies in knowing that if he carries on for a while on the same tack he'll snap the audience's capacity to keep up with his theme. So he breaks into the stage action, using something extraneous (a spectator's funny way of laughing, for example, or imitating the way La Malfa* speaks). Then the comic casts out the hook again, for a bigger laugh (although he can fish for laughs by casting out the hook more than once

---

*Ugo La Malfa: economist and statesman, leader of the Italian Republican Party (PRI) and Minister of Foreign Trade and the Budget until his death in 1979.

before provoking one big laugh) . . . One could talk endlessly about techniques of laughter. In Nancy Lecoq gave veritable lessons about techniques of laughter: head laughter, throat laughter, silent laughter, side-splitting laughter, rolling in the aisles . . . I think, however, the audience's real way of laughing can be divided into just two types: when it is symptomatic of involvement in the play and when it is not. The difference lies between the mechanical reaction of laughing and the relationship through which an audience collaborates in building the play. The first is about the star-satisfaction of the comic who sees the effects of his technique and is pleased with himself, and it is quite different from the comic's reaction to a sort of confrontation which prompts him immediately, on the spot, into developing what he is saying, preferably through improvisation, and the action he is building up on stage with the audience. The comic provokes the audience's laughter with his resources, but audience laughter is a response which itself recharges the comic – it's not just a technique – maybe even feeding the yeast of his stage reactions in the course of a given play, or maybe just adding to the further exercise of his craft . . . All popular theatre requires the audience to be 'inside', and take part in the rhythm of laughter.[12]

The texts in performance

Fo has excavated the texts which he uses as a basis for his performance in *Mistero buffo* from a wide variety of Latin, Provençal, Italian, Middle English, and even Yugoslavian, Czech and Polish sources, but the criterion behind his choice and adaptation of the texts is based on a desire to highlight their popular aspect as vehicles of the people's struggle against capitalistic and ecclesiastical oppression. This frequently involves a process of stripping down rather than augmentation, paring away the additions and superimpositions of subsequent adaptors of the original texts (who include even Dante), rescuing the material from the appropriations of 'cultural aristocrats'. In *Rosa fresca aulentissima* (*A Fresh Delicate Rose*) for example, Fo is dealing with a story which is presented in school textbooks as a coy, courtly love story of a boy whose physical lust is checked by the polite blandishments of the girl who is the object of his lust. Fo restores the tale to a brutal example of sexual oppression in which the boy, a rich tax collector, is able to have his way with the girl, and owing to a special wealth protection law, can even charge her with rape, rather than vice-versa.

Mistero buffo has frequently been attacked from academic quarters as well as from Vatican sources. In a book entitled *Giullari e Fo* (1978), Michele Straniero retitles the play 'Mistero Bluff', and sets out to debunk Fo's spurious sense of history, producing a list of historical inaccuracies and anachronisms which occur in *Mistero buffo* (such as, for example, the fact that the term 'mystery' is not found in the Mass but in the Rosary), and accusing Fo of falsifying historical facts and simplifying the popular elements of his source material. Straniero maintains that Fo, in his zeal to reappropriate popular culture from the mystifying hands of bourgeois commentators, ignores or multilates texts which are of bourgeois origin, in what he describes as 'inviting young people to burn books instead of reading and criticising them and discussing the difficulties of cultural mediation, together with the importance of mastering sources like these which the bourgeoisie tends to keep to itself.'[13] Fo regards such arguments as arid and over-academic, while pointing out that many of the historical inaccuracies that Straniero picks up are deliberately ironic anachronisms: 'Only a person as deficient in irony as Straniero wouldn't notice they were put there deliberately.'[14] In reply to the 'book burning' charge, Fo points to the lengthy bibliography included in the published edition of the play, the fact that some of his material, such as the Apocryphal pieces, are in fact culled from bourgeois sources, the numerous university theses on mediaeval theatre sparked off by *Mistero buffo*, together with the increase of sales of books on the subject.

There is no doubt that Fo's intentions in *Mistero buffo* are didactic and educational, but in performance he stresses the entertainment and amusement to be gained from his mediaeval popular sources, and one is more than willing to forgive him a few ironic anachronisms. Performances of *Mistero buffo* frequently last up to four hours – no two performances are ever the same, and the critic Chiara Valentini has estimated that if all the pieces Fo has performed in *Mistero buffo* were placed end to end, the performance would last an entire day. Fo performs alone on a bare stage, dressed in black sweater and trousers, with no lighting effects and the aid of only a microphone slung round his neck to carry his voice to the outer reaches of the vast halls, sports stadiums, converted cinemas, deconsecrated churches, public squares and open spaces he has performed the play in. He keeps up a constant patter of witty repartee, constantly ad-libbing with the audience, rather like a thinking-man's Lenny Bruce, displaying a staggering physical dexterity, continually changing character, and running through an enormous variety of grotesque, vain, pathetic and comic characterisations of human folly, using his hooded eyes, Chaplinesque mouth, and physical largeness and gaucheness in a mimic style often reminiscent of Jacques Tati. (Fo studied with the French mime Jacques Lecoq in the 1950s, and Lecoq taught him how to use his large frame, long limbs and big feet to advantage, and his lollopping physique together with his vastly expressive face seem capable of evoking any number of physical idiosyncracies.)

Fo establishes an instant rapport with his packed audiences of enthusiastic and predominantly young supporters who often spill onto the stage at the actor's invitation. Using the familiar, informal *tu* form, he ad libs, (in one performance in Vicenza during a thunderstorm he conversed with the thunder, addressing it as the voice of God), and jokes with the spectators. One particularly noteable performance took place in April 1974, in a field opposite the newly occupied Palazzino Liberty, which Fo and his group La Commune had virtually squatted in and adopted as their home theatre. The audience was estimated at about 30,000 and as Fo recalls:

> At least 30 per cent were people from the local area: housewives, old age pensioners, workers, entire families, and hundreds of children, who caused inevitable confusion during the performance, running around, getting lost . . . I had to interrupt the play every ten minutes to find the mothers of kids who were up on the stage crying desperately.[15]

Typically, Fo used the situation to improvise a discussion about the necessity for more state-run crêches. A sense of solidarity develops between actor and audience, also due to the fact that audiences often have to undergo a police search before entering the theatre because of Fo's status as a politically subversive figure in Italy. *Mistero buffo* is a prime example of 'epic' theatre in the true sense of the word, at once a recreation of popular history and culture and an affirmation of the political potency of this recreation.

The TV performances

For the television transmission of *Mistero buffo*, which took place in April and May of 1977 (in four parts), and which can be regarded as a definitive version of the play, Fo was filmed in performance on his home base in the Palazzino Liberty, in front of a live audience, with whom he improvised, swapped quips, and went through his array of political caricatures, such as his satirical portrait of the then Italian Prime Minister, Giulio Andreotti. A definitive performance then, in the sense that it was transmitted to an audience of some 5 million, and that Fo has only rarely performed *Mistero buffo* since then, but subject to the spontaneous developments which always take place in a live performance of the play. A live audience has always been an important aspect in Fo's shaping and reworking of the play, both in terms of the method he adopts in trying out his texts as public readings and listening to audience suggestions, and in terms of the adaptations he makes as a result of this audience feedback. As Fo has said,

> *Mistero Buffo* has always relied on improvisation, since the audience is involved in it and doesn't play a passive part, since it imposes its rhythms, and provokes off-the-cuff lines. This type of theatre is recreated from performance to performance, and is always different, and never repetitive.[16]

The television performance is worth describing in some detail, since the highly idiosyncratic and virtually untranslatable language of the play, and the demands it makes on the actor, make it an unrepeatable performance, an 'epic' and 'total' theatre experience which establishes Fo as an actor/dramatist of unique status. *Mistero buffo* is also the lynch-pin of Fo's prodigious output of theatre works, propagating most of the theatrical and political concepts which are embodied in a different dimension in his other plays.

Zanni's Grammelot

The piece with which Fo opens *Mistero buffo* is a *lazzo*, or improvised sketch from the commedia dell'arte, as it was performed by one of its greatest exponents. Zanni, Fo explains in his introduction to the piece, represents the plight of the peasants of the Po valley, who were displayed by the 'origins of capitalism' in the Middle Ages, and forced to abandon their land because they couldn't face the competition of imported produce. So Fo as Zanni represents a starving peasant who, in his hunger, imagines that he is eating himself – which Fo represents in minute gestural detail. He then mimes Zanni's dream, in which he prepares an enormous Pantagruelian feast, stirring an enormous bubbling pot of *polenta*, frying chicken, eggs, cheese and sauce, making the sounds of the boiling pot, the sizzling meat and the rising steam, representing the pans and the cooker with gestures in mid-air, and then abruptly making everything disappear, as Zanni, awakening from his dream, hunts down and captures a fly, dismembers it and eats it with all the relish of someone devouring the feast he has dreamed up previously, distending his stomach grotesquely. The ironic epicureanism of the sketch conveys a desperation and self-parody which combines hunger and anger. Fo's onomatopoeic utterances and mimed gestures are a prime example of what he refers to as a theatre of *gesto mimico* (mimed gesture), which

> originates from an extremely old tradition, but which has been renewed

through the generations, and allows past and present to coexist simultaneously, while amplifying the point being made on stage by continually fixing it on the level of technical experience, projected out to the audience without verbal retractions connected with lighting or atmosphere.[17]

Zanni's Grammelot is followed by another *Grammelot, The Story of Saint Benedict of Norcia*, about a wall-builder who founded an order of levitating monks who become concerned about their bellies when their cook also starts levitating, which induces the monks to abandon the spiritual sophistication of contemplating their navels in favour of cultivating the land in order to fill their stomachs.

The Massacre of the Innocents

In *The Massacre of the Innocents* Fo represents a number of different characters, presenting a mad woman who has substituted a sheep for her dead baby, and who is accosted by a soldier who takes the sheep for a baby. The woman then tells her story to a statue of the Madonna, and the Madonna unsuccessfully attempts to console her. Fo alternates between the mother, the ruthless and merciless soldier, and the Madonna with impressive speed and physical differentiation, while emphasising the peasant environment of deprivation of the distraught mother, who at the end goes off rocking the sheep and singing it a lullaby. Fo avoids sentimentality both through the grotesqueness of the situation he depicts, and the 'chorality' of his performance, in which he is continually swopping characters like a quick-change artist. The unusual pathos and sense of tragedy of this piece is immediately juxtaposed with a comic, grotesque, almost Beckett-like performance, *The Morality of the Blind Man and the Cripple*.

The Morality of the Blind Man and the Cripple

This sketch is attributed to Andrea della Vigna in the fifteenth century, but exists also in French and Belgian versions. A blind man and a cripple join forces, the latter riding on the former's back, and run into Christ on his way to Calvary. They try to flee and hide from Christ, since they don't want to run the risk of being cured of their afflictions by a miracle, which would oblige them to look for work with a master and lead considerably harder lives. In their attempt to avoid Christ's glance, the blind man trips and the pair fall in a heap at the feet of Christ, who heals them and leaves them in disgrace.

Here a grotesque situation of peasant degradation exists alongside a revolutionary message which advocates by implication the overthrow of the *padroni* – the masters and landowners, while also pinpointing the charlatanry of contemporary beggars in a way which echoes Peachum's rabble of false cripples and afflicted in Brecht's *Threepenny Opera*. In the piece Fo 'doubles up' between two very distinct and separate physical types – the blind man who has lost his dog, and the cripple who has lost his cart, presenting them comically, and almost naturalistically, although he frequently speaks the words of one character while physically representing the other, which is an example of his concern with presenting a theatre of situation rather than identifying with the characters he plays. It is characteristic that he does not represent Christ in the piece, but makes him a described objective presence whom his two protagonists are trying to avoid, and thus the focus of the piece is not 'supernatural', concentrating exclusively on the misery and deprivation of their plight.

The Wedding Feast of Canaan

Like the previous piece, *The Wedding Feast of Canaan* presents one of Christ's miracles from the people's point of view, playing down the supernatural overtones to stress the joyous, Dionysian, pagan view of the gospels, presenting Christ as a catalyst for festivity and enjoyment and even Bacchanalian excess. The piece begins with an argument over who is going to present the story, between a stiff, refined archangel who wants to present the correct, official and celestial version of the miracle, and an ape-like, drunken, shambling wedding guest who wants to tell the story from a more earthy, boozy and materialist point of view. In this dialectic, the Drunk, a character linked to Fo's line of peasant protagonists like the Blind Man, the Cripple, and Zanni, prevails through brute force and vulgarity and chases the archangel off the stage, after plucking some of the feathers out of his wings. The Drunk then narrates the wedding feast from a fool's point of view, emphasising the pleasure principle, and relishing his description of the epicurean delights of the feast (echoing Zanni's dream about his meal) and expressing the full 'tragedy' of the discovery that the wine has turned into vinegar (and not run out as in the official version, which is changed to the focus of a *contadino*, or peasant farmer). He describes Christ's entrance like that of a magician, and goes into a rapturous, onomatopoeic and alliterative description of the miracle and the resulting wine which he proceeds to get drunk on. Commenting on Christ's insistence that his mother try the wine as well, he reflects that if Adam had had a good glass of wine in his hand when he and Eve were tempted by the serpent and the apple, or if the apple had been made into good cider, the Fall of Man could have been avoided, along with the necessity to work. This hedonistic and decidedly secular irreverence, which includes the Drunk's vision of heaven as a vat of wine, is free of the socialist condemnation of the excesses of alcohol as an escape from the rigours and constraints of working-class life which one might expect. Fo, in the tradition of the Lombardian travelling players, embraces an almost utopian vision of communal festivity in which the joys of food and drink play an important part.

Mistero buffo was shown on Italian television at the same time as Franco Zeffirelli's comparatively pious and reverent film version of the gospels, *Jesus*. Fo and Zeffirelli had a debate about their disagreements over interpreting the gospels, which was set up by the newspaper *La Repubblica*. Zeffirelli maintained that *Mistero buffo* was too 'scurrilous' to be shown to 'unprepared television audiences', and that its 'elitist' political satire would be over the heads of television audiences. It is difficult to see how popular forms and traditions can be regarded as elitist, and Fo defended his position by attacking the lack of a popular viewpoint in Zeffirelli's film:

> Zeffirelli's most serious defect is the fact that he has stifled the festivity, joy and fantasy which exist in all Christian popular tradition and also in the gospels, where there are moments of great festivity and real community. The miracle of the wedding feast of Canaan, for example, the transformation of water into wine. This is one of the greatest passages in the gospels, and it's

strange that Zeffirelli censored it. In his *Jesus* there's no miracle of Canaan, and it's a serious omission, because the audience doesn't get the idea that Christ is also the god of joy and spring, the social and religious continuation of Dionysus . . . His film was a ruling class operation, because he has cut out all the popular content of the gospels.[18]

Fo's emphasis on community and festivity is part of a political vision of popular culture in which the spirit of enjoyment and even excess plays an important part. The 'popularity' of *The Wedding Feast of Canaan*, and the fact that it is frequently requested by live audiences, is ample proof of the success and comprehensibility of Fo's cultural operation. 'Popular culture,' he has stated, 'doesn't mean just taking things that are of the people *per se*. It means taking everything that the masters have taken from that culture and turned upside down, and revealing their origins and developments.'[19] *The Wedding Feast of Canaan* is an outstanding example of this operation, while Zeffirelli's film is a perpetration of the 'masters' ' viewpoint of that culture.

The Origin of the Giullare

La nascita del giullare (*The Origin of the Giullare*) is a key text of *Mistero buffo*, and derives from a twelfth century Sicilian text of Eastern origin. It reveals the peasant origins of the *giullare* and the secular, down to earth, popular nature of their treatment of Christ and supernatural religious events. A serf discovers a mountain and cultivates it with crops until a landowner tries to confiscate the now fertile land, calling on a bishop to lend his support to the appropriation and give it the sanction of the Church. When the peasant still refuses to give up his land, the landowner rapes the peasant's wife in front of his children. The peasant's family deserts him, and he is about to hang himself, having lost his land as well, when a man arrives and asks him for water. The peasant obliges, offering him some food as well. The man then reveals that he is Christ, confirming the peasant's growing suspicions, and promises to perform a miracle which will give the peasant 'a new language' which will 'cut like a knife', deflating and mocking the class of landowners and overlords. Christ makes the peasant a *giullare*, and instructs him to spread the message of his oppression and that of his class throughout the country.

So the mission of the *giullare* is political rather than religious, despite its sacred origins, and his message is the subversive mockery of the ruling class. Fo performs the piece in the first person as the *giullare*, presenting Christ as an ordinary person without supernatural trappings. The *giullare* originates from poverty, degradation and anger, which gives his satire a strong cutting edge. As Fo explains:

All the forms in which the *giullare* expresses himself are intrinsically satirical, because of the very fact that he . . . originates from the people and takes their anger in order to give it back to them, mediating it with the grotesque, and with rationality, so that the people can become aware of their own condition. When I relate the origin of the *giullare* in *Mistero buffo*, I'm able to tell the story in a convincing way because I believe in it, I believe in the mission which the *giullare* originally chose for himself as the jester of the people. I also believe in it because I've experienced what it means to be the jester of the bourgeoisie. When we put on plays for . . . occupied factories, our greatest joy was being able to follow our comrades' struggles from close at hand, and then to make use of them.[20]

Fo identifies with the *giullare*, and sees his role as the modern equivalent of the mediaeval *giullare* playing to an industrial working-class audience instead of mediaeval peasants. In fact in *The Origin of the Underling*, his companion piece to *The Origin of the Giullare*, Fo makes a historical leap in order to relate the predicament of the mediaeval peasant to that of the modern working class, breaking out of the story to mime a worker on the production line programmed as to when he can go to the toilet so as not to slow down the conveyor belt. This serves to contextualise the predicament of the mediaeval peasant as the original form and the cultural heritage of the modern working class.

The Origin of the Underling

This text is presented in virtually its original form, as used by the *giullare* Matazone da Caligano. It relates the creation of the peasant-serf 'from an ass's fart' after Adam has refused to lend his rib, so the master can have someone to do his unpleasant work for him. The master teaches the serf, under the guise of religious instruction, that his lot is to be a vulgar, repellent creature, who nevertheless has an eternal soul, through which he can transcend the misery of his fate. Then an angel appears to instruct the landowner how to treat the serf, concluding 'How can this idiotic serf have a soul when he was born from an ass's fart?', thus revealing the overlord's religious blackmail and sowing the seeds for the peasant's revolt and rejection of his lot. Fo sees a strong affinity between the underling and the *giullare* in the fact that both are soulless and see through the overlord's religious duping. The origin of the underling is also the origin of the *giullare*:

> The *giullare* was an underling; he was oppressed – maybe he was even born from an ass like the underling, as the *giullare* Matazone describes the first underling born on this earth. If the *giullare* had a soul, he would feel it like lead, and wouldn't be able to fly because the soul would weigh him down, and he'd say, as Bonvesin de la Riva suggests, 'You should thank God you haven't got a backside, soul, because I'd kick it till it was black and blue.' It's because he was born without a soul that the *giullare* can refuse to accept the blackmail of 'having a good conscience', and prick and gnaw away at the overlord with his satire, and arm the oppressed against him.[21]

The Resurrection of Lazarus

The chameleon-like capacity of Fo's mimicry is taxed to the utmost in *The Resurrection of Lazarus*, where he represents an entire crowd of people straining to see Christ's miracle of raising Lazarus from the dead. First he portrays the cemetery guard receiving the first arrivals, and then, through a series of one-line utterances and physical changes, the curious, pushing and voyeuristic crowd gathering and renting chairs for a ring-side view, with brief vignettes of a sardine-seller and even a pickpocket. As Fo states in his spoken introduction to the piece:

> The text of *The Resurrection of Lazarus* is a virtuoso's battle horse because

the *giullare* often found himself having to play as many as 15 or 16 characters one after the other, with no way of indicating the changes except with his body – by striking a posture, without even changing his voice. It's the kind of piece which calls on the performer to improvise according to the audience's laughter, cadences, and silences. In practice, it's an improvisation which requires occasional ad-libbing.[22]

The piece is a satire on the 'mystical experience' of a miracle, and Fo's performance emphasises the fairground spectacle aspect of the miracle, which is seen from the peasant spectators' point of view, complete with references to the smell of the decomposing body and the worms inside it, as the cries of the market sellers mix with the sounds of bets being made on the outcome of the miracle, and the final cries of admiration and astonishment are mixed with the shouts of the person whose pocket has been picked, in a truly 'choral' finale. Here the allusiveness of Fo's performance is paramount, as he suggests characters and situations with a few swift gestures and changes of position, which rely on the audience's imagination to fill in the details. Here the audience is virtually presented with a mirror image of itself in terms of assisting at a prestidigious spectacle in which the spectator plays an active role. As Fo has explained:

> I am able to express my personal resources as a comic, because I *believe* in the *giullaresque* function of the comic. The ability of the mediaeval *giullare* to play as many as 15 characters . . . depended on the necessity of doing everything on his own. It wasn't just exhibitionistic wishful thinking. We know that the mediaeval *giullari* performed their plays alone from the stage directions in the texts and their allusions to doubling. Even the most able inventions of the *giullare* required audience participation. The play of allusions and the collaboration of the audience who picked them up, redoubled the poetic and comic charge. So what has been referred to as a 'didactic operation' wasn't really so at all, at least not in the sense that the audience was indoctrinated. Rather their imaginations were stimulated – this was the only way they could reach an awareness of their origins, their past, and their culture.[23]

When Fo and the Associazione Nuova Scena first began working on *Mistero buffo* in 1969, the original intention was to have the plays performed by more than one actor, but this idea was rejected as impracticable after experimentation, as it detracted from the necessary allusiveness of the performance of the *giullare*, and broke the rhythm and flow of the pieces, as well as filling in too much unnecessary detail by introducing minor subsidiary characters who frequently had very little to do and distracted attention from the principal comic's performance. By performing alone, Fo brings a predominantly imaginative element to Brecht's idea of didactic entertainment, which requires not only rational detachment from the audience in *Mistero buffo*, but also an imaginative filling-in and fleshing-out of details and situations rather in the same way as listening to a radio play requires (hence no costumes and no lighting effects), and where there is no space or time for the actor to detach himself from the characters he is playing, who are often only fleeting vignettes in a narrative.

Boniface VIII

Fo's allusive mimic capacity also relies on the audience's imagination in *Boniface VIII*, where, as the critic Paolo Puppa has described,

> On a completely bare stage, the audience's imagination is directed towards real objects which are conjured up with a minimum of signs; everything that is named is shown. The pope's charismatic dressing-up is shown in this way, while he recites an ancient extra-liturgical chant, assisted by priests and attendants . . . The aesthetic aspect . . . is exalted in tandem with the political connotations, since the self-investiture lays bare the power which it accumulates by building up its own connotations.[24]

Boniface VIII is introduced by an account of that pope's celebrated Good Friday orgy in 1301, with an array of prostitutes, bishops and cardinals. Candles are extinguished at three metres distance by farts. The piece presents Pope Boniface preparing for a ceremony, singing a hymn, and praying – the prayer becoming a response to an interrogation by Christ, who finally, appearing invisibly, kicks the pope. Fo mimes in detail Boniface's fastidious dressing-up, choosing caps, mirrors, gloves and cloaks, in an illustration of the capacity of fascistic authorities to oscillate between supreme arrogance and potency and abject self-deprecation and servitude. When Boniface is confronted by Christ carrying the cross, played by Fo as a country bumpkin, in the line of the *giullari*, he becomes mincing and masochistic, releasing a monk he has imprisoned and even kissing him for Christ's benefit, although he is unable to disguise his disgust. Fo's Boniface could almost take his place unnoticed in Pasolini's *Salò*; as Puppa points out, Fo's Boniface 'dressing-up' is almost a direct Italian equivalent to Hitler's preparation for public appearances in Brecht's *Arturo Ui* – both lay bare the narcissism which lies behind the temptations of absolute power.

Fo takes a number of historical liberties in *Boniface VIII*, for which he has been severely criticised, but the implied political leap of the imagination in the piece, especially in his anachronistic reference to a peasant communard movement in the same historical period, is executed with such theatrical skill that his detractors are inevitably disarmed. Zeffirelli's comments on the piece are a typical example:

> Satire about the church and the papacy's bad worldly operations is as legitimate as any other form of satire, but it's a different matter when it's extended to the subject of the gospels. I don't think it's right to elaborate the contents of the gospels in a satirical way.[25]

Fo's satirical Christ is unacceptable to Zeffirelli, although he is forced to admit that 'Fo is one of the greatest Italian theatrical phenomena and his performances are always brilliant. I am also aware that the scurrility of his theatre derives from the roots of our theatre, from Plautus and the commedia dell'arte.'[26] – an opinion which leads Fo to discriminate between 'those who become militants of the proletariat, and those who become militants of the Vatican'.[27]

Texts from the Passion

The television version of *Mistero buffo* also included four 'Texts from the Passion': the first of these, *Death and the Madman*, presents a Madman playing a Tarot-like card game while the inn-keeper of the hotel where he is staying announces that thirteen people have come for supper. Meanwhile the Madman wins a large sum of money, and the game culminates in his drawing the card of Death. At this point Death enters in the form of a beautiful virgin, grieved by her task of coming to take Christ away. The Madman proceeds to seduce her and divert her from her duty. The role of the Madman, (*Il Matto*), combines the characters of the *villano* (underling) and the *giullare*, and is a prototype of the protagonist of Fo's later play, *Accidental Death of an Anarchist*, who is also called *Il Matto* (the Maniac) and wreaks similar havoc in a much more modern political context. In *Mistero buffo* he is part fool, part idiot, part pagan and part charlatan, a profane character-actor who is also capable of laudable motives – his attempts to seduce Death are a ploy to warn Christ.

Mary Comes to Know of her Son's Sentence, performed by Franca Rame, relates the attempt by the friends of the Madonna to conceal Christ's crucifixion from his mother, who finds out what is going on only when she sees Veronica with the imprint of Christ's face after the scourging and the crowning of thorns. This piece is a prototype of a series of mother figures whom Franca Rame has performed in Fo's plays since the 1960s, highlights of which were gathered together in a television show, *Parliamo di donne* (*Let's Talk About Women*), which was broadcast by RAI (Radio e Televisione Italiana) as part of the 1977 Fo season. Rame's mother figures, who will be dealt with later in this study, have a toughness, political awareness, and sense of sisterhood which sometimes risks sentimentality in their more tragic manifestations – a factor which in Fo and Rame's collaborations after *Mistero buffo* becomes a springboard for parody of the archetypal Italian *mamma* – but here Mary's total acceptance of Mary Magdalene and her determined desire to find out the truth about what is happening to Christ make her a very gutsy figure. The piece ends with Mary's realisation that Christ is about to be crucified, but is cut off as she rushes off in desperation to look for him, and there is no direct presentation of her maternal emotion (unlike Brecht's *Mother Courage*, for example).

In *The Madman beneath the Cross*, the Madman presents the stripping and preparation of Christ for the crucifixion as a theatrical spectacle, while the Roman soldiers bet on the number of hammer blows needed to nail him to the cross. The Madman and the Soldiers then play cards for Christ's clothes in a kind of grotesque 'Strip Jack Naked', and the Madman reveals that he has collected the thirty pieces of silver that Judas has thrown away, and offers them in exchange for Christ's body. When Christ voices his refusal of the Madman's offer, the latter concludes that Christ is mad. At this point the Madman-Samaritan becomes angry and embittered, declaring that the only really appreciable action Christ performed was driving the money-lenders from the temple, through which he is seen to be a representative of the militant proletarian in his ingenuous but well-motivated desire to reroute the course of history and justice.

In the fourth text from the passion, Franca Rame returns to perform *Mary's Passion at the Cross*, in which, rather like Fo's Madman, but in a more distraught fashion, the Madonna tries to bargain with the Roman soldiers to save Christ from being crucified. Graphically envisaging the crucifixion, she offers a silver ring and gold earrings to the soldiers, who claim that they are just doing their job, and that to accept her bribes is more than their job is worth. The Archangel Gabriel appears to attempt to explain to Mary the purpose of her son's death, and it is left ambiguous as to whether the Archangel's appearance is a 'real' supernatural manifestation or a hallucination of the grief-stricken Madonna. Mary accuses him of not understanding the condition of being a mother, since he was a mere messenger at the Annunciation, and Gabriel apologetically reminds her that her grief, 'your sacrifice and your son's sacrifice will split the heavens, and enable men for the first time to enter into paradise'.[28] Gabriel has the last word, and the implied irony and the avoidance of sentimentality, are immediately apparent.

At the end of the second television transmission of *Mistero buffo* Fo added a *Grammelot* of English origin, dating from the end of the sixteenth century, *The English Lawyer*, the story of a man on trial for raping a girl of the nobility. Like *A Fresh Delicate Rose*, the piece turns the tables on plaintiff and defendant, the English lawyer in a brilliantly histrionic display proving that the girl is to blame for the rape because her physical attributes and provocative appearance induced the 'poor' young man to rape her – an argument which is still frequently used in Italian rape cases in the present day.

Mao Tse-tung and a Chinese *Mistero buffo*

Fo's concern with re-representing inherited culture from a popular point of view which clashes with official received ideas of the gospels and the history of the Catholic church is a process he regards as needing constant renewal, and his use of the popular theatrical roots of the Christian tradition is continually aligned with popular working-class culture:

> Unfortunately centuries of history haven't supplanted the necessity of teaching the people to become conscious of their condition. Mao Tse-tung insisted that party intellectuals should make it their concern to retrieve and research popular culture, which has been submerged and camouflaged by priests, aristocrats and the like, and give it back to the people for them to make use of. But as soon as they start making use of it on their own, they tend to gloss it over again, and superimpose all the tricks and forms which are inherent in the fact that the ruling class has always imposed this culture, it becomes necessary to take it back and clean it up again in a continual process which is carried out in collaboration with the people. The problem of the history of the origin of man, his exploitation and the historical development of this, is fundamental to all workers' struggles – this applies to each and any member of the proletariat who is capable of carrying out the revolution which is constantly being talked about.[29]

Fo is not pontificating if one considers the mindlessly grotesque films, television shows and live entertainment which are continually on offer for working-class spectators in Italy, which includes the type of 'popular spectacles' offered by the Italian Communist Party in their summer celebrations, the 'Feste dell'Unita', which frequently cater to the lowest common denominator of popular culture, the variety show.

The success of *Mistero buffo* on Italian television, and the high audience figures, which were helped along by the free 'scandal' publicity afforded by the Vatican's outrage at the play, brought Fo across to the widest possible range of audiences. The television version of *Mistero Buffo* formed part of a 20 hour retrospective of Fo's major plays, and as a result Fo virtually dropped the play from his ample repertoire, performing it mostly abroad, until three years later, in keeping with his belief in the necessity for a constant renewal of his diffusion of popular culture, he returned to the Italian stage (or rather 'fringe' network) with a second edition of *Mistero Buffo*, entitled *La Storia della tigre e altre storie (The Story of the Tigress and Other Stories)*, first performed in 1980, in the same theatrical conditions as *Mistero buffo*. Interviewed in Rome during his premiere of the piece in a converted cinema rented by a feminist organisation, *Casa della donna*, Fo commented on the need for the 'community spirit' of performing to live audiences in a politically-charged situation:

> People are tired of solitude, which television only serves to make more acute. And cinema is no substitute for cohesion or collective movement. The theatre, on the other hand, gives people the opportunity of really meeting one another, especially the type of theatre that we and other rank-and-file groups put on, where there's a real sense of involvement and participation. And in recent years the need to get together has increased considerably.[30]

The Story of the Tigress is based on a story which Fo heard in Shanghai in 1975, as related to a Chinese audience of 20,000, by a local country story-teller who performed in a minority dialect, which was translated into Mandarin and then into Italian for Fo, who subsequently took Michelangelo Antonioni to task for his voyeuristic view of China presented in the documentary *Cina-Chung Kuo*. The dialect of the piece reminded him of his own adapted Padano dialect in *Mistero buffo*, and so he set about preparing a Padano version of the story, trying it out in public, reshaping it, and in fact ultimately expanding it from 15 to 45 minutes, sharpening the details, presenting a 'final' version before a script of the piece even existed:

> The audience's participation was a decisive factor. I've had the right sort of support from my audiences in a very precise way, and I've also noticed where there were lapses and slips, and passages which needed cutting and adjusting.[31]

The story concerns a Chinese soldier from Mao's army who is wounded during the war of liberation against Chiang Kai-shek, with gangrene setting in. He tells his comrades to leave him in a cave, where, like Romulus and Remus, he is looked after by a tigress and adopted into her family, teaching them how to cook meat in exchange for learning the laws of survival in the jungle. When his wound finally heals, he persuades the tiger family to accompany him to his home town, and the tigers help the local inhabitants to get rid of the last vestiges of Chiang Kai-shek's army by intimidating them with their roars. After the war is won, the Popular Government takes over the town's administration, and are intimidated by the tiger family, whom they try to have sent to the zoo, since they maintain that the tigers are a redundant force under the peace-time regime. The villagers are not happy with this proposed solution, and at the end they use the tigers to chase away the new administration. The piece ends with a tedious polemical speech by one of the new administrators, exhorting the people to obey him, a speech which is punctuated by an almighty roar from the family of tigers. In the Chinese context of the fable, as Fo explains in his spoken introduction to the piece, the tiger represents the spirit of self-management, self-determination and endurance, which aligns the story with the context of occupied factories where Fo frequently performs:

The tiger has a very precise allegorical significance: they say that a woman, or a man, or a people, have the tiger when they are confronted by enormous difficulties, and at the point where most people are inclined to flee, scarper, run away and abandon the struggle, piss off and even reach the point of denigrating themselves and everything generous they've done before, they insist on standing firm and resisting . . . Another clear allegorical meaning the tiger has, which is perhaps fundamental, is this: a person has the tiger when he never delegates anything to anybody, and never tries to get other people to resolve his own problems . . . The person who has 'the tiger' gets directly involved in the situation, participating in it, controlling it, verifying it, and being on the spot and responsible right up to the end.[32]

The reference to striking workers is obvious. Fo's introduction spells out the contemporary political implications of the fable and indicates his continuous involvement in working-class political struggles from the inside, as well as his role as a cultural spokesman for the extra-parliamentary Italian left.

From the performance point of view, *The Story of the Tigress* is a tour de force. Fo plays the soldier with his gangrenous leg, and the tigress, relishing her roars, snarls and growls, which he modulates through a whole range of emotions, even representing the deer she brings back for her cubs, whose childlike playfulness he represents charmingly without ever stooping to the compromise of getting down on all fours. He even represents a bullet coming out of the soldier's gun, and winds up the piece as a pompous party bureaucrat personifying the denial of the spirit of the tigress, which charges the whole piece, in an exhilarating way. One of the most hilarious sequences in the play is when the tigress gives roaring lessons to the soldier's countrymen. As Renzo Tian describes it:

Dario Fo does all this . . . without using words. At the most there are some fragments of words. He moves a few centimetres and becomes the teacher, then becomes the pupil, strains his vocal chords to an almost frightening extent, saws the air with his long paws, does both the real roars and the apprentice ones, and multiplies his hands, legs and utterances to let us 'see' rather than just hear the roaring class. And he succeeds. He succeeds because he has adopted everything that's been going round the theatre theory scene about gesture, mime, the *giullare*, body language, metaphor and audience involvement, and he incorporates it all into the sole ingredients of dust and sweat, without mediators, without indirect asides, and without playing his cards close to his chest.[33]

Fo's onomatopoeic language, which here even transcends *Grammelot* in its representation of the world of the tigers, not only manages to translate the context of the Chinese fable into an easily comprehensible contemporary Italian context, but also can be understood by a multinational audience, as the English critic John Francis Lane, reviewing the Rome performance of the play, testifies:

It is an invented language which he speaks as if he (and we) spoke it naturally. It isn't too difficult to understand, even if the pace at which he rambles on requires a great deal of concentration on the part of listeners of any language background . . . As happened a few weeks ago, when I watched Fo perform for an audience of British theater (sic) people who didn't understand Italian and weren't getting much help from Fo's official translator, he revealed an ability to communicate concepts and images with characters and events and ideas. One man in three hours runs the whole gamut of theatrical experience from primitive self-expression to the latest invention of media sophistication.[34]

Much of the international success of Fo's work is due to the fact that he is an 'animal of the stage', as the Italian expression goes, capable of communicating through sound and gesture in a way which leaves language barriers behind. As Fo himself has said, referring also to Franca Rame's performances and the plays they have collaborated on together:

> We're often asked why our plays are performed so frequently abroad. Part of the answer is this: we talk about real things, which we re-interpret in an ironic and satirical vein. We talk about Italy, but in countries like Germany and France, talking about Italy means talking about their problems.[35]

The 'other stories'

The three other stories in Fo's second edition of *Mistero buffo* are adapted from the Apocryphal gospels, and hence much more similar to the first edition of the play than is *The Story of the Tigress*.

The first of these, *The Child Jesus' First Miracle*, presents Christ as a Palestinian immigrant in Egypt who, out of bbredom and loneliness, starts performing bizarre tricks like projecting lightning from his eyes, working up to his first miracle, which is a political act – he changes the son of the owner of the city into a terracotta pot, because he never allows the other children to play with him and ride his horses. Mary persuades Christ to change the boy back to his original form, since she and Joseph have just found a job and have no wish to be on the run again. Another of Fo's 'Gospels of the Poor', which invariably have a political twist to them, is *The Sacrifice of Isaac*, in which the sacrifice is revealed to have been based on a bet between God and the devil as to the extent of Abraham's love for God. This is revealed to Isaac only after the Angel has appeared to stop Abraham carrying out the killing. The piece ends with Isaac throwing a stone which lands on his father's head, claiming that it has come from heaven and is for his own good, using the same logic as his father has in preparing him for the sacrifice. The piece illustrates Fo's irreverence for the official gospels, which he uses as a basis for religious satire, and here attacks the traditional notion of patriarchal power invested in the father figure. *Daedalus and Icarus* deals with the same theme of the power fathers exert over their children, dealing with Icarus and Daedalus lost in the labyrinth they have built themselves for Gnossus, and ending with Icarus' tragic fall as he tries to fly. The piece is based on a story by the Greek satirical poet of the second century BC, Luciano di Samosata, whom Fo claims was one of the first ever satirists, and a big influence on Rabelais, whose influence in turn is omnipresent in *Mistero buffo*. Fo uses *Daedalus and Icarus* to stress the importance of the imagination and inventiveness, and to attack resorts to surrogate substitutes for the imagination like drugs, horoscopes and UFOs. In exhorting his audience to seek out more creative activities, Fo himself presents a formidable example.

The Obscene Fables

Il fabulazzo osceno (*The Obscene Fable*) is the third edition of *Mistero buffo*, based on more secular sources, which Fo first performed in March 1982. It consists of a group of three stories, all tried out and developed by Fo in public with an audience, which deal with popular sexuality and scatology in a way which was usually censored by Mediaeval church and state authorities, but which was preserved through oral tradition. Fo recounts how he was unable to find any academic source material for the stories, and hence has added his own embellishments to the pieces, which convey a popular spirit of bawdry and earthy humour similar to that of Boccaccio, but with more political bite. The *fabulazzo osceno* is a Franco-Provençal story (which Fo plays in roughly the same dialects he uses in *Mistero buffo*, with a bit of Provençal dialect thrown in to tease the audience) of the type known as *Fablieux*, and Fo stresses that they are obscene in the erotic and anti-scandalous sense, as opposed to mere dirty stories. As the American critic Joel Schechter, whose commentary on Fo's performance of the plays in Gubbio I am indebted to, has explained in his excellent article, 'Dario Fo's Obscene Fables':

> Few of the tales that Fo recites can readily be found in books. He discovers them in obscure sources, invents details, and turns them into performance scenarios. In doing this he brings to the public some chapters of Italian history and folklore that went unrecorded because the scholars who preserved past culture favoured the ruling class; it was not in their interest for stories of political and sexual unrest to survive . . . Fo notes that Popes and noblemen in the middle ages were free to write obscene literature, and circulate it among their friends, while stories for the general public survived – if they survived at all – through the oral tradition of minstrelsy in which Fo places himself.[36]

The first piece, *Il Tumulto di Bologna* (*The Bologna Riot*), is 'obscene' in the sense that it deals with excrement, which the local peasants of Bologna in 1334 used as weapons in their revolt against papal legates and the Provençal troops protecting the Pope. Fo mimes with relish the local peasants throwing buckets of shit over the walls of their fortress, and the high-ranking Vatican officials being splattered by it, changing from the role of a detached narrator to those of the gleeful participants in this ultimately successful peasants' revolt, and of the disgruntled and finally banished Vatican troops.

The second piece, *La parpàja tòpola* (*The Butterfly–Mouse*) is a twelfth century sexual fable about a wealthy but simple-minded goatherd who is tricked on his wedding night by his wife, who has been married off to him to avoid scandal arising from the fact that she has been having an affair with the local parish priest. When her new husband finally returns from a put-up wild-goose chase on their wedding night, she, tired from her frolicking with the priest, tells him she has left her sex at her mother's house, and when he insists, she instructs him how to go about getting it. The goatherd goes to his mother-in-law's house, and is given a cardboard box with a cloth and a mouse in it, and told not to open it until he gets back to his wife. But he is impatient, and unwraps the parcel, and the 'sex' ('topola' is a pun on the Italian word for mouse) escapes. At the end of the story the goatherd's wife takes pity on him and tells him the mouse has come home of its own accord, showing him where her vagina is. Fo originally intended this piece to be performed by Franca Rame, but she demurred due to 'certain passages which were so crude in their erotic satire, and so ruthless in their paradoxicality, that they made me feel uneasy. I would have had to do violence to myself to manage to play it: the perennial condition of sexual inhibition of a woman faced with the blackmailing myth of modesty and shame.'[37] The piece is a satire on Victorian-type sexual repression and euphemisms, which frequently amount to the imposition of ignorance, and Fo's performance is in itself a revolt against censorship and sexual oppression.

Fo prefaces his third story in *Il fabulazzo osceno* with an improvised monologue about the P2 scandal in Italy, which he performed on its own in an extended form in Pisa in 1982, after the secret lodge P2 had been exposed and shown to include some of the most prominent Italian politicians, businessmen, industrialists and even entertainers, making it a type of secret Mafia which contained more power and influence than the Italian government. In this *P2 Prologue*, Fo simply talks to his audience, acting out situations and inventing allusions and analogies as he goes along – it is spontaneous theatre. He is particularly scathing about the role of entertainers in the Lodge, and the theatrical overtones of Italian public life:

> P2 is a totally Italian story, with all the drama of espionage, slaughter and crime, but also all the ridiculousness of farce. An example? One of the members of P2 was Claudio Villa, the king of song, who immediately admitted everything, since he's no politician and so has nothing to be ashamed of. Well, Gelli (the head of P2) took Villa into P2 for just one reason: women. The king of song directed a revue company and Gelli invited them all to his house in Arezzo, to have a few dancing girls . . . Don't you find it funny (*buffo*) that a Masonic Lodge doesn't allow women to be members, and yet Gelli used his secret lodge to get some dancing girls? Don't get me wrong, having dancing girls can be a wonderful thing, but can you imagine a country where secret sects are used to get access to women? . . . Compared to these masons, terrorists are mere amateurs. They don't just strike at the heart of the state, they've taken over its eyes, brain, heart, stomach and all the rest.[38]

Fo goes on to describe scenes which recall the orgies of *Boniface VIII*, and uses the political scandal to tease out sexual high-jinks in order to prove his point about the double-standards of sexual repression and the sexual decadence of church and state authorities in whose interest sexual repression operates. Here Fo reveals the real 'living newspaper' aspect of his theatre, in which he is continually editorialising and improvising sketches based on events in the news, which he changes in every performance, providing a live running commentary and dramatisation of political news.

The piece which follows the *P2 Prologue*, *Lucio e l'asino* (*Lucio and the Donkey*), has sexual overtones similar to those between Bottom and the Queen of the Fairies in *A Midsummer Night's Dream*; a poet suffering from 'phallocratophantasmagoria' tries to perform an Ovidian transformation of himself into an eagle, imitating Jove's famous miracle, in an attempt to increase his sexual prowess. He mixes the wrong potion, however, and ends up as a donkey, who is robbed by brigands and forced to carry the beautiful daughter of a wealthy family. Fo portrays the randy, constantly sexually aroused donkey with vigour and high comedy, using onomatopoeic sounds to parody male sexual ambition in a way which echoes ancient Greek comedies like *Lysistrata*. As a donkey, the poet is constantly kicked in the testicles by all and sundry, but manages to rescue the girl and return her to her parents, who seek to gratify his insatiable sexual appetite with horses. After they discover his ability to write, they sell him to a circus, where he is rented out to an aristocratic lady for sexual purposes, which leads to his employment in the circus in a love-making act with a slave girl. He then discovers the antidote for his metamorphosis and is changed back into a man. He seeks out the lady with whom he made love as a donkey, only to be rejected by her on the grounds that he is no longer an exceptional representative of the Priapic principle, but merely a man like any other. This fable originates in the second century BC, and was written by Luciano di Samosata, a Greek satirical poet who lived in Italy, and whose writings were later an influence on Machiavelli, Rabelais and Voltaire. The 'obscene fables' reveal Fo in a more 'scabrous' vein than *Mistero buffo*, exploring a more Rabelaisian vein of satire than the religious subjects of the earlier texts, while also illustrating how he has ventured into the field of sexual politics, a process which started with his television compilation *Parliamo di donne* in 1976, and which has become a dominant feature in his subsequent collaborations with Franca Rame.

Il fabulazzo osceno concludes with a revised and adapted version of Franca Rame's monologue about the 'suicide' of the German terrorist Ulrike Meinhof, *Io, Ulrike, Grido . . .* (*I, Ulrike, Cry . . .*), which was first performed on a stage covered in cellophane in Milan in 1977 to commemorate the first anniversary of Meinhof's death. Here it is presented as an 'obscene tragedy' and used to focus on political torture and the 'obscene' Italian *legge sui penitenti*, a law which offers reduced sentences to terrorists who give information to the state about terrorist activities, (like British supergrasses) which often leads to the conviction of innocent people. The monologue, based on letters and documents by and about Ulrike Meinhof, is a bleak, static and intense depiction of her attempts to stay sane and rational in prison, and overcome the oppressive torture of sterile, white silence by painting the colours of West German consumerist capitalism and speculating about the 'state clean-up' which will harness dissent and stamp out all forms of protest and political opposition in West Germany after the Stammheim deaths. The Fos are careful to point out that they do not agree with the ideology of the Baader-Meinhof group, but use the monologue as a vehicle to condemn the sense of apathy and impotence which has blighted much of the post-1968 revolutionary Left and extra-parliamentary political groups both in Germany and Italy since the late 1970s.

This piece is a rare example in the Fo canon of direct political address in a non-comic form, and illustrates a growing sense of disillusionment with the heady, optimistic and positive form of communal didactic theatre of the early days of *Mistero buffo*, which runs parallel with a more general decline in political protest and Left-wing constructivism in Italy since the late 1970s, a factor I shall return to in the latter part of this book.

Mistero buffo and its many offshoots, together with the countless improvised routines and sketches on topical events which Fo frequently makes up on the spot, reveal him as the 'theatrical animal' that he is, and show his unique capacity for turning a one-man show into a piece of epic and total theatre. His presence as an actor, director and frequently designer, charges his plays with a dynamism both stylistic and political which is often far less apparent in the printed texts of his plays (most of which are in fact only written down after Fo has knocked them into shape through performance, and exist as records of performances rather than constructed literary texts). *Mistero buffo* is an unrepeatable experience tailor-made for and by Fo, which fortunately surmounts language barriers (at least to a certain extent), as a performance by another actor in translation would be virtually inconceivable. This has, however, happened on two occasions in Brussels – first in November 1972, when Arturo Croso performed *Mistero buffo* in French and Flemish at the TRH and then in February 1983, when Charles Cornette performed selections from *Mistero buffo* under the title *La Jonglerie* at the Atelier rue Ste-Anne.

There have also been at least two attempts to stage *Mistero buffo* in English. Some of the pieces were performed in a puppet show format by Malcolm Knight and his Maskot Puppet Theatre in Scotland and at the 1983 Edinburgh Festival, relying on rod and glove puppets to illustrate the gestural range of Fo's monologues in Knight's own translation. In 1984 a young, six-member English and American collective theatre group called the 1982 Theatre Company did an 'ensemble' version of *Mistero buffo*, which included one performance at the Half Moon Theatre in February 1984. The group worked from a very accurate, literal translation of the pieces by Ed Emery, who also translated the Fo Riverside Theatre Workshops and has done a number of other Fo plays in English. The 1982 Theatre Company adapted *The Hymn of the Flagellants, The Slaughter of the Innocents, The Marriage at Canaan, The Morality Play of the Blind Man and the Cripple, The Birth of the Peasant* and *The Birth of the Jongleur* into a condensed, 90 minute production which maintains the spirit of the original from an oblique, contemporary standpoint, with little attempt made at finding an English equivalent of Fo's *Grammelot*. Using a collective style reminiscent of Paul Sills' Story Theatre and the Bread and Puppet Theatre (appropriately, as this latter group was also an influence on Fo's stagecraft), and performing without sets and costumes, the group simplified Fo's texts into a modern English idiom, frequently resorting to corny jokes and slapstick devices in a limited but likeable dramatisation of the monologues. Many of Fo's necessary explanatory and introductory prologues to the pieces were maintained, while an extract from the Wakefield Mystery Cycle's *Shepherd's Play* was interpolated to illustrate similarities between Fo's sources and the English Mediaeval Mystery Play tradition. These similarities involve not only features of dialect, but also the religious mystification of texts by academic commentators, as the group indicated by reading a footnote from the English texts which suggested that the Shepherd's expression of misery at his plight was merely intended to reflect the greater sufferings of Christ. Ensemble 'alienation devices' were incorporated, like performing the *Morality of the Blind Man and the Cripple* with two actresses, and staging the conflict between the Angel and the Drunk in *The Marriage at Canaan* as a battle between two actors trying to upstage each other. By drawing on English theatre traditions such as pantomime and music hall double acts, the group's performance was rooted in a 'popular' format. A modern political parallel illustrating 'state brutality similar to that of the sixteenth century' was made by reciting Franca Rame's account of her improvised *interventi* at the gates of the Fiat factory in Turin in 1980 after the wholesale sackings there. While sacrificing most of the onomatopoeic richness and mimic range of Fo's performance of *Mistero buffo*, the 1982 Theatre Company production did demonstrate that by approaching the pieces from a respectful distance, an English equivalent to Fo's 'popular theatre', albeit impoverished, is possible.

2: BIOGRAPHY AND OUTPUT 1951-1967

Our theatre became more and more provocative, and left no space for 'théâtre digestif'. Reactionaries raged, riots broke out in the audience more than once, and fascists tried to provoke riots in the auditorium . . . Our theatre could be criticised on all counts, but it has to be admitted it was a 'living' theatre, which dealt with 'facts' that people wanted to know about. This, together with the direct language we used, made it popular theatre.

(Franca Rame, Preface to *Le commedie di Dario Fo*.)

English speaking audiences are likely to be familiar with five of Dario Fo's plays at the most: *Accidental Death of an Anarchist* (*Morte accidentale di un anarchico*, 1971), *Can't Pay? Won't Pay!* (*Non si paga! Non si paga!* 1974), *Female Parts* (*Tutta casa, letto e chiesa*, 1977) – all three of which have received numerous productions in the UK, the USA, and Australasia – *Mistero buffo*, which Fo finally performed in London at the Riverside Studios in April 1983 to considerable acclaim, and *Trumpets and Raspberries* (*Clacson, Trombette e Pernacchi*, 1981).

These five works represent the tip of the iceberg of Fo's output, to say the least, since over a 30 year period of activity he has written, directed, designed and acted in some 40 plays, as well as numerous short sketches and occasional political pieces. From the comic radio monologues of *Poer nano* (*Poor Dwarf*, 1952) to the scurrilous, 'obscene' popular monologues of *Il fabulazzo osceno* (1982), Fo has produced a vast repertoire of ensemble plays, revue sketches, farces, clown shows, political documentaries and agit-prop musicals, as well as writing numerous songs for his own plays, and for popular Italian singers such as Enzo Jannacci, Ornella Vanoni and Giorgio Gaber, and performing 'living newspaper' sketches for political demonstrations in piazzas, streets, sports stadiums, converted cinemas, occupied factories and even de-consecrated churches. His output forms an extraordinary mosaic of popular political theatre which can be divided into three parts, corresponding to his three decades of activity: His initial exploration of revue and French farce and Italian neo-realist cinema; his adoption of the role of 'court jester to the bourgeoisie' with the Compagnia Fo-Rame, with which he achieved an enormous popular success working within established commercial theatre while exploring political issues which frequently encountered censorship problems; and finally his break with this 'bourgeois theatre' in 1968, in order to propagate popular political theatre on an alternative circuit, playing to non-theatregoers and producing topical plays of an agit-prop nature which became internationally acclaimed and made him the most well-known living political playwright in world theatre.

Early influences

Dario Fo was born on March 24th, 1926, in Sangiano, a small town in the province of Varese on the shores of Lake Maggiore in Lombardy. His father, Felice Fo, was a socialist employee of the Italian state railways (at a time when the Italian Communist Party was yet to be formed) who worked as a station master and was frequently transferred from one station to another along the Swiss border, but still found time to act in an amateur theatre company which performed plays by Ibsen, among other authors. His mother, Pina Rota Fo, came from a peasant family, and is the author of a book of reminiscences of life in the Lake Maggiore area between the wars, *Il paese delle rane* (*Land of Frogs*, 1978). Dario was the eldest child of the family, followed by a brother, Fulvio, who became a theatre administrator, and a sister, Bianca Fo Garambois, who has written two books about the Fo family's experiences: *Io, da grande mi sposo un partigiano* (*When I Grow Up I'll Marry a Partisan*, 1976) a book of childhood war-time reminiscences, and *La ringhiera dei miei vent'anni* (*The Gallery of My Twenty Years*, 1981), about the Fo family's life in Milan in the 1950s and her experiences in the rag trade and as a theatre costumist.

The Lake Maggiore region was a seminal influence on Fo's subsequent career in the theatre by virtue of the *fabulatori* and *cantastorie*, travelling story-tellers and ballad singers who wandered through the towns around the shores of the lake, telling stories to the local fishermen and peasant farmers about fantastic undersea adventures. Fo was an attentive listener to these stories, many of which he learned by heart, while he also picked up a large repertoire of fishermen's tales, as his sister recalls:

> He would often sit on the steps of the jetty where the fishermen mended their nets and told stories about the legends of the lake. At night in bed he would repeat them to Fulvio and me, reconstructing them in his own fashion, and passing them off as true. Stories about green, mossy, enchanted towns buried under the waters of the lake, inhabited by giant silver fish with human heads.[1]

Fo also studied and imitated the gestures and actions of the *fabulatori*, and at the age of seven built a puppet theatre with his brother, inventing stories, making sets and creating characters for their home-made marionettes, which he animated in the courtyard of their house. Later he came to be considered by the local people as an expert in the techniques of the *fabulatori*. Fo's own account of how he achieved this status and the *fabulatori*'s influence on his subsequent popular, 'illegitimate' theatrical vision is worth reporting in full:

> I lived in a town of smugglers and fishermen, to whom it wasn't enough just to have guts, you had to have a lot of imagination. People who use their imagination to break the law always keep part of it in reserve to entertain themselves and their friends. In that sort of environment, everybody's a character in, as well as the author and the protagonist of any story he tells. I built up a collection of these stories from the time I was seven, when I started hanging out with these smugglers and fishermen. I didn't just learn the content of their stories, but also their way of telling them. It's first and foremost a particular way of looking at and interpreting reality. The way these people used their eyes, classifying people in a flash into characters or a chorus, into story-builders or story-repeaters (authors and actors), was my main weapon when I arrived in the city (for us the city meant Milan). My

fellow townspeople who I got on best with were the *fabulatori*, who went around the part of Lake Maggiore where I lived, telling stories in the piazzas and the *osterie* – stories they hadn't got from books, but had made up themselves. They were stories which arose from an observation of everyday life, full of a bitterness which they channelled into satire. Their 'fables' would start off from any old story, and then pick up momentum until they often reached the point of hyperbole. They always told their stories in the first person. One fellow had got angry and cast out his line too far and got it snagged on a bell-tower hidden on the bottom of the lake. Another was in a race and had forgotten to untie his moorings and came in second. Another one was trying to be cunning betting on a snail race, and when his snail came in first, he smashed it against a stone, and then got all upset and didn't have the heart to scrape it up and eat it . . .[2]

In almost all of Fo's plays, first-person story-telling plays a prominent part, and in the French language edition of *Mistero buffo* (1973), Fo referred to the stories of the *fabulatori* as a 'structural storehouse' (*blocco strutturale*), a model and constant background source of reference for the satirical stories, fables and tales which form the backbone of both his monologues and his more conventionally-staged ensemble plays.

One of the towns Fo lived in as a child was Portoraltravaglia, a colony of glass-blowers which was reputed to have the highest percentage of insane people in Italy. 'It was here,' Fo has recalled, 'that I began to see the figure of the madman as something familiar. This intuition I later found writ large in popular theatre, where the madman is a fundamental character'[3] (as he is in a number of Fo's plays, from *Mistero buffo* to *Accidental Death of an Anarchist*). While he was accumulating these local, indigenous theatrical stimuli, Fo was also sketching and painting, and by 1942 he had made up his mind to study at the Brera Art College in Milan. After his first year at the college, war broke out, and Fo returned to Varese to help his father in the Resistance, assisting escaped English, American and South African prisoners of war to cross the border by disguising them as Lombardian peasants. Subsequently, while his father was still underground working with the partisans, Fo decided to join the anti-aircraft division of the navy, in the hope that he would be given an immediate discharge owing to the lack of munitions, but found himself sent to a camp in Monza where Mussolini arrived to give instructions about going to Baden Baden to retrieve dead Italian soldiers. Fo made false documents for himself and some companions and deserted, wandering at large for a time before joining a parachutist squadron, which was later to lead to accusations against him of subscribing to the fascist movement. In fact Fo deserted again after less than two months and tried to regain contact with the Resistance movement, without success, wandering through the countryside and sleeping rough. 'At the end it was like coming out of a nightmare,' he has recounted, 'an absurdity which seemed endless. This is another reason why I get angry when I'm accused of having been a Republican. I see it as an insult against all those years of suffering which my family, my friends and the people of my town had to go through.'[4]

In 1945 Fo returned to the Accademia di Brera, but also enrolled at the Milan Polytechnic in the faculty of architecture – a decision which helped shape his later work as a stage designer and playwright, and another feature which links him with the English political playwright with whom he has most in common, John Arden. Fo was particularly interested in vernacular and popular architecture, and began a thesis on Roman architecture, but later abandoned his studies seven examinations short of a degree, disillusioned by what he saw was expected of architects in a postwar environment of building speculation and cheap, impersonal housing. After suffering a nervous breakdown, Fo was advised by a doctor to pursue what he found enjoyable, which resulted in his gravitating towards the theatre. In this period he began painting and moving in artistic circles, reading Gramsci, Brecht and Mayakovsky, who were to become his chief sources of inspiration when he moved into the theatre. He also discovered the Neapolitan farces of Eduardo De Filippo, after whom he was later to become the most successful popular actor-playwright in Italy. (One of Fo's favourite later stories is of how he and Eduardo were almost run over while crossing the road together in Milan, and Eduardo cheerfully accused the driver of the offending car of trying to kill two birds with one stone.) Fo also recalls how he used to hide in the stalls of the Piccolo Teatro of Milan to watch the director Giorgio Strehler, another major figure in the postwar Italian theatre, who was at first one of Fo's main influences, but later his chief rival, conducting rehearsals. Fo was impressed by Strehler's sense of stagecraft, and also his anti-naturalistic, anti-Stanislavskian use of actors in creating a theatre based on situation, and the two colleagues later discussed Brecht's theatre of alienation, although Fo was subsequently to regard Strehler as having reduced Brecht to a bourgeois, 'théâtre digestif' format. Fo also met some of the important figures of Italian neo-realist cinema, such as Roberto Rossellini, Gillo Pontecorvo, and Carlo Lizzani, with whom he was later to work in Rome. He also acquired a reputation as an improviser of stories and player of practical jokes, most notably one in which he announced the arrival of Picasso in Milan, and organised a reception with flowers and reporters at Milan station. The part of Picasso in this mock-masquerade was played by one of the Brera caretakers, who failed to turn up to the reception for Picasso, at which various happenings, including an impersonation by Fo of an old Milanese drunk who had known the artist in 1911, were staged until the police intervened. Fo also made occasional visits to Paris, where he was particularly impressed by cabaret.

Radio origins

Fo had written his first farce in 1944, and after the elections of 1948, which were a severe disappointment for the Italian left (although not a member of the Communist Party, Fo moved in predominantly left-wing and PCI circles, worked for the party, and read the periodical *Politecnico*) he mounted a stage production in Luino of a play called *Ma la Tresa ci divide* (*But the Tresa Divides Us*), which he wrote, designed, and played the part of an Angel in. The play tells the story of a contested cow in a wild, surreal environment of live farm animals and racing motorbikes, and a white town and a red town argue for the rights to the cow's milk. The plot bears a faint resemblance to Brecht's *Caucasian Chalk Circle* but in form appeared to be more similar to Fo's student pranks, although Fo directed satire against the Catholic church, the Christian Democrat party and the elections through the character of the Angel.

In 1950 Fo approached the actor Franco Parenti, noted for his performance in Strehler's Piccolo Teatro production of Goldoni's *Harlequin, Servant of Two*

Masters and for a radio comedy entitled *Anacleto the Gas Man*, who had become disillusioned with the art-house, predominantly stylistic concerns of the Piccolo and moved into Revue. Parenti was organising a variety show of radio actors in Intra, and Fo asked him if he could take part in it. Parenti accepted him, and a collaboration between the two actors began which lasted until 1954. For the show, Fo drew on his rich stock of material from his home town, telling stories which, as Parenti recalls, 'were absolutely original, with an extraordinary humour, wit and personification. When the show was over, we'd go for walks round the lake and he'd tell me more stories, and in this way we originated a project in which we would work together on a new type of revue, one which didn't copy reality, but which involved people and took a stand.'[5] This first revue, in which Fo had his first experience as an actor in front of an audience, embarked on a series of what the participants referred to as 'punitive expeditions' in Piemonte, Lombardy and Veneto, and took the form of variety shows performed outdoors with a minimum of scenery, which required a special emphasis on mime and gesture.

As a result of his theatrical exposure with Parenti, Fo was accepted by the RAI, the Italian national radio network, to do his own solo radio comedy series, *Poer nano* (*Poor Dwarf*), for 18 weeks at the end of 1951. *Poer nano* went out on the air on Saturday evenings after Parenti's *Anacleto the Gas Man*, and in it Fo built up a series of reversals of biblical, historical, and even Shakespearian stories, turning accepted commonplaces upside-down. This series of adult fairy tales represented Fo's first experience as a fully-fledged author-performer, and the 'poor dwarf', the narrator, presented the point of view of the underdog, as in the story of Romulus and Remus who build Rome because other children's mothers won't allow them to play with children raised by a wolf. The story of Hamlet is presented as that of a prince who kills his father in order to continue his affair with his mother, who is in fact his stepmother. Hamlet's uncle tries to get him to marry Ophelia, who is the uncle's transvestite mistress, while the ghost of Hamlet's father, who only appears to Hamlet when the latter is drunk, is in fact Horatio dressed up in a sheet who is trying to steal Hamlet's stepmother's favours. Similarly, Othello is not a Moor but an albino who is offended because Desdemona won't give her sexual favours to his old drinking companion, and Romeo is the victim of a sadistic Juliet who keeps him in her garden with savage dogs. 'The key point of these stories was always paradox, opposites and contraries,' Fo wrote in his preface to the book which included the most successful of the pieces, *Cain and Abel* and *Samson and Delilah*, published in 1976 and illustrated in comic-strip form by his son Jacopo:

> Cain was the victim and not the executioner, the Almighty knew everything but was absent-minded and caused chaos and confusion which his son had to remedy – witness the story of original sin . . . these reversals were not done just for their own sake, but were a sacrosanct refusal to accept the logic of convention, a rebellion against the moral contingent which always sees good on one side and evil on the other . . . The comedy and the liberating entertainment lies in the discovery that the contrary stands up better than the commonplace . . . There is also the fun of desecrating and demolishing the sacred and untouchable monuments of religious tradition.[6]

Here we see the iconoclasm against established forms of Catholicism which was later to inform the more grotesque satire of *Mistero buffo*, while the radio experience of *Poer nano* gave Fo valuable experience in acting from a text without gestures, and in developing the tonalities of his remarkably deep, sharp and resonant voice in order to discriminate acoustically between the various characters, a technique which later came into its own in *Mistero buffo*.

Revue and *avanspettacolo*

In 1952, Fo performed *Poer nano* on stage at the prestigious Teatro Odeon in Milan, offering him his first opportunity to flesh out his religious satire and championing of the underdog with gesture and action in the official Italian theatre. In the same year, he acted in a revue entitled *Cocoricò* together with Giustino Durano. *Cocoricò* reflected the current Italian trend of 'colossal', American-influenced, 'imported revue', with a superficial, mildly satirical content. In the early 1950s the most prominent revue company in Milan was I Gobbi (The Hunchbacks), who reacted against the musical spectacularity of 'imported revue' and opted for a more intellectual, satirical cabaret form of 'chamber revue' which could perhaps be compared with the Cambridge Footlights and *Beyond the Fringe* in the UK. *Cocoricò* did contain some degree of social comment as, for example, in a 20 minute sketch about the situation of black people in the USA, but by and large it was a conventional revue. The following year Fo, Parenti and Durano formed their own revue company, calling themselves I Dritti (The Stand-ups, a joke at the expense of I Gobbi), and wrote, directed and performed in a revue called *Il dito nell'occhio* (*A Finger in the Eye*) which opened at the Piccolo Teatro in June and later toured all over Northern and central Italy. Fo designed the sets and costumes as well as co-writing and co-directing, and the lighting was done by Strehler, while the French mime Jacques Lecoq was choreographer and created a number of mimes. The cast also included a Milanese actress, Franca Rame, who came from a popular touring theatre family, the Teatro Famiglia Rame, and whom Fo had first met while performing in a summer revue Called *Sette giorni a Milano* (*Seven Days in Milan*), a 'girlie' show with a troupe called the Sorelle Nava. Fo and Franca Rame were married in June 1954 and the following year had a son, Jacopo.

Il dito nell'occhio broke new ground in the revue field for its political satire and irreverent comedy, and critics called it an 'anti-revue'. The theatrical tradition it belonged to was that of *avanspettacolo*, as opposed to cabaret, although French commentators in Fo's work were later to see many resemblances between it and French cabaret. But as Fo explained to an American interviewer:

> I've never done cabaret, but rather a form of theatre tied to popular traditions; if anything, in the framework of *avanspettacolo*. (A kind of variety theatre performed between two movie showings. It was very much in vogue in Italy between 1930–1940.) All our comics, from Petrolini himself, to Ferravilla and Scarpetta have all contributed to this type of theatre.
>
>   When, for example, we did *Il dito nell'occhio* . . . the ambience was not that of a cabaret – the space itself, 700 seats, the stage being twelve to thirteen yards wide, the complete set, the number of people acting (there were twelve of us), and finally, the concept of the piece, which, yes, was a string of sketches, but had a logical continuity of its own . . . It had little to

do with the French or German tradition in cabaret. That is, it was something better than cabaret, which forces one to adopt a certain unnatural format: a café performance requires a very private and intimate form of speaking. With us, instead, everything was flung out: the action, the amount of physical expression inherent in our way of acting . . . (and) pantomime . . . Moreover, there was a popular element that consisted of the storyteller's visual narration . . .[7]

The revue consisted of 21 sketches which ran through a potted satirical history of the world, but using the reversal technique of *Poer nano*. The expression 'a finger in the eye', which comes from the title of a regular column in the Italian Communist Party newspaper *L'Unità*, roughly corresponds to the English concept of 'nose-thumbing', and the revue overturned the perspective of school history books, as in the sketch about the Trojan war in which the idea for the Trojan horse originates from an unknown soldier. (In 1954 Fo was to declare that his favourite playwrights were Chekhov and Shaw, and here one can see some influence of the Shaw of *Ceasar and Cleopatra*.) 'The basic idea was to dismantle the mythical mechanisms imposed by fascism and retained by the Christian Democrats,' Fo later said. 'Like the myth of the hero, in which history is made up of prominent figures, and the myth of the family, and morality, and culture as the product of an intellectual elite, of patriotism, efficiency, virility, and history as the "school of life".'[8] Fo's sets and costumes also broke with traditional forms of revue. The split-level set allowed two playing areas and took the form of a parallelepiped with a curtain – a kind of stage within a stage in which scene changes took place in full view of the audience. All the cast wore a basic black costume over which they put a few additional items to suggest a historical period and the nature of their characters.

Il dito nell'occhio, apart from being the last play in which Fo played a supporting role, was also important for the influence of Lecoq, a mime who, unlike the 'deaf-mute', 'white' mime of Marcel Marceau, espoused 'black' mime, which incorporated language, song and dance. Lecoq had been in Italy since 1948, assisting on two of the first Italian productions of Brecht, and in *Il dito nell'occhio* he provided what one critic called a 'perfect geometrical mechanism',[9] schooling the company in rhythmic gestures, and teaching Fo a considerable amount of mimic and vocal technique to shape his spontaneous improvisations. Lecoq trained Fo to use his physical defects (long arms and legs, uncoordinated body and flat feet) to advantage rather than hiding them, instructing him in the different forms of laughter, while also introducing him to *Grammelot* and character-transformation, ingredients which were to come into their own in *Mistero buffo*.

Musical activities and the cinema

In 1953 Fo also began his activity as a song-writer, in collaboration with Fiorenzo Carpi, who was to provide the music for all of Fo's plays up to 1967. Their first song, *La luna è una lampadina* (*The Moon is a Lightbulb*) remains one of Fo's most well-known individual songs – a piece of whimsy which Fo sang in a raunchy, vaguely rock 'n' roll vein. The protagonist has been betrayed by Lina, who has gone off with a wealthy barber, leaving him to lament under her window. But instead of complaining about a broken heart, he complains about his sore feet, and the fact that he will have to walk home because the last trams have left. The anti-romantic irony of this song is typical of Fo's early songs about the Milanese *Mala* (underworld) written for Ornella Vanoni and Enzo Jannacci (with whom Fo adapted a sketch from *Il dito nell'occhio* about a chicken thief imprisoned for offences against the fascist regime, and for whom he later wrote an entire musical show). The language of these early songs has been described by Lanfranco Binni as expressing

> an instinctive positiveness expressed with immediacy, naturalness and irony. It is the type of language which we can find in Jannacci's most popular songs, and it is no coincidence that Dario Fo struck a chord with him which led to an important collaboration. It is a language which expresses detachment from the world of the bourgeois city, with its luxurious shop windows in the centre of town, in favour of the squalor of the industrial outskirts where the streets are populated by 'poor sods' who are viewed as basically defeated people who nevertheless have a humanity which is absent from the cold bourgeoisie with a purse where their heart should be. A language which instinctively finds emotional truth and knows which side is right, but which does not yet see the 'rich' and 'poor' divided into classes, into the 'bourgeoisie' and the 'proletariat'.[10]

Fo's songwriting comes into more prominence in the second revue on which he collaborated with Parenti, Durano, Lecoq and Carpi, *I sani da legare* (*A Madhouse for the Sane*) which opened at the Piccolo Teatro a year after the critical and commercial success of its predecessor. The second revue consisted of 24 sketches about contemporary life in the big city – which is never mentioned by name, but easily recognisable as Milan – from daybreak to nightfall. With more immediate subject matter, the revue was more forceful in its political satire than *Il dito nell'occhio*, and ran into censorship problems from Italy's equivalent of the British Lord Chamberlain, the Ministero dello Spettacolo, at a time when Mario Scelba was Minister of the Interior, and administering a repressive, violent police force made up of ex-fascist recruits, and the new American ambassador, Clare Booth Luce, was pressurising the Italian government to stamp out the spread of communism. This situation occasioned a sketch in the play about McCarthyism in Italy, while another sketch entitled 'The Compromise', about a dissident Soviet scientist who is killed by his orthodox son, ends with a characteristic Fo touch – a film director rushes onstage to ask how the scene has gone down with the censor. The repressive political climate of the time was typified by the *legge truffa* (fraud law), a proposal to give a party who obtained 50% of the vote a two-thirds majority in parliament (Italy has proportional representation), which was reminiscent of the strategy which Mussolini used to seize parliamentary power in 1923. In this political climate, in which police frequently appeared in the audience to check the cuts which had been enforced on *I sani da legare*, many critics seemed to be cautioned into giving the play a lukewarm reception.

Formally very similar to *Il dito nell'occhio*, the play concentrated on the underdogs of Milan – tramps, thieves, unemployed, poker players, production line workers, and lovers, while satirising middle-class charitable institutions, journalists and film-buffs. Stylistically, the influence of the French absurdists was apparent, while the poet Salvatore Quasimodo described the play as mixing decadent French surrealistic elements with 'a form of popular theatre',[11] acknowledgement of a feature which was to become more and more predominant in Fo's subsequent work.

Due to the financial failure of *I sani da legare*, I Dritti broke up, after discussing doing a Milanese adaptation of Brecht's *Threepenny Opera*, a project which Fo was to realise almost 30 years later, while Strehler premiered the play at the Piccolo in 1955. Durano returned to more conventional revues, while Parenti, after having difficulty getting back into radio drama in the RAI, went on to do traditional French farce, only venturing back into political theatre briefly in the 1970s with a production of Mayakovsky's *The Bath House*. Fo decided to move with his new family to Rome and try his hand as a screenwriter in the cinema.

Despite working on a high salary with prominent screenwriters like Pinelli (Fellini's scriptwriter), Age and Scarpelli, and living next door to Rossellini and Ingrid Bergman in Rome, as well as designing film sets, Fo's three year stint in the Italian cinema capital did not yield any substantial results. In 1956 he co-wrote and acted with Franca Rame in *Lo svitato* (*The Screwball*), which was directed by Carlo Lizzani, a film influenced by the comedies of Jacques Tati, in which Fo plays the part of a disoriented hotel porter cast adrift in a neo-capitalist Milan of skyscrapers and modern technology. Fo's essentially improvisational, theatrical style of acting was at odds with the concise, naturalistic needs of the cinema, and the prominent Italian film critic Tullio Kezich described the film as 'a satirical film which misses all its probable targets.'[12] Although the film can still occasionally be seen on private Italian television channels, it achieved little apart from giving Franca Rame a certain degree of prominence, and when she was offered parts in a series of farces at the Arlecchino Theatre in Milan in 1958, the Fos returned definitively to the city which has been their base ever since. 'For me the lesson of the cinema,' Fo later recalled, 'meant learning from a technical point of view what people had already grasped: a story divided into sequences, a fast pace, cutting dialogue, and getting rid of the conventions of space and time. Working on screenplays gave me an apprenticeship as a playwright and I was able to transfer the lessons of the new technical means to the theatre.[13]

The early farces

For his return to the Piccolo Teatro in Milan, with the newly-formed Compagnia Fo-Rame, Fo put on four one-act farces under the general title of *Ladri, manichini e donne nude* (*Thieves, Dummies and Naked Women*), three of which Fo wrote, while the fourth was an adaptation of a farce by Feydeau with the title *Non andartene in giro tutta nuda* (*Don't Go Around Naked*), which was later substituted by a fourth Fo play. At a time of unprecedented economic stability in Italy with the beginning of what was to be called the 'economic miracle', Fo turned his attention to the relatively frivolous area of sex comedy, although all four pieces show his concern with developing a theatre of situation, and at the time they were regarded as an indigenous response to the predominantly literary, pessimistic plays of Ionesco, Adamov and Beckett. One of these pieces, *Non tutti i ladri vengono a nuocere* (*Not All Burglars Have Bad Intentions*), a boulevard farce of mistaken identities, was revived in Rome in 1980 – an indication that these early farces are by no means ephemeral – when a reviewer wrote: 'Seeing this risqué type of theatre now, one laughs at the way we used to laugh, in rediscovering the heretical humour of a stage which was still not very permissive . . . it re-evokes the late *dolce vita* atmosphere of the Kinsey report and the scandal magazines.'[14] This play also has the distinction of being, together with a later short Fo farce, *La Marcolfa* (also revived in Rome in 1980), what is probably the first of Fo's plays to receive a professional English language production, translated and directed by Maurice Edwards, at the off-Broadway theatre the Cubicolo, where it ran for nine performances in August 1969. *I cadaveri si spediscono, le donne si spogliano* (*Corpses Are Despatched While Women Strip*), a 'thriller farce', was Fo's first play to be transmitted on Italian television (in 1959, stripped of the second half of its title), and deals with a transvestite detective investigating a divorce agency – divorce did not become legal in Italy until 1974 – which is in fact a cover for a human mincemeat factory. This piece has also received an American production. Some of the stage business in these short pieces like characters losing their clothes, furniture and objects becoming animated, and injections in the backside, were to recur even in Fo's most recent work like *Clacson, trombette e pernacchie* (*About Face*, 1981).

In 1959, Fo was commissioned by the Teatro Stabile of Turin, where his brother Fulvio was working as an administrator, to write and direct a play to open its new season. The theatre's artistic director, Gianfranco De Bosio, was one of a group of postwar directors who had pioneered the plays of Brecht in Italy, and had also done research into one of the major figures of the commedia dell'arte, Ruzzante, a major influence on Fo's work, and *Mistero buffo* in particular. For the occasion, Fo excavated some of the nineteenth century popular farces which the Teatro Famiglia Rame had performed, rewriting and restructuring them into four one-act plays which De Bosio co-directed. The title of the plays, *Comica finale* (*Comic Finale*), derives from that of the brief improvised topical farces which travelling players performed at the end of a tragedy or 'serious' play, and which belong to a tradition of popular theatre akin to that of the 'comic interlude' in Shakespeare's time. The recourse to this popular tradition was reflected in *Comica finale* by having a wagon onstage with painted backdrops, and in the opening song, *Ma che aspettate a batterci le mani* (*What are you waiting for - clap!*) the audience are exhorted to put out their flags on their balconies for the arrival of the 'charlatan kings'. The tradition is that of the *guitti*, popular strolling players similar to the *giullari*, and the *lazzi*, improvised comic routines which formed interludes in the repertoire of the *comici dell'arte*. The first of the four farces, *Quando sarai povero sarai re* (*When You're Poor You'll Be King*) is important insofar as it reflects a carnival tradition, that of the 'Feast of Fools', in which the roles of rich and poor, nobleman and servant, are reversed, and the poor man is 'king for a day', which is a basic influence in Fo's work. *La Marcolfa* also echoes this tradition – the eponymous servant is courted by all and sundry in an aristocratic household when it is discovered she has the winning lottery ticket, but she opts for her good-for-nothing fiancé. *Un morto da vendere* (*A Dead Man for Sale*) is based on a newspaper article about a simpleton who beats some cheats at cards, and when they try to 'rub him out' they discover that he is a dangerous criminal – a situation which could be seen as a precursor to the 'Death and the Madman' sequence in *Mistero Buffo*. The final piece, *I tre bravi* (*The Three Suitors*), turns on a misunderstanding between three daughters of a wealthy landowner and three applicants for menial jobs, whom the daughters take for suitors, a situation which finds its antecedent in Plautus' *Miles Gloriosus*, on which the film director Pasolini later based one of his highly literary, neo-classical stage plays, which belong to a highly verbal theatrical tradition completely different from that of Fo's work. 'These farces,' Fo has said, 'were an important exercise for me in writing a theatrical text. I learnt how to dismantle and re-assemble the mechanisms of comedy, and to write directly for the stage without any literary intermediary. I also realised how many antiquated, useless things there were in many plays which belong to the theatre of words.'[15]

The 'bourgeois period'

In September 1959 the Compagnia Fo-Rame began a series of full-length plays, six in all, which were performed every season at the Teatro Odeon – the equivalent of a London West End theatre, although it could boast that it was the first theatre to bring Eduardo De Filippo to Milan – which brought Fo and Rame considerable success in the Italian theatrical establishment. The first of these plays, *Gli arcangeli non giocano al flipper* (*Archangels Don't Play Pinball*), remains one of Fo's most accomplished farces, a three-act play with music, based on a short story by Augusto Frassinetti, with whom Fo had written the screenplay for the film *Lo svitato*. *Gli arcangeli* was Fo's first play to be performed outside Italy, receiving productions in Yugoslavia, Poland, Holland, Sweden and Spain, and at the time of writing plans are underway for the first English language production of the play by the Yale Rep at New Haven in 1984. The play has also been revived a number of times in Italy, most recently in Milan in 1980 and Rome in 1983, where it was presented as a 1950s period piece. It is also Fo's first play to combine political-satirical content with a Brechtian form (evident in the play's songs but also in its reliance on paradoxical situations to make its points), in which he abandons the revue-sketch and short farce form for a consistent plot line and character development which almost makes it a 'well-made play'. For its satire on government bureaucracy (the protagonist discovers that he has been registerd by mistake as a hunting dog and is sent to a kennel) and government ministers (the protagonist steals a minister's clothes on a train, impersonates him at a reception, and receives a bribe for his troubles), the play ran into censorship problems, as did most of Fo's work before 1968. 'I took the starting point of the play from current events,' Fo has recalled, 'and the striking contradictions which illustrated the more paradoxical contradictions of the Christian Democrat state, and I took the subject into areas which would clash with audiences on the commercial circuit. Having accepted this circuit and these audiences, we had to put across political and social truths under the guise of satiric licence.'[16]

The play is set in the industrial outskirts of Milan, and deals with a group of *balordi*, or 'louts', vaguely resembling English Teddy Boys, enabling Fo to mine a rich vein of Milanese street slang. The *balordi* are petty criminals who live on their wits, and resort to theatrical con-tricks reminiscent of those of Fellini's early films like *Il bidone*. *Gli arcangeli* is also notable for the first reference in Fo's work to the *giullari*, in the following exchange between Il Lungo and the Blonde (Franca Rame), a streetwalker who is used by the *balordi* to set up a fake newspaper personal column marriage with Il Lungo:

LANKY: Being a fall-guy is more or less my job.
BLONDE: You mean you work as a fall-guy?

LANKY: Right – have you heard of the *giullari*?
BLONDE: Of course I have. (*Eruditely, like an encyclopedia.*) The *giullari*
        used to make royalty laugh – isn't that right?
LANKY (*laughing*): Exactly. The same goes for me too, except for one thing.
        Since royalty doesn't exist any more . . . I make my coffee-bar
        mates laugh. I'm a poor man's Rigoletto.[17]

The *balordi* are cheerful, optimistic Milanese cousins of the doomed,
down-and-out *ragazzi di vita* of Pasolini's gritty, naturalistic early novels and
films, and the play follows Il Lungo's successful attempt to extricate himself
from this desperate demi-monde of pranks and petty crime, get his papers in
order, and find an identity for himself. The critic Paolo Puppa has commented
that the play breaks new ground in

> presenting, for the first time, a *socially determined group* as opposed to a
> previous concentration on fixed absurdist types. They are good-natured,
> sulphuric louts, a kind of proletariat of the outer suburbs who survive on
> expedients. Coming from the tradition of naturalistic melodrama . . . They
> present a type of neglected underworld, cheerful and desperate at the same
> time.[18]

The influence of Brecht, and of *The Threepenny Opera* and *Arturo Ui* in
particular, is strongly apparent in Fo's second play for the Odeon, a black
comedy described as 'a play in 3 acts and 2 interludes' which again deals with a
criminal underworld. *Aveva due pistole con gli occhi bianchi e neri* (*He had Two
Pistols with White and Black Eyes*, 1960), is partly based on a couple of
newspaper crime stories, and its farcical plot turns on a 'double' and a series of
mistaken identities in a way which closely resembles Fo's later play *About Face*
(1981). Political satire is more predominant (although the play is far from being
a piece of agit-prop) at a time when Fo and Rame were drawing closer to the
Italian Communist Party, and there were deaths in Sicily and Reggio Emilia
after clashes between workers and police, a general strike which caused the
Christian Democrat government to fall, while the trade unions were gaining in
strength. Grafting a topical newspaper story onto a situation taken from
American *film noir*, the play deals with a priest in a mental hospital who has
lost his memory and is appropriated into a hoodlum gang. In an interview
published in the American *Drama Review*, Fo claimed that the play 'satirised
latent fascism. It was the story of a bandit whose two-sided character was
portrayed through the use of doubles, in the tradition of Greek and Roman
theatre. Censorship had become just about intolerable, and we almost ended in
jail for having refused to submit the text for approval by the authorities,
knowing that permission could be obtained only after they mutilated the work
beyond recognition.'[19]

Fo's play for the Odeon the following year, *Chi ruba un piede è fortunato in
amore* (*Stealing A Foot Makes You Lucky in Love*) was a sentimental comedy
with an imbalance between a highly farcical form and slight content, and was
judged harshly by left-wing Italian theatre critics. A modern version of the myth
of Apollo and Daphne, with a series of running gags punning on the word
'foot', it could be compared with the neo-classical plays of Shaw and Giraudoux
in form. It is centred on a naive, honest taxi driver (Apollo), who is cast in the
same mould as Il Lungo and the Bandit-Priest, who gets unwittingly involved

with big-time building speculators. Despite the topicality of the play at a time when the Italian economic boom was in full swing and building speculation was rife, the bourgeois comedy form of the play did not help its satire to hit its mark, and the play remains one of Fo's minor works. An English version of it was performed at the 1983 Edinburgh Festival by the Channel 5 Theatre Company, using what Joseph Farrell described in *The Scotsman* as 'the Frankie Howard (sic) slapstick approach', and resulting in 'a mess of asides to the audience, improvised gags, over-the-top acting and curious accents . . . There is little that is memorable, and it is not particularly funny.'[20]

The television fiasco

In 1959, as a result of Italy's first centre-left government coming into power, Fo and Rame had been invited by the more permissive second channel of RAI-TV, the Italian state television network, to present some of their one act farces on national television. RAI is controlled by the Italian government, and tends to reflect the opinions of the Christian Democrat party, but with the entry of the smaller left-wing parties into the government, its policy relaxed somewhat, particularly in the second channel, with programmes like *Tribuna politica*, introduced in 1960, which gave a hearing to the parties of the Italian left. Fo was appointed artistic director of the musical revue programme *Chi l'ha visto?* (*Who's Seen It?*), and then, in 1962, to write and perform sketches and songs in the highly successful musical variety programme *Canzonissima*. Fo took advantage of the popularity of the programme to produce satirical sketches and songs which attacked building speculation, working conditions in factories, prisons and the Mafia, which almost immediately caused censorship problems, despite the considerable public appeal of the series. The Fos' conflict with the programme's producers culminated in them walking out of the studios before the eighth programme of the series was about to go on the air, refusing to accept the cuts ordered in sketches which referred to current strikes and the like. The Fos were then sued by RAI, who subsequently destroyed all the recordings they had made for *Canzonissima*, and effectively excluded from Italian television for fourteen years. Fo has described an incident which led to the vetting and cutting of their transmissions:

> There was one sketch which caused an avalanche of protest. It showed a worker who was in the habit of kissing the effigy of his boss as if it were a saint. This worker had a fat aunt who weighed a ton, and who came to visit him one day in the factory. It was a canned meat factory. The aunt tripped and fell into a machine, and came out as mincemeat because they couldn't stop the production line. The worker was given 150 cans of meat which he kept in a cupboard at home and showed to his friends every so often, telling them 'This is my aunt' . . . There were no reactions against this from aunts, but a lot from canned meat producers and industrialists in general.[21]

This type of grotesque humour satirising capitalist exploitation of workers and reflecting the grim reality of Italian factories, in which accidents were a common occurrence, was a foretaste of the political satire of Fo's post-1968 plays, and was evidently too close to the bone for television programme controllers in 1963. It was as if Monty Python had got together with Red Ladder in a prime-time comedy show on BBC 1. *Canzonissima* and its 15 million spectators gave Fo his first direct experience with the potentialities of the mass medium, and he used the opportunity to undermine the diversionary, drugging effects of the entertainment industry, especially in musical programmes, and to expose and condemn the social injustices and exploitation which lay behind the 'economic miracle' which TV was a part of, giving Italian viewers their first taste of a brand of humour which derived from the popular origins of theatre.

Historical drama in an epic context

Fo returned to the Teatro Odeon with a play which for him was a radical new departure – a two act piece about Christopher Columbus entitled *Isabella, tre caravelle e un cacciballe* (*Isabella, Three Sailing Ships and a Con man*). This play appeared in the same year as Strehler's celebrated production of Brecht's *Galileo* at the Piccolo, and there are evident resemblances to Brecht's play, although the way their protagonists clash with the political regimes in each case is quite different. Fo's play was primarily an attempt to demystify and debunk the traditional history-book image of Columbus, as it was reflected, for example, in the naming of a street after him in EUR, the fascist-designed modern business and government ministry area of Rome. Fo was undoubtedly influenced by Maxwell Anderson and Kurt Weill's *The Nina, the Pinta and the Santa Maria*, again using songs to comment on the action, but used the historical format as a framework in which to couch comments on contemporary Italian social and political problems. As he has commented:

> I wanted to attack those Italian intellectuals who, with the centre-left and the Socialist Party in the government, had discovered power and its advantages and leapt on it like rats on a piece of cheese. I wanted to dismantle a character who had been embalmed as a hero in school history books, whereas he is in fact an intellectual who tries to keep afloat within the mechanisms of power, play games with the King and be cunning with power figures, only to end up reduced to a poor sod. I'd started to view the present with the tools of history and culture, in order to assess it better, and in this play I invited the audience to use these tools.[22]

Fo uses the mechanism of the play-within-a-play to present Columbus through a further filter of Brechtian detachment. The protagonist is an actor condemned to death under the Spanish Inquisition for performing a play by Rojas. At the gallows he improvises a play about Columbus and Isabella which is exempt from censorship according to a law which allows a condemned prisoner to do anything he likes at the gallows – a tongue-in-cheek self-reference (both the actor and Columbus were, of course, played by Fo) to Fo's own problems with censorship. After a performance of the play at the Teatro Belli in Rome, Fo and Rame were physically attacked by a group of fascists, who tried to pelt them with rubbish, while another performance was called off due to a bomb scare. Fo received threatening letters, and was even challenged to a duel by an Italian cavalry officer. Fo agreed to the duel as long as it was fought along the lines of Thai boxing, at which he was a regional champion, and the challenge was never taken up. Franca Rame was charged with giving offence to the Italian armed forces in the following dialogue:

ISABELLA: You are allowed certain concessions, such as looting and
plundering. That's covered by the war law. Then there's those
four rallying words – King and Country! Family and Morality!

> The blood that our sons spill so generously – you'll fall right on
> your feet.
> FERDINANDO: Not just on my feet – I'll be up to my neck in the shit.
> ISABELLA: So that's why all you soldiers always walk with your chins
> up . . .[23]

The final line of this exchange, which was later used by Fo in a slightly transposed form as the final line of his play *Accidental Death of an Anarchist* to attack the Italian government's manipulation of scandals, here had to be modified by adding, 'I mean here in Spain, of course.'

The final song of the play expresses clearly where Fo's sympathies lie: 'The really cunning person is always the honest man/Not the opportunist,/but the man who come what may/is always on the side/of the underdogs,/of the just.'[24] In many ways, not least its focus on the plight of the underdog who is finally executed, and its use of a devious, double-dealing intellectual as its protagonist, the play has affinities with the historical, Brechtian works of John Arden, especially *Armstrong's Last Good Night*, which appeared in the UK the following year. Despite a cool reception from the critics, *Isabella* broke box office records in Italy at a time when the theatre was in dire economic straits, and having achieved considerable popularity and notoriety in Italy, Fo became the most widely performed living playwright in Europe the year after.

In 1963 Fo also wrote *La fine del mondo*, or *Dio li fa, e poi li accoppia* (*The End of the World, or God Makes Them and then Matches Them*), which remained unperformed until February 1969, when it was produced at the Teatro Belli in Rome by the film and TV director Jose Quaglio, supervised by Fo, and with music by Fo's old collaborator, Fiorenzo Carpi. The play presents a contemporary Adam and Eve, who survive a world cataclysm by hiding in a sewer, and believe they are the sole remaining people in the world until they encounter a corrupt General of counter-espionage and an Angel. Meanwhile the world is being taken over by cats in the absence of human power figures, and here the influence of popular puppet shows on Fo's work is apparent. The play's situation accommodates a series of discussions about sexual relationships, an area which comes to prominence in Fo's work after 1976, while Fo updated the piece to make comments through the General on current political events and scandals, as well as offering assessments on the state of the left in Italy since the Historical Compromise, a proposal by the PCI leader Berlinguer that the Communist Party cease being an opposition party and negotiate entering the government, which caused a number of splinter groups to leave the party. As a reviewer of the 1979 production of the play commented, its rather flimsy science-fiction metaphor is too generalised to sustain the political points the play makes, and it remains a curiosity piece, with its faint echoes of Beckett:

> Fo's metaphor does not have anything like the gloomy tragedy of Beckett,
> though it has all the signals or signposts: rubbish bins, for example, or tape
> recorders, which recall and pay hommage to *Krapp's Last Tape*, which also
> announced the end of the world . . . Sometimes playing tricks with
> commonplaces results in sinking into the swamp the commonplaces invite.[25]

Graveyard humour and witchcraft
Meanwhile, back at the Odeon, Fo produced *Settimo:ruba un po' meno* (*Seventh*

Commandment: Thou Shalt Steal a bit Less) for the 1964 season, returning to farce in a contemporary setting in a play specially written for Franca Rame, whose performance as Isabella had been one of the high points of Fo's previous play. The play again attacks building speculation, but with considerable impact, as in the scene where Enea, the female gravedigger protagonist, witnesses a clash between armed police and striking demonstrators, which, although it takes place offstage, is the first time an event of such immediate political implications was to appear on an Italian stage. The play charts the political education of Enea, played by Franca Rame in a departure from her previous 'vamp' roles, and a step towards 'epic acting' in which situation takes precedence over psychology. After she is made aware of the building speculation scandal in which the graveyard's director is immersed, Enea does a brief stint in the 'elevating, emancipating' profession of prostitution, and then disguises herself as a nun in order to get hold of compromising documents for blackmail purposes. This takes her into a mental asylum, and Fo presents us with a highly ironical and satirical scene in which mental patients act out a 'game of the nations', representing the jostling for political power positions between various countries, including England, represented by 'an inmate with a grotesque mask resembling a lion, and a large military hat with flags and pennants all over it, and three Tudor lions on the front: all of which resembles the warlike divinity of the Chinese theatre in the guise of a clown, with 'typical commedia dell'arte trimmings'[26] as Fo's stage direction indicates. The scene bears a striking resemblance in its grotesque pageantry to the World War One human chess game in Joan Littlewood's *Oh What a Lovely War*, although Fo was probably more influenced by the Peking Opera, which had performed in Milan shortly before he wrote the play and had impressed him with the simplicity and evocativeness of its stagecraft, at a time when he was impressed by the progress of the Chinese cultural revolution.

The last play that Fo wrote, directed and performed with the Compagnia Fo-Rame for the Teatro Odeon was *La colpa è sempre del diavolo* (*Always Blame the Devil*), which anticipates *Mistero buffo* both in its mediaeval setting and its satire on established forms of Catholicism as manifested in its most vicious form in Mediaeval times by witch-burning. However, satire of religious corruption is at the basis of almost all of Fo's plays, many of which include a burlesqued representative of the Catholic church as an almost instant source of comedy. As Fo has commented:

> Unlike *Mistero buffo*, *La colpa è sempre del diavolo* is not a *giullarata*, and not a reconstruction of Mediaeval texts, but a totally invented story in a farcical vein, which takes advantage of its Mediaeval setting to tell a few truths about Catholicism, like showing that the authorities maintained that the gospels were too embarrassing to put into practice, as well as too dangerous, because if they were applied they would take away all their privileges.[27]

La colpa è sempre del diavolo is important in marking the beginning of Fo's research into Mediaeval theatre* but was a critical flop, being judged an unintegrated combination of a demystifying historical format and contemporary social comment on subjects such as the Vietnam war, which did not quite hang

---

*At about the same time John Arden was doing similar research in the UK. One of Fo's source books for *Mistero buffo* was *Early English Stages* by G. W. C. Wickham, under whose supervision Arden did research at Bristol University.

together structurally or conceptually. The plot concerns Amalasunta (Franca Rame), a kind of twelfth century 'con woman' who is wrongly accused of witchcraft, and sets about becoming a witch for real, enlisting the aid of a devil-dwarf Brancaleone (a famous name in Mafia circles), played by Fo in a guise he later elaborated and perfected in his political satire about the Italian government minister and sometime prime minister Fanfani, combining his head with the body of another actor in a mimic technique which owes something to the influence of Lecoq. Fo also used an old Venetian dialect which was a forerunner of the Padano of *Mistero buffo*.

Popular music, an adaptation, and circus satire

During the run of *La colpa e sempre del diavolo*, Fo went to see *Bella ciao*, a performance of songs of popular origin by the Nuovo Canzoniere Italiano, which marked a revival of peasant and working-class political songs and popular culture which immediately interested Fo. When he was approached by the musical group and asked to collaborate on a new show, he accepted willingly, and the result was *Ci ragiono e canto* (*I Think Things Out and Sing about Them*), which played in Turin and later in Milan in 1966. Fo directed the show, and rewrote some of the popular musical material, but it was an uneasy collaboration, as the musicians and singers in the group, many of them amateurs, often resisted Fo's attempts to theatricalise the songs, and choreograph them in terms of the action of work rhythms, which Fo insisted that many of the songs were based on, and affected their musical setting:

> Pausing for breath in a work song determines not only its rhythm, but also its melody. One could say that every type of work which differs from another because of its particular gestures inevitably determines a musical difference in the songs.[28]

Fo's ideas as a director led to clashes with the musical uniformity of the group he was working with, while he was also very much against the current of Italian theatre at a time when mildly outrageous figures of the avant-garde, like Carmelo Bene, with his semi-pornographic rehashes of Shakespeare, and Leo de Bernardinis, with his underground jazz concoctions, were coming into prominence, and the Living Theatre had toured Italy and exerted considerable influence in propagating a research into physical theatrical form and an emotive relationship with the audience, creating an elitist ghetto of conceptual theatre. Fo, on the other hand, was excavating popular forms from the past, which appealed to him because they gave him the opportunity of getting across to a wider, non-theatre-going audience, as well as for their political importance in retrieving popular culture. As he stated in an interview in 1967:

> I maintain that in the theatre, the more one approaches the new by way of experimentation, the more there is a need to seek out roots in the past, by which I mean the relevant aspects of the past – above all those which are attached to the roots of the people, which derive from the people's manifestations of life and culture, . . . and which enable the expression of new research and new investigations on the basis of the 'new within the traditional', which I am concerned with.[29]

The first part of *Ci ragiono e canto* presented popular festival songs and ironic popular songs about war (somewhat in the manner of the songs in *Oh What a*

Lovely War), while the second part contained work songs, a representation of the apocryphal gospel version of Christ's passion (which Fo would later take up again in *Mistero buffo*), while the finale was the anarchist song *Our Home is the Whole Wide World*, sung in chorus with the audience, a *coup de théâtre* which Fo later used in an ironical form to conclude the first act of *Accidental Death of an Anarchist*.

In 1966 Fo travelled in Eastern Europe, the USA and Cuba, studying the new forms of theatre in these countries, remaining unimpressed by much of the new avant-garde, experimental theatre he saw, regarding it as sterile, formal and technical experimentation which too frequently used new material for its own sake. In Cuba he was impressed by the poverty of means young theatre practitioners employed, making do with simple props and costumes, and the gestures of ritual. On his return to Italy he was invited to adapt and direct the French playwright Georges Michel's *The Sunday Walk* at a small experimental theatre in Milan, the Durini. As he was to do in his later adaptations, Fo completely gutted Michel's text, a gentle satire about a petit bourgeois family going through its provincial rituals without acknowledgement of the violence and turmoil in the outside world, and changed the play's references to the Algerian war and the OAS to the Vietnam war and clashes between police and demonstrators. As the continually changing, updated texts of his own plays prove, Fo runs completely against the grain of any literary theatrical tradition, and takes an essentially practical, pragmatic approach to texts, and in this case he also used Michel's play to experiment with stagecraft: the production included a beat group on a circular platform centre stage, performing songs specially written by Fo, as well as non-naturalistic lighting effects, costumes and action, while the actors performed more than one role apiece. Fo also used the play to make a savage attack on the cosy domestic security afforded by electrical appliances, a theme he was later to take up in his own plays. The critic of the magazine *Il Dramma* commented at the time that 'Fo has saved all the intelligence of the play and replaced its delicacy with a bitter polemical thrust.'[30]

For his final play in the mainstream, establishment Italian theatre, *La signora è da buttare* (*The Old Girl's for the Scrapheap*), which opened at the Teatro Manzoni in Milan in September 1967, Fo used a clown show, revue-sketch format (again reminiscent of *Oh What a Lovely War*) to satirise pre-Kennedy America (personified by the 'old girl') and the Vietnam war. The American critic A. Richard Sogliuzzo, in what was the first critical article about Fo to appear in English (in 1972), has described the play as follows:

Set in an American circus of the 1860s, *The Lady is to be Thrown Out* progressed like a circus performance: acrobats, clowns, dancers, tightrope walkers, and trapeze artists rushed on and off. A hundred mechanical contraptions whirred and hummed. The pace was frenetic; the joy excessive, manic. Fo and his company sang, danced, joked, performed on the high wire, executed impressive feats of acrobatics. His verbal banter, spiced with his Milanese argot, delighted the audience, but in the end it was gesture and movement that prevailed over language. Among that gesture and movement were an avalanche of teeth pouring out of Fo's mouth, an oxygen mask that became a serpent, shoes propelled by themselves, hands flying through the air, and performers sitting in mid-air with their coat-tails folded under them, plus an endless array of surrealistic sight gags. Gradually, however, one realised that the joy was fraught with tragedy, clearly evident in the death of a dove at Dallas. The lady to be eliminated was the owner of the circus, an aged female P.T. Barnum, representing American capitalism. A moment before her death, she was elevated above a sink in a Statue of Liberty pose, and then ascended to a heaven packed with consumer goods, a touch of mock ritual denigrating both Church and State. Fo's circus was a metaphor of the industrial state, a vast bureaucracy of machines and trapezes in which man had yielded his individuality to the collective pandemonium, a puppet in a tyrannical circus of injustice, prejudice, crime, and war.[31]

Although this is a description of the updated TV version of the play in 1976, it gives an accurate picture of the bustling pace and circus techniques, in what is an example of what Fo called 'theatre of provocation', with its form akin to that of agit-prop. Italian theatregoers in 1967, however, did not take kindly to the play's grotesque, black political satire, illustrated in one scene where Fo ridicules forensic research, tracing an absurd trajectory of the bullet which kills the Bride in White (a representation of Kennedy in Dallas), hitting a stray dog, a chauffeur and an ice-cream van on its way to its target. Fo was almost arrested for 'offences against foreign heads of state' in the play's references to President Johnson, and the play satirised American imperialism, racism, justice and absurd forms of entertainment like the 'flea-tamer' who tries to take out a flea's appendix. In using a clown show format (the cast included I Colombaioni, a duo of circus clowns) consistency of characterisation is eliminated in a style which moves further towards the epic theatre which Fo espoused, in which the actor plays not a character but a 'mask'. As Fo told an American interviewer when the play was being prepared for Italian TV in 1976:

> . . . this means that the actor must be the exclusive renderer of whatever happens, that he does not have to wear a robe to become a character, but to become a mask . . . The mask is the dialectical synthesis of conflicts, whereas a character carries with him conflicts without ever achieving their synthesis . . . the actor is an individual entity, while the mask is collective, because it tells of a general concern . . . it is the voice of the story, not the means of acting it out. It is not I who identify with what I present on stage. Rather, I can criticise, suggest conflicts, contradictions, hypocrisies, and comment under any circumstance. This is the epic fact, the estrangement.[32]

In both its epic style and its political-satirical content, *La signora e da buttare* shows that Fo's theatre could no longer be contained within the structure and fulfil the expectations of the conventional bourgeois Italian theatre, with its subscription-payers and predominantly safe diet of revived classics or modernised classical stories, for which the irrepressible energy and zest of Fo's play was too much. Although the play ironically received a prize of eight million lira (£4,000), which Fo donated to university theatre research, it was to prove to be his last for establishment theatre. After touring *La signora* in Scandinavia, Fo disbanded the Compagnia Fo-Rame, and set about forming his own alternative theatre outlets which could reach audiences outside the predominantly snob environment of Italian theatre-goers. 'For years I have been the court jester of the bourgeoisie', Fo later told an Italian journalist in what has become a famous utterance, 'hurling invective in their faces, which they responded to with ignorant laughter. Now I will become the jester of the proletariat. They will become the recipients of my invective.'[33]

3: THEATRE IN THE SERVICE OF CLASS STRUGGLE 1968-1973

My opinion of Dario Fo and his work is so negative that I refuse to talk about him. Fo is a kind of plague on the Italian theatre. I should say the worst possible things about him, but this doesn't seem an appropriate time. (Pier Paolo Pasolini in *Panorama*, after Fo's arrest in Sassari, November 1973.)

The events of May 1968 in Paris had rapid repercussions in Italy, where they were compounded with the implications of the Vietnam war, the cultural revolution in China, and the various guerilla movements in Latin America and Africa in changing the state of play for Italian intellectuals. Those on the left were no longer content with compromising with a centre-left government, and took to the streets with students and workers, initially backed by the Italian Communist Party. Franca Rame had become a member of the PCI in 1967, while Fo, though remaining outside the party, supported its tenets from a distance, aligning himself with Gramsci's emphasis on the importance of popular culture and the guiding role of the intellectual in reaffirming that culture. Strehler, following the example of Jean-Louis Barrault at the Theatre d'Odeon in Paris, resigned from the Piccolo Teatro in Milan, and set about forming his own collective theatre company outside the state structure. Fo and Rame approached the PCI, assuming that it was backing the new breakthroughs brought about by the student revolt, with a view to setting up a theatre cooperative which would operate through ARCI, the party's cultural, recreational wing, and play in the *camere di lavoro* and *case del popolo*, PCI community centres and workers' clubs. As Fo was later to say in an interview with the French newspaper *Liberation*:

> the bourgeoisie accepted even our most violent criticisms of them as long as we criticised them inside their own structure, in the same way as the king's court jester was allowed to say the most incisive things to the king, as long as he said them at court, to the courtiers who laughed, applauded and said 'My, how democratic this king is.' This was a way for the bourgeoisie to show itself how sympathetic and democratic it was . . . But once you go outside this dimension and go and talk to the peasants and the workers, to the exploited, and tell them a few home truths, then you're not accepted . . . If your work's run by the boss, it becomes the boss's work, whereas if it's run by the working class, it's the work of the proletariat, even if it's contradictory and incomplete.[1]

This type of shift from the 'official' theatre to an 'unofficial', alternative circuit was shared by a large number of left-wing European writers after 1968, including John Arden in the UK, who in his play *The Bagman* expressed a predicament very similar to that outlined by Fo above – the necessity for self-management, and for siding with the 'thin men' against the 'fat men', in order to combat what Marcuse has called the 'repressive tolerance' of the establishment. The Fos thus attempted to use the theatrical talents which had brought them enormous success in Italian mainstream theatre, to support class struggle and the revolutionary process which they saw, in the heady and euphoric atmosphere of 1968, as a real and viable alternative to state reform:

> When we got involved with ARCI, it was in the hope that the spirit of 1968 was moving things in a new direction, even though we were well aware of what cooperatives meant, and who was behind the *case del popolo*, and in whose interests they were. We had the illusion that working on a grass roots level we could change the organisational structures, and that the PCI had adopted a revolutionary line from the pressure of the student movement and the workers. We saw it as the only possible solution, the only representative of the working class.[2]

Nuova Scena: a new theatre for a new audience

In 1967, Peter Brook's *US* had played in Italy, and had a resounding impact in theatrical circles for its earnest and thought-provoking attempt to bring home the implications of the Vietnam war to middle-class intellectuals . A young Milanese theatre group, the Teatro d'Ottobre, were so impressed by *US* that they spent several months working on an Italian adaptation of the play, exploring forms of collective, cooperative theatre which American groups like El Teatro Campesino and the Bread and Puppet Theatre had also spread to Italy. Fo approached the Teatro d'Ottobre and invited them to play a part in Nuova Scena, the new cooperative he had set up as a private club in order to avoid state censorship and discourage the presence of police in the audience. In October 1968, Nuova Scena performed Fo's new play, *Grande pantomima con bandiere e pupazzi piccoli e medi* (*Grand Pantomime with Flags and Small and Middle-sized Puppets*) at the Casa del popolo of Sant'Egidio in Cesena, a modest beginning for what became a historical event in the context of Italian political theatre. Almost no critics attended the first night, and the audience consisted mostly of local people and PCI sympathisers. The form of the play, with its revue-length sketches which made historical leaps in a matter of moments, and used a two-level stage with actors in black leotards who doubled a large number of emblematic roles, was a return to the 'rough theatre' (to use Brook's term) of *Il dito nell'occhio*, but with an increase in political charge which made it resemble more the 'Red Revues' of Piscator. Characters were replaced by generalised 'masks' representing Capital, the Confederation of Industry, High Finance, the Church, the People, Rebels and Peasants. The use of puppets, masks, pageantry and masquerade elements resembled commedia dell'arte, and although Fo stipulated in his opening stage direction that this was the case, it is worth stressing, as A. Richard Sogliuzzo does, that the stagecraft of this and subsequent Fo plays stems from a popular, pre-commedia tradition:

> Because of his extensive use of mimicry, masks and puppets, Fo's theatre is

mistakenly characterised as stemming primarily from commedia dell'arte. But commedia satirised social stereotypes, whereas Fo's political satire (broad comedy and highly presentational), originated in the period between the tenth and twelfth centuries. the post-feudal age when the Italian peninsula experienced a burst of political freedom; jesters roamed the land with a repertoire of gags and skits celebrating the end of feudalism, and ridiculing the remaining feudal overlords and the Church.[3]

Grande Pantomima ridicules the Church, the Monarchy, the Army and Industralism, representatives of which are born from a giant puppet representing fascism. The play pits these caricatures against a dragon, representing the people, in a constant duel which takes us through a potted political history of Italy from fascism to the economic boom and the age of consumerism, while suggesting that the shadow of fascism still hangs over the contemporary political scene. Despite its sprawling, rather inchoate form, it makes its points with wit and economy, as in the satire of the use of natural disasters like earthquakes to re-entrench and make political capital for the ruling class, which uncannily predicts the aftermath of the earthquake in Southern Italy in 1981:

> KING: Yes . . . a great disaster . . . a veritable cataclysm, with several million victims – that'll give us an excuse to organise a campaign of solidarity, fraternity . . . At times like this, everybody suddenly becomes charitable, and the people forget all their resentments in a flash . . . The king – that's me – and the queen – that's her – visit the site of the disaster and console the poor desperate survivors . . . I usually kiss a couple of orphans. Then the queen bursts into tears, and I shed a few tears myself, in front of the television cameras – and hey presto, it's game, set and match. The nation is overwhelmed by emotion, and cleaves to their national father-figure, and zap, the revolution is put down![4]

The play also hits out at other topical targets, as in its satire of the mass media for its vampirism of popular culture, and its creation of the 'society of the spectacle' to distract the people from examining their social problems and acting accordingly, and mindless advertising jingles are repeated throughout, counterpointing ironically with events like clashes between armed police and demonstrators. As well as attacking such contradictions inherent in the political actions of middle-class intellectuals, the play also initiates a series of representations in Fo's work of the monotony and exhaustion suffered by workers on production lines, in an absurd Monty Python-like sketch in which workers are tested for foot prehensibility so they can work on a double production line. The play is deliberately left open-ended, in order to stimulate what became known as the 'third act' in the work of Nuova Scena – debates and discussions with the audience about political issues and popular culture.

Towards the end of 1969 there was some dissension among the ranks of Nuova Scena due to a certain amount of resentment by some of its members about the dominating role played by Fo and his wife, a conflict which was never resolved. The company divided into three groups, one consisting of Fo on his own performing *Mistero buffo*, another, coordinated by Vittorio Franceschi, writing and performing their own material, while Franca Rame participated in a third group which performed two plays written by Fo, *L'operaio conosce 300 parole il padrone 1000 per questo lui e il padrone* (*The Worker Knows 300 Words, the Boss Knows 1000 – That's Why he's the Boss*), and two one-actors, co-written with Fo by Franco Loi, under the umbrella title *Legami pure che tanto io spacco tutto lo stesso* (*Chain Me Up and I'll Still Smash Everything*). *L'operaio* dealt with the necessity of retrieving working-class culture, and included criticisms of the PCI which were not taken kindly. The situation of the play is that of a group of workers who are cleaning out an old library in a *casa del popolo* which is being converted into a recreation centre and billiard hall. They start leafing through the books and quoting Mao Tse-tung, Lenin and Gramsci, and as they are stacking the books into large boxes, four of them 'come alive' and scenes from the books are acted out. In dealing with Gramsci's visits to factories while he is trying to form the PCI, the play expresses what has become a cornerstone in Fo's aims in reviving popular theatre:

> The worker is knowledgeable, because he's the vanguard of the people, and the people have a vast culture . . . A large part of it has been destroyed and buried by bourgeois aristocrats and religious power, but it is our duty to rediscover it.[5]

Another section of the play presents the monologue of the wife of Michele Lu Lanzone, which became a performance vehicle in its own right for Franca Rame, and was frequently presented in the Fos' later 'direct intervention' plays. A Sicilian woman in a mental asylum relives her trade unionist husband's death at the hands of the Mafia after he discovers a spring in a region stricken by drought, and his comrades find his dead body plugging up the spring. The play ends with a reconstruction of Mayakovsky's 'suicide' after his satirical plays have virtually been silenced by the Soviet state theatre, and describes his performances in Soviet factories in which his poem on the death of Lenin becomes a rallying point. The case of Mayakovsky is clearly used as a model for the socialist satirical theatre Fo was inclining towards. The main point of the play was expressed in an old and neglected Communist Party slogan: 'If a poor man asks you for charity, give him tuppence for bread and threepence to buy a book.'[6] The PCI was angered by the play's exposure of a few sore points in its current party policies about culture, and saw Fo as biting the hand that was feeding him.

Legami pure . . . consists of the two one-act pieces *Il telaio* (*Fruit of the Loom*) and *Il funerale del padrone* (*The Boss's Funeral*), both of which deal directly with working-class situations in contemporary Italy. In the first, a communist family who do domestic piecework with weaving looms discover that they have to work sixteen hours a day to meet their overheads, and is a grotesque comedy of domestic chaos which culminates with the Father, exhausted by the work and shocked by the fact that his daughter is sleeping with her boyfriend (a satire on the outmoded male-dominated attitudes present in the PCI), goes beserk, smashes the looms (which are imaginary, represented by mime) and hits his wife on the head. The mother (played by Franca Rame) is staunch in her belief that it is important to follow the precepts to be found in the Communist Party newspaper *L'Unità* even though she never has the time or energy to read it. After she is knocked out, she dreams of a Communist Party shake-up:

Kick out all the deviationists, whether they're politically motivated or just hangers-on makes no difference . . . This isn't a party for just anyone, pigs and dogs . . . It's not enough just to be exploited, you have to be totally and constantly committed – not just go to Mass on Sundays![7]

These ironic references to the Catholic Church as a source of comparison with the PCI, together with the play's criticisms of the *Feste dell'unità*, an attempt to bring popular culture to the masses by the PCI which frequently pandered to the lowest common denominator of mass-media entertainment, led to further attacks on Fo and Nuova Scena.

In *The Boss's Funeral*, which was loosely based on the situation in an occupied factory at the time, a group of workers in an occupied textiles factory are about to be evicted by a Police Inspector (who appears in the auditorium of the theatre) and decide to put on a play about the funeral of their boss. By showing a group of workers portraying themselves and a group of caricatured 'Influential People', Fo uses a makeshift agit-prop street theatre format which reflects the Carnival 'Feast of Fools'. The play-within-the-play satirises industrial pollution and the often appalling working conditions in Italian factories where explosions and accidents are a frequent occurrence, and culminates in a scene which extends the disputed meat-factory sketch in *Canzonissima*. A group of executioners are about to kill a worker, who has been chosen by drawing lots, in order to keep the factory accident figures to a constant daily average, but at the last minute the actors, adapting a 'reality' device from the Roman theatre of Seneca's time, substitute a butcher who is about to kill a live goat as part of his daily work. This gives rise to an argument among the actors about the justification of this type of theatrical device (at a time when directors like Jodorowsky and Ortiz in the USA were killing live chickens on stage), and the play is cut short in order to pursue a debate with the audience. Loose and minimal in its form, the play shows Fo approaching the type of caricatured street theatre which he was later to use in his own idiosyncratic way in the 'roadshows' which he performed in actual occupied factories. By this time the PCI were unable to tolerate further the 'provocativeness' of Fo's plays, and refused to allow him to continue using the *camera del lavoro* in Milan. Meanwhile disputes within Nuova Scena on the political line of the company and its organisation on cooperative terms reached a head, and it split up, one group going its own way and leaving Fo, Rame and a few others to go theirs. But as Fo later recalled in an article published in 1976:

When we were at the *camera del lavoro*, at a certain point we were kicked out with the excuse that our theatrical criticisms were dividing the working class, whereas in fact it was a space which originated and developed in a way that was too autonomous, and caused trouble because thousands of people with direct connections with the working class were starting to come along . . . on their own initiative because they felt it was their theatre.[8]

The Nuova Scena period produced little of lasting value apart from *Mistero buffo* and *The Boss's Funeral*, which subsequently received a number of productions outside Italy, and the ARCI initiative was short-lived as the PCI's policies were clearly too moderate to accomodate a writer and performer of the status of Fo, who tended to cause controversy in any theatrical context. ARCI subsequently invited the Piccolo Teatro to put on two plays at the *camera del lavoro*, but after this it became virtually unused, while Fo sought his own outlets to get across to left-wing and working-class audiences.

La Comune and *Accidental Death of an Anarchist*

In 1970 Fo formed a new group, the Colletivo teatrale 'La Comune', which organised its own playing spaces within the environment of the 'extraparliamentary' left, which had grown along with a spreading disillusionment with the PCI. The PCI in turn was attempting to get rid of what it saw as 'revolutionary extremist' and 'Chinese styled' elements, like the group which had formed around the newspaper *Manifesto*, who had approached the party in the wake of the student movement. After the 'hot autumn' (*autumno caldo*) of 1969, in which the Italian left went on to the offensive, the student movement began to dissipate, the militants on the outer left, while still trying to maintain contacts with the working class, tended to split into relatively small groups reflecting Marxist-Leninist, Maoist and other ideologies. 1969 had also seen the first outbreaks of terrorism in Italy, a further incentive for the PCI to exert a 'clean-up' operation, although many of these terrorist attacks, like the bomb in the Banca Nazionale dell'Agricoltura in Piazza Fontana in Milan in December 1969, on which Fo was to base his play *Accidental Death of an Anarchist*, proved to be the work of right-wing terrorists. In the context of this shifting ground among the Italian left, La Comune stated its aims as 'putting our work at the service of the class movement, which doesn't mean slotting into existing set-ups, but contributing to the movement, being present in it, changing with it and its struggles and real needs.'[9]

In October 1970 La Comune took over an abandoned workshop in via Colletta, in a working-class suburb of Milan, which was to be their base for three years. They converted it into a type of community theatre which became a rallying point for various extra-parliamentary groups, but the Fos were careful not to become mouthpieces for any of these groups, remaining part of an autonomous cultural organisation which was involved in a Marxist-Leninist movement of working-class struggle in its broadest sense. In any case, Fo's work entered its most overtly political, revolutionary phase, as the first play La Comune presented at the Capannone di via Colletta showed. Entitled *Vorrei morire stasera se dovessi pensare che non é servito a niente* (*I'd Die Tonight if I Didn't Think It'd Been Worth It*), it was put together and presented after only a day's rehearsal, as a response to the events of 'Black September'. The play combines readings, songs and mimes, based on accounts by Italian partisans of their experiences, with readings and performances of personal testaments by members of the Palestinian Liberation Movement. The play has a direct, 'living newspaper' form, in the vein of 'theatre of intervention', commenting on political events in the Middle East and relating them to the situation in Italy. It typified what Fo was later to state in an interview with the Italian *Playboy* magazine:

> Our theatre is a throwaway theatre (*un teatro da bruciare*), a theatre which won't go down in bourgeois history, but which is useful, like a newspaper article, a debate or a political action.[10]

Fo's next play took this type of theatre much deeper and much closer to home, and went further than didactic documentary theatre, 'which shouldn't be just a documentary theatre of cold information,' as he has stated, 'a theatre which, for all the respect I have for Piscator, doesn't get to the bottom of things. There must also be a vast mechanism to make people laugh about dramatic events.'[11]

Morte accidentale di un anarchico (*Accidental Death of an Anarchist*) did precisely this; 'a grotesque farce about a tragic farce', it opened at the via Colletta theatre in December 1970, a year after the Piazza Fontana bombs had shaken the Italian public and revealed a network of corruption, intrigue and unexplained contradictions in its wake. Fo's play was a response to what had become known as the 'strategy of tension' in Italy, in which the new Christian Democrat government, having deposed the centre-left coalition, tried to crack down on the left and dissipate its forces. Since 1969, according to statistics quoted in *Accidental Death of an Anarchist*, there had been 173 bomb attacks in Italy, 102 of which had been proved to have been organised by fascists, while more than half the remaining 71 appeared to have been organised by the right with the intention of bringing suspicion and blame on the left. In this situation, La Comune set about providing a theatre of 'counter-information' against the widespread discrediting of the left in the press and on television, which had reached its apex in the case of Giuseppe Pinelli, a Milanese anarchist railway employee charged with placing bombs in the Milan railway station in 1969, and then charged with the bombing in Piazza Fontana which had killed 17 people and injured 100. Pinelli had been charged together with Pietro Valpreda, a Rome anarchist ballet dancer, who languished in prison for nearly ten years (and whose prison notes were later published in an English translation), and on 15 December 1969, Pinelli died after 'falling' from a fourth floor window of the Milan police station where he was being interrogated. As Fo wrote in his introduction to *Accidental Death of an Anarchist*:

> In the spring of 1970 the comrades who came to see our plays urged us to write a full-length play about the Milan bombs and the murder of Pinelli, discussing their causes and political consequences. The reason for this was the fearful vacuum of information about the problem. After the initial shock, the press was silent, and the official left-wing newspapers, especially *L'Unità*, hadn't put themselves out beyond the odd sporadic comment like 'It's a disconcerting business'.[12]

Shortly after this a book entitled *La strage di stato* (*The State Massacre*) appeared, published by the left-wing editors Samona-Savelli and written anonymously, documenting all the principal facts of the Pinelli 'defenestration' and the 'strategy of tension'. This, together with legal documents and court transcripts of the Pinelli enquiry, became the source material for Fo and La Comune for their play, 'a farce . . . as painfully grotesque as the action of the magistrates and the contradictions in the official statements.'[13] At the same time as the play opened, a law suit instigated by Inspector Calabresi, who had been in charge of the Pinelli case (and who was later assassinated in 1972), against the extra-parliamentary left newspaper *Lotta Continua*, which had accused him of causing Pinelli's death, had just opened. This meant that Fo's play became a direct source of information and a discussion point for the whole Pinelli affair, which had had a severe impact on the Italian left. The play was constantly up-dated, and each performance included reports on the day's hearing in the *Lotta Continua* case, and in its various versions, over a period of four years, the play was seen by more than a million people, and became Fo's most celebrated work after *Mistero buffo*.

In *Accidental Death of an Anarchist* Fo created for himself one of his most extraordinarily comic and 'histrionic' roles, that of a 'Maniac' (*Matto*) who infiltrates the Milan police headquarters and goes through a number of impersonations in order to force the police to admit to the ludicrous illogicality of their version of Pinelli's 'leap' and to confess their responsibility for his death. The Maniac ('I'm a maniac, not a fool – watch your terminology,'[14] he says at one point) combines some of the blustering farcical antics of Il Lungo's encounter with state bureaucracy in *Gli arcangeli non giocono al flipper* with the Mediaeval figure of the disconcerting, truth-telling Madman in *Mistero buffo*, but above all he is a representation of Fo himself in his multifarious guises as clown, political pamphleteer, *giullare*, stand-up comic, quick-change artist and satirist. In the first scene he is interrogated by an Inspector after being charged with impersonating a psychiatrist, and admits that he has got his training from being a mental patient in a number of asylums, and that he suffers from 'impersonation mania', otherwise known as 'histrionic mania':

> from the Greek 'istriones', meaning actor. Acting's a hobby of mine you see, but I never do the same part twice. I'm a great believer in living theatre, so I need a company of real people who don't know they're acting. I wouldn't be able to pay them, anyway, since I'm always broke. I did apply for an Arts Council grant, but I haven't got the right political connections . . .[15]

The thinly-veiled meta-theatrical distinction between character and actor was not intended to bluff Italian audiences, and nor was Fo's attempt to provide a 'historical' framework to the play in a spoken prologue which stated that the action takes place in New York in the 1920s and refers to the death by defenestration of an Italian anarchist called Salseda, an actual historical event which is used merely as a source of ironic detachment and not sustained through the play. After the Maniac theatens to jump out the window if the exasperated Inspector lets him go, he impersonates a certain Inspector Pietro Anghiari (a jokey reference to Fo's previous unperformed play about this historical character from the crusades), and succeeds in creating an argument, which later comes to blows, between the Inspector and a 'Sporty' Inspector by joking about the latter's fascist connections.

The Maniac, having stolen the Inspector's coat and briefcase, impersonates an examining magistrate who has come to re-open the inquiry into the anarchist's death. In this guise, he forces the Sporty Inspector and the Superintendent, (who is clearly based on Calabresi, although Fo deliberately doesn't give his characters names), to act out their roles in events leading up to the anarchist's death. The Maniac plays the part of the anarchist, correcting the police's version from the transcripts of the interrogation which he has stolen from the Inspector's office. The police's version of the anarchist's death is that it was caused by a 'raptus': 'an exasperated form of suicidal anguish which can affect psychologically normal individuals if provoked by some form of violent anxiety or desperation.'[16] In trying to ascertain the cause of this anxiety or desperation, the Maniac proceeds to pick holes in the police's two different versions (both of which are based on actual police statements to the Italian media), pointing out their glaring inconsistencies, and intimidating them into admitting that their actions were not free of guilt. He then reveals that the government wants both

Dario Fo performing the '*lazzo* of the fly' in 'Zanni's Grammelot' from *Mistero Buffo*.

Dario Fo in *La storia della tigre*.

Franca Rame in
Tutta casa, letto e chiesa.

Yvonne Bryceland in *One Woman Plays* (National Theatre, 1981).
Photo: Laurence Burns.

Dario Fo and Nicola de Buono in *Non si paga! Non si paga!* (1980).

Maggie Steed, Christopher Ryan, Alfred Molina and Sylvester McCoy
in *Can't Pay? Won't Pay!* (Criterion Theatre, London, 1981).
Photo: Donald Cooper.

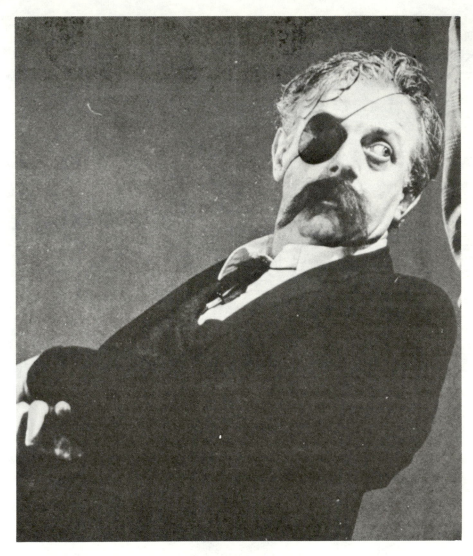

Dario Fo in *Morte accidentale di un anarchico.*

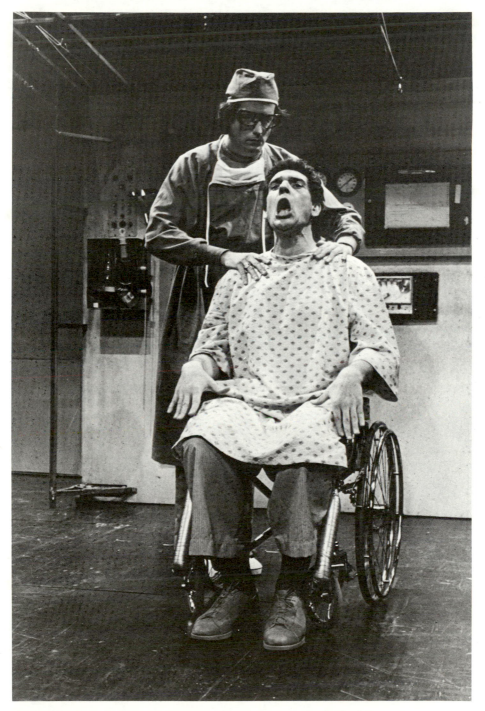

Warren Keith and Andreas Katsulas in *About Face* (Yale Repertory
Theatre, 1983).
Photo: George G. Slade.

Dario Fo in *Fanfani rapito*.

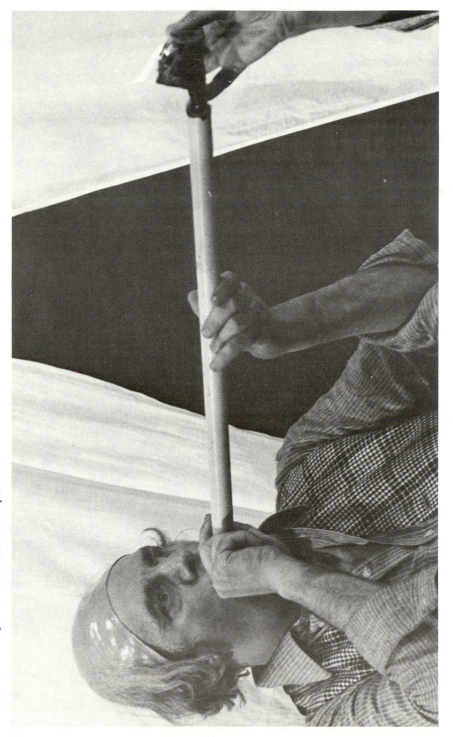

Dario Fo in *La marijuana della mamma è la più bella.*

Dario Fo and Giorgio Biavati in *Clacson, trombette e pernacchi*.

the Superintendent's and the Sporty Inspector's heads, and quotes 'an English saying that goes like this: "the master sets his mastiffs on the serfs. If the serfs complain to the king, the master kills the dogs to appease them."[17] He then plays on the two policemen's despair to induce them to jump out the window like the anarchist (proving the 'raptus' theory), and they are about to do so, such is the skill of the Maniac's persuasions, when they are interrupted by a Constable. At this point the Maniac says he has been bluffing them, resorting to the same 'tricks and traps' they used on the anarchist in faking a story that the Rome anarchist ballet dancer (Valpreda) had confessed he had planted the bombs. As for the English saying: 'if anything, it's the other way round – if the dog dies, the king immediately sends telegrams of condolence to the master, and smothers the dog in decorations!'[18] He then reverses his strategy and sets about trying to help the police to come through unscathed by juggling their two versions to prove that their interrogations had no effect on the anarchist's death. In a brilliantly farcical build-up to the end of the first act, the Maniac goads the police into inventing a story which depicts them as kindly sympathising with the anarchist and trying to cheer him up and make him 'feel at home' (since the anarchist group he belonged to was infiltrated by police informers). This culminates in the Maniac, the Superintendent, the Sporty Inspector and the Constable lustily singing the anarchist song *Our home is the whole wide world*, an ironic *coup de théâtre* which some of the audience remembered from *Ci ragiono e canto*, and pushes Fo's 'satirical license' to the utmost in giving the police a dose of their own medicine.

In the course of helping the policemen to construct a version of the anarchist's 'fall' which exonerates them from any suspicion, the Maniac comes up with the following hilarious theory after the Constable states he tried to save the anarchist from jumping by grabbing his foot, but was left with only a shoe in his hand:

MANIAC: But in this statement here, there's clear indication that when the anarchist was on the ground dying in the courtyard, he still had both his shoes on. On-the-spot witnesses testified to that, and there was a reporter from *L'Unità* among them, as well as a few other passing journalists!

INSPECTOR: That's odd . . .

MANIAC: It certainly is! The least this speedy Gonzales could've done in the circumstances was to rush down the stairs, get to a landing on the second floor, stick his head out the window as the suicide came flying past, slip the shoe back on his foot in mid-flight, and then shoot back up like a rocket to the fourth floor to be there at the same time as the falling man hit the ground.

SUPERINTENDENT: There you go again, being sarcastic!

MANIAC: I take your point – I just can't help it, I'm sorry. So, we're stuck with three shoes. You don't happen to remember if he was a triped by any chance?

SUPERINTENDENT: Who?

MANIAC: The railwayman, the suicide – if he had three feet, it logically follows that he'd've been wearing three shoes.

SUPERINTENDENT (*annoyed*): No, he was not a triped.

MANIAC: Please don't get in a huff – don't forget you can expect
             anything from an anarchist, even that! . . . It's possible that
             one of his shoes was too big for him, and he hadn't got any
             stuffing handy, so he slipped on another, smaller shoe first,
             and then put on the one that was too big.
INSPECTOR: Two shoes on the same foot?
MANIAC: Why not? What's so unusual about that? It could've even been
             a galosh – you know those rubber overshoes people used to
             wear?
SUPERINTENDENT: 'Used to' is right.
MANIAC: Some people still wear them – do you know what I think?
             What came off in the constable's hand wasn't a shoe at all, it
             was a galosh!
INSPECTOR: No, it's too ridiculous for words – an anarchist wearing
             galoshes? No self-respecting anarchist would be seen dead in
             those antiquated, conservative things . . .[19]

This scene illustrates the absurd logic which Fo, in the guise of the Maniac in
the guise of an examining magistrate, uses to point out the grotesquely farcical
lengths to which the Italian police went to exonerate themselves from any
responsibility for Pinelli's death, and to justify not following up any right-wing
leads in their investigations of the Piazza Fontana bombs. The bombs in fact
were subsequently proved to be the work of two fascists, Franco Freda and
Giovanni Ventura. The ensuing trial dragged on for more than twelve years,
with the police attempting to prove that the fascists were working in
collaboration with anarchists. Valpreda, who had been depicted in the Italian
press as a 'monster', was never completely exonerated, being accused of
'subversive associations' largely in order to cover up the incompetence of the
Italian police and its collusion with right-wing elements in dealing with the case.
(There were various unexplained incidents such as the facility with which
Ventura and Freda were able to escape from custody and leave the country.) It
is important to stress that the police characters in *Accidental Death of an
Anarchist* are no mere caricatures or stereotypes – a factor which makes many
foreign productions of the play inaccurate. Although Fo makes them the butts
of comedy and farce, this is inherent in the inconsistencies of their statements
and behaviour, which is in fact that of devious, dangerous types who show the
abuses of power the police exerted in brazenly cracking down on the Italian left,
frequently without a shred of evidence, often resorting to wildly trumped-up
accusations. Nor does Fo show any undue sympathy for the anarchists, whom he
depicts as an insignificant group of extremists whose organisation was so chaotic
that they were incapable of planning or carrying out an operation on the scale of
the Piazza Fontana bombings – an operation which, as one of the Inspectors lets
slip, required 'military precision'. The play's audience was aware of the gravity
of the 'strategy of tension', and it is a measure of Fo's achievement that he was
able to turn the play's situation into a vehicle for madcap farce and popular
comedy, distancing the tragic implications in order to forestall the audience's
empathy (one of the reasons the Maniac continually changes his disguise) and
make them think seriously about the political implications of the play. As Fo
later wrote in his preface to a sequel to the play, 'this monstrous tragic farce
which goes under the name of "state massacre", presented courtesy of the

'democratic' organs of the state . . . had the programmed result of a vast "isolation campaign" of workers' struggles and the "obliteration" of their more militant activists.'[20]

The play's indictment of police behaviour takes a more serious turn with the entry of a woman Journalist, who is based on Camilla Cederna, a reporter for the weekly magazine *L'Espresso*, who unearthed some embarrassing facts about the Pinelli affair. Her hard line of questioning, however, is counterbalanced by a lot of farcical, slapstick stage business caused by the Maniac's change in disguise to hide the presence of the 'examining magistrate'. He dons a false moustache, an eyepatch (from under which he produces a glass eye), and a 'false' artificial hand and leg to become 'Captain Marcantonio Piccini from forensic research'. While the Journalist reveals disquieting facts like the bruise on the back of the anarchist's neck which had nothing to do with his 'fall', and the police calling an ambulance five minutes before the alleged time of this 'fall', the Maniac substantiates her interpretation of events while pretending to be protecting the police. This is made more difficult by the entry of the Inspector who interrogated the Maniac at the beginning of the play, a forensic expert who brings in a facsimile of the Piazza Fontana bomb. The Inspector recognises the Maniac, and has to be gagged and even injected by his colleagues to prevent him giving the game away to the Journalist, a double bluff which occasions stage business deriving from Fo's earlier farces. The play uses a provocative, Pirandello-like device after the Journalist questions the police about their use of intelligence infiltrators in left-wing extra-parliamentary groups:

SUPERINTENDENT: . . . I don't mind telling you we've got a few planted in the audience tonight, in the normal way – would you like to see them?
He claps.
We hear voices from various points in the stalls.

VOICES: Yes sir! What are your orders?
The MANIAC *laughs and turns to the audience.*

MANIAC: It's all right, don't worry, they're only actors. The real ones are sitting tight and keeping out of sight![21]

This emphasises in satirical form the constant threat of police intervention Fo and his company underwent during the tour of *Accidental Death of an Anarchist*. Despite the fact that it was frequently performed in large arenas like sports stadiums, which required the use of microphones by the actors in an atmosphere that emulated that of a rock concert, there were police searches of the audience at the door, the Flying Squad intervened more than once, and there were anonymous bomb threats, proof of both the vulnerability of La Comune and their predominantly left-wing audiences, and the disturbing impact of the play on the police and right-wing factions in Italy.

The farcical capers of the play's situation reach a climax when the Maniac is stripped of his 'forensic' disguise, and proceeds to impersonate a Bishop who is collaborating with the police. This disguise - which was cut in English versions of the play – enables Fo to broaden the implications of the play's situation, satirising the church and discussing the implications of scandal, which as the Bishop states, is used as 'the fertiliser of social democracy'.[22] The Bishop refers to the Profumo scandal in Britain as an example of the 'catharsis of indignation' which scandals cause, and their use by governments to re-entrench the powers-that-be by creating red herrings which distract the political consciousness of the people who are content to see the state washing its dirty linen in public. The Inspector who has recognised the Maniac produces a gun, and handcuffs all the other characters so he can unmask the 'Bishop'. This ruse backfires, since the revelation of the Maniac's psychiatric record means that under Italian law he cannot be incriminated: 'Italian lunatics are like the sacred cow in India – you so much as touch them and you get lynched!'[23] The play ends with the Maniac producing a detonator for the facsimile bomb, as well as a tape recorder with which he has been recording the entire proceedings, and theatening to circulate the tape in order to 'cause a scandal . . . Give Italians a chance to emulate their English and American social democrat counterparts! Then we can face the world and tell them the real reason we walk around with our noses in the air – because we're up to our necks in the shit!'[24] This is Fo's definitive conclusion to the play, but as Chiara Valentini has commented:

> Like *Mistero buffo, Anarchist* grew and developed over a period of years, enriched continually by new situations and characters, in this case taken not from Mediaeval texts but from the current events of the strategy of tension which Italy was experiencing day by day. As a member of the audience ironically commented during a discussion after a performance at Forlimpopoli, 'what Fo has shown us this time is a *mistero buffo*, only we can understand this mystery perfectly.'[25]

In the course of its extensive tour of Italy, the play's title was changed to *Accidental Death of an Anarchist and Other Subversives* to incorporate the death of the well-known left wing publisher Giangiacomo Feltrinelli, who was found dead under an electricity pylon with unexploded dynamite next to his body which appeared to have been 'planted'. It is worth describing the original ending of the play, as two different endings were mixed up, changed and re-elaborated in the London production of the play. In the first version, after the Maniac produces the detonator to the bomb, he threatens to blow up the police and the Journalist and jump out the window. There is a blackout and an explosion offstage, and noise from the courtyard below indicates that the Maniac has jumped. The Journalist interviews the Superintendent and the Inspectors about this new 'jump', and they immediately come up again with the 'raptus' theory. After the Journalist rushes off to take the news to her newspaper, a man with a beard, who 'resembles' the Maniac, enters, revealing that he is the 'real' examining magistrate, and proceedings begin over again before the play is thrown open to the audience for discussion. In his second version, Fo clearly pruned this ending since the explosion of the bomb seemed an inappropriate stage device to resolve the situation, as did the destruction of the illusionistic framework of the play by having the Maniac actor reappear. In leaving the ending relatively unresolved, the play avoided any sort of catharsis. As Fo later explained:

> We don't want to liberate the indignation of the people who come along. We want them to keep their anger inside them, and not be freed of it, so that they can take action on events, and get involved in the struggle . . . Anger and hatred must become conscious action in collaboration with others, and not the individual letting off steam in an impotent way. The great weapon of satire and the grotesque – a weapon always used by the people in their

struggle against the dominant classes – finds further verification in its enormous possibilities of penetration.[26]

To close the play by tying up loose ends would be mirroring the use of 'catharsis' in state scandals, and Fo wanted the 'stink' provoked by the Pinelli affair and the strategy of tension to remain in the air. In leaving the audience's anger and indignation without an outlet, Fo and La Commune hoped, as Brecht did in his didactic plays, to stimulate a desire for political change. Discussions after the play tended to deal with the need for a revolutionary strategy and a 'counter-power' developed on Marxist-Leninist lines against the Christian Democrat state. Thus it is incidental that *Accidental Death of an Anarchist* remains one of Fo's most accomplished and widely-performed plays for the ingenuity of its farcical form, and its Ortonesque madcap comic situations and dialogue. The play was written as a response to a political need in the Italian left, and remains part of Fo's 'throwaway', journalistic theatre of 'counter-information', written for a specific purpose to discuss a particular and pressing political problem.

Political documentaries

Part of La Commune's attempt to stimulate revolutionary strategy and build a revolutionary party involved research into the history of the Italian working-class movement, about which they produced a couple of pamphlets, before beginning research for a new play based on a book by Renzo Del Carriera, *Proletari senza revoluzione (Proletarians without Revolution)*. The result, *Tutti uniti! Tutti insieme! Ma scusa, quello non è il padrone? (United We Stand! All Together Now! Oops, Isn't that the Boss?)*, which Franca Rame considers Fo's best play after *Mistero buffo* and *Accidental Death*[27], was first performed in March 1971. The play dealt with the history of Italian working-class struggle from 1911 to 1922, the period of the Great War, the reformism of the Italian Socialist Party, the activities of Gramsci and the birth of the Communist Party, and the advent of fascism. The play's intention was to illustrate Gramsci's dictum of 'knowing where we come from in order to know where we're going to', and it is one of Fo's more didactic plays, using placards, songs and discussions, but going beyond the somewhat arid seriousness of *L'operaio conosce 300 parole*, in using comedy and farce. In dealing with the betrayal of the workers' struggles by the PSI and the trade unions during the Turin factory occupations of 1920, the play covers similar ground to that of Trevor Griffiths' play about Gramsci, *Occupations*. Historical events are filtered through Fo's central character, Antonia (played by Franca Rame), who changes from being an ingenuous representative of the world of high fashion into a revolutionary activist. Her character is based on the commedia dell'arte mask of the *'etourdie'* (scatterbrain), a type of vamp who, as she becomes politically conscious, uses her 'mask' in a calculated way. Her husband, Norberto, a militant in the revolutionary wing of the Italian Socialist Party, is killed by a fascist squadron, and Antonia, pretending to be a police informer, inveigles her way into police headquarters in 1922, when a top-level collaborationist meeting is taking place between a trade unionist, an industrialist's wife, a police superintendent, a colonel and a fascist and avenges her husband by shooting the fascist. The body is dumped in the same rubbish tip where Norberto was shot along with twenty other comrades. The play ends with a monologue by Antonia, in which she regrets the fact that she has killed 'the dog instead of the masters', realising that killing a fascist won't change the system, and that anger without rationality is no means of constructive action. The play drew implicit parallels between the Socialist Party before the Livorno split and the current reformist policies of the PCI in the 1970s, and urged a divided and increasingly ghettoised left to 'build the revolutionary party', to use the words of the Trotskyist militant in Trevor Griffiths' play *The Party*, which dealt with similar arguments to Fo's play in a contempoary 1970s setting.

Between 1971 and 1972, La Comune intensified its political interventions, using the via Colletta theatre as a forum for political discussions, and continuing its criticism of the policies of the PCI. The level of these debates was taken to an extreme in *Morte e resurrezione di un pupazzo* (*Death and Resurrection of a Puppet*), an updated rewrite of *Grande pantomima* . . . in which Fo, wearing a mask, played the part of the PCI leader Palmiro Togliatti, who had died in 1964. The play contrasted Togliatti's policies with those of Lenin and Mao Tse-tung, presenting him as an epitome of the PCI's revisionism, in an aggressively satirical puppet show which attacked American imperialism, the upsurge of fascism in Italy, and right wing terrorism, using a format similar to that used by the Bread and Puppet Theatre. The play's hard-line satire and criticism of Togliatti were later reconsidered by La Comune, who admitted that the play was a 'tactical error' in its attack of a figure who had had a considerable grass-roots, popular following. This play was followed by *Fedayn*, which was an advance on the Palestinian documentary *Vorrei morire* . . . in that La Comune worked directly with eight members of the Popular Democratic Front for the Liberation of Palestine, who appeared in the play, which was subtitled 'The Palestinian People's Struggle through its Culture and Songs'. A series of autobiographical accounts by Palestinian guerillas (translated into Italian by Franca Rame) with mimes and songs, the play's support of the PLF line in the interests of internationalism provoked considerable controversy among the Italian left, especially for its criticism of the Al Fatah movement. La Comune eventually issued a statement admitting they had 'confronted the internal problems of the Palestinian resistance movement too directly, in a situation of general lack of information.'[28] This play was followed by another documentary drama about the death of Feltrinelli, *Traliccio di stato* (*State Pylon*), written and staged by La Comune and the mime Albert Vidal, and in which Fo's role was that of an advisor.

At about this time La Comune's political activities extended into the area of providing help for political prisoners detained under suspicion of terrorist and related offences. This organisation, called Soccorso Rosso (Red Aid), in which Franca Rame was particularly militant until the early 1980s, wrote letters and sent packages and books to prisoners as well as maintaining contacts with their families and lawyers, and had about 3,000 members culled from La Comune's audiences. Funds for the organisation were collected after performances at the via Colletta. Needless to say, La Comune did not receive state funding, but were sufficiently popular and successful to be able to donate the proceeds of many of their performances to occupied factories and other deserving causes. In 1972 legal proceedings were brought against Fo and Rame, accusing them of using Soccorso rosso to foment prison revolts, but charges were later dropped due to lack of evidence.

La Commune's political activities during this period tended to overshadow their theatrical output, which largely consisted of cannibalised, revamped versions of previous Fo plays. *Ordine per DI0.000.000.000 (Order, for Mammon's Sake*, 1972) was an example of this, being an extended rewrite of *Il Telaio*, expanding it into two acts, and adding two extra characters, a prostitute and a revolutionary son, as well as more intensified attacks on the PCI. Although it was generally considered to be one of Fo's weakest plays, it is worth recording comments made in a review of the play by Dacia Maraini, a feminist novelist and playwright, and founder of Italy's first feminist theatre, La Maddelena in Rome. Maraini's comments indicate the unique position which Fo's work occupied in contemporary Italian political theatre, which was virtually a vacuum:

> It can't be said that Fo hasn't dealt with current topics in this play. If an Italian theatre exists, it should be produced exactly like this. This is theatre which takes a stand, and uses polemics, both cultural and political, insults, revolt, gripes, falling in love, rational and reckless frenzy, self-observation and observation of others. If there were a hundred plays like this every year, one could say the Italian theatre was alive. Probably ninety-nine of these plays could be discarded. . . . In compensation, however, we would have the delight of feeling that inside the enormous, semi-paralysed, gaudy but bloodless body of Italian theatre, hot and surging blood had started to flow again. Since there are unfortunately only two or three plays like this a year instead of a hundred, they end up being regarded with suspicion, from the viewpoint of the orderliness and refinement of museum theatre.[29]

Political repression against La Comune was growing alongside the political controversy of their plays, and in the summer of 1972 they were evicted from the via Colletta due to police pressure on the owners of the building, and left without a base for two years. Disagreements within La Comune were also beginning to become more apparent. Later Fo and Rame were also evicted from their appartment by a Jewish landlord who refused to have tenants who were sympathisers of Fedayn.

Three years after the Piazza Fontana bombs, Fo wrote an updated version of events with the intention of continuing the 'counter-information' of *Accidental Death of an Anarchist. Pum, Pum! Chi è? La Polizia! (Knock Knock! Who's There? Police!)*, which was written in a week, continued the story of police cover-ups and corruption since the Pinelli affair, documenting the events which had occurred since the previous play. The sequel is set inside the Ministry of the Interior, and Fo plays the part of the Chief of Confidential Affairs, in a performance in which he remains on stage throughout the play. *Pum, Pum!* lacks the fictional, farcical mechanism of its predecessor, being more of a comic documentary reading (in which all the actors had their scripts on stage, a distancing device which Arden also insisted on for his *Non-Stop Connolly Cycle*), and is predominantly a 'word play'. It moves at a frantic pace, as phone calls, telegrams and telexes come into the ministry announcing the latest turn of events, and there is this time no attempt to fictionalise the protagonists of these events, who are referred to by name throughout. 'We want to demonstrate,' said Fo in his spoken introduction to the play, 'with this morass of news and information, that the state is criminal, and there's no getting away from it. We believe there is only one valid signpost – the one Lenin gave us when he said we have to smash the state.'[30] Despite occasional scrappiness, the play was virtually a monologue for Fo in which he drew analogies between the hypocrisy of Christian Democrat politicians and Scapino's performance in Molière's *Tartuffe*, demonstrating the thesis that Italian politics, being a form of theatre in itself, needed no theatrical mediation. *Pum, Pum!* led to further political harrassment of La Commune – after opening in Rome while Valpreda's trial was going on, they moved to the Cinema Rossini in the outskirts of Milan, which they were forced to occupy after police put pressure on the owner to evict the 'subversive' Fo. The poster of the play, drawn and designed by Fo, showing a blood-spattered family (somewhat in the style of a Ralph Steadman cartoon), was charged with 'offences against the armed forces'.

In March 1973 Franca Rame was abducted by a group of fascists at gunpoint, dumped in a van, raped, beaten up, burnt with cigarettes and slashed with razor blades and then left in a park. She was later to use this experience as the basis for a monologue, *Non mi muovo, non urlo, sono senza voce* (*I Can't Move, I Can't Scream, My Voice is Gone*) which was premiered in London in May 1983. At the time, she prepared an 'intervention' play called *Basta con i fascisti!* (*Stop the Fascists!*), an audiovisual piece comparing fascism past and present, which she toured around La Comune's circuit. La Comune also tried to organise anti-fascist demonstrations, including one in the Milan Palazzo dello Sport, but were refused permission by the local council. Meanwhile, dissension within La Comune was getting worse, recalling the situation before the break-up of Nuova Scena. Eventually, a faction who were members of *Avanguardia Operaia* accused the Fos of suffocating the creative activities of the others and took control of the company. The situation reflected the inevitable conflicts between Fo's status as an actor and the political line of the group. This conflict was summed up as follows in 1975 by the American translator and critic of Fo, Suzanne Cowan:

> as intensely involved in political work as the troupe is at all times, one cannot avoid the feeling that its effective communication with the masses of working people is to some extent obstructed and overshadowed by the presence of a great performer. No matter how democratic, how sincerely 'anti-status' he may be, a Star must in some ways inhibit the performance of mundane, everyday political tasks. And it is only through such unglamorous organisation work that political change can, in the last analysis, take place. Revolutions nearly always have their flamboyant heroes, moments of pageantry, theatrical climaxes. But revolutions are not *theatre*. At times Fo seems to lose sight of this distinction, and tends to upstage both the working people who make up the majority of the mass movement of which his theatre is a part, and the members of his own company.[31]

This may well be the case, but since Fo's profession is that of an actor and playwright, and he has become one of the most accomplished and talented members of this profession in Europe since the war, it tended to be his plays and his performances which drew crowds and made La Comune the political force that it was. In the event, other members of La Comune took possession of the vast amount of theatre equipment which the Fos had accumulated in twenty years of theatre activity and after the split produced little theatrical work, being racked by further splits, leaving the Fos to proceed on their own from scratch.

The 'roadshows' and Fo's arrest

Fo and Rame, together with the Sicilian *cantastorie* Cicciu Busacca, who had
participated in a third edition of *Ci ragiono e canto* in 1973 (a second had been
produced in 1969 with a more contemporary focus, adapting industrial workers'
songs), bringing an authentically popular element into the songs, and Piero
Sciotto, who became a key figure in Fo's company as actor-manager until 1981,
continued their activities on a reduced scale, maintaining the banner 'La
Comune'. They began performing a series of what Fo has referred to as *messe
da campo* (roadshows), following the example of the *Teatro Campesino*, touring
around Lombardy and Veneto performing to local people and at demonstrations
and political trials. The main play they performed was a short piece entitled
Mamma Togni, a monologue performed by Franca Rame about a peasant
woman weighing more than 90 kilos whose husband and son had been shot by
the Germans during the war, and who single-handedly broke up a fascist
meeting in Milan, physically attacking the speakers, and became a 'mother' to
the Italian anti-fascist movement. Then, in September 1973, Allende was killed
in Chile and Pinochet's military government took power. The 'new' La
Comune decided to write and perform a play on the subject, at a time when
fears of a similar coup in Italy (which had frequently been expressed by
Feltrinelli) were still being expressed. The result was one of the most dramatic
plays Fo has produced, not in terms of its form or even its content, which were
rough and ready, in the 'roadshow' style, but in terms of the impact it had on
audiences. *La Guerra del popolo in Cile* (*The People's War in Chile*) was
constructed along similar lines to *Vorrei morire . . .* , with performances of first
hand accounts of the Chilean situation, songs written by Fo about the Colonels,
Santiago stadium and Victor Jara, while the play incorporated *Mamma Togni*, a
ballad by Busacca about a unicorn who symbolises the need for revolution, and
a monologue by Franca Rame in the guise of a Chilean Christian Democrat
'procuress' who backs the *coup d'état*, weeping and invoking the pope. The play
toured extensively around Italy, and restored the considerable audiences La
Comune had previously enjoyed, largely due to the controversy and scandal
provoked by the final part of the play, which Chiara Valentini has described as
follows:

The first sign that something was wrong was a voice with a southern accent
which suddenly burst from the battery microphone Dario Fo was wearing
round his neck. 'Hello, hello. This is Dragon. Orders from Dragon to move
the squad north.' This interrupted Fo's monologue about Augusto Pinochet,
and he blinked and tried to explain it away: 'These cops are everywhere.
They even pump their radio messages through our microphones.' Then he
carried on as if nothing had happened. After a while the interferences started
up again. Agitated orders and coded sentences came through. Suddenly a
youth shouted through a megaphone, 'The telephones aren't working'. Then a
voice from the stalls said 'The radio's gone dead.' 'Come on, comrades, it's
nothing. Just keep calm', exhorted Fo from the stage, but his voice became
more and more strained as he pressed on with his lines. Someone in the
audience seemed to get an attack of nerves, and started up a long monologue:
'It's not as if we're in Greece or Chile. We've got a Communist Party, the
unions – a coup's impossible.' Tension spread through the audience. Suddenly
a police inspector came in, and leapt on to the stage: 'I must interrupt this

show. The following persons are to accompany me to the police station.' He began listing the names of the most well-known representatives of the extreme left present in the auditorium. The tension reached breaking point, and various people started muttering 'coup d'état'. Someone started singing the Internazionale, and immediately everyone leapt to their feet, raised clenched fists, and sang at the top of their voices in what they thought would be their last expression of freedom. (At this point the 'police inspector', another 'policeman', and the members of the audience who had started the 'incident' got up on stage and joined in the singing.) The audience were stunned for a moment, then they realised that they'd been had. In Turin a youth ate ten pages of his diary, which were full of what he thought were compromising addresses. In Merano a student tried to jump out of a window, breaking the glass. In Nuoro, where two coach loads of Sardinian shepherds had arrived from Orgosolo, someone flashed a cheese knife when they saw the fake inspector.[32]

While the play was being performed in Sassari, Sardinia, in November 1973, Fo, who had refused to allow 'real' police to enter the theatre, was arrested for 'verbally violent resistance of a public officer', and the rest of the company organised a demonstration outside the Sassari police station until Fo was released 24 hours later. The event created considerable polemics in the Italian press and mass media, where Fo became the centre of attention, opinions about him tending to fall into two camps. Among the number of intellectuals interviewed at the time about Fo, there were those like Natalia Ginzburg and Franco Zeffirelli who saw him as a talented actor who had been led astray by revolutionary politics. As Zeffirelli stated:

> Fo is a very great actor, director and clown, the last great clown of our time. I don't judge Fo's works from a political point of view; to me it's enough that his work is good, which it is, on an artistic level . . . Dario Fo's plays are liked much more by the bourgeoisie than by workers.[33]

The other, more partisan, point of view was that Fo was predominantly a political animal who was becoming dangerous to the Italian political establishment because of his capacity of drawing enormous crowds and engaging them in political debates which attacked the government and state authorities; in short the view that Fo was being treated as a 'subversive'. As Fo's lawyer, Sandro Canestrini, stated after his arrest:

> The fact is that Dario Fo has for some years been more than just an actor. He's a politician, a man engaged in a tough battle against the authorities. It's logical that the authorities are using all their weapons, even the most reckless and openly illegal, to silence him.[34]

As La Comune was still a private club, under Italian law the police had no right to enter the theatre in Sassari. A relatively minor incident became blown up in the Italian mass media at precisely the time when Fo and La Comune needed the free publicity, which put them back into the forefront of public attention and drew more audiences to his plays for both his formidable powers as an actor and for the revolutionary political line of his plays.

4: POLITICAL THEATRE ON SHIFTING GROUND 1974-1983

The Palazzina Liberty and *Can't Pay? Won't Pay!*

All the revolutionaries and militant workers of Milan got into the habit of coming to the Palazzina (a theatre or a non-theatre, according to your point of view), where state authorities were . . . subjected to mass criticism, all as well orchestrated by Fo as his plays. Although the Palazzina no longer serves this purpose, due to the vagaries of the (Italian left) movement, militant theatre continues. (Piero Sciotto, 'Con Dario Fo', March 1977)

After Fo had successfully toured *Mistero buffo* in France in 1974, La Comune, which had become 'Il Collectivo teatrale "La Comune" diretto da Dario Fo', set about finding a base for itself in Rome. They presented a list of 20 disused buildings owned by the Milan council to a Socialist Party assessor, and obtained permission to examine them. They then chose the Palazzina Liberty, a dilapidated, rat-infested art nouveau building in the middle of a public garden in Porta Vittoria, a working-class area of Milan, and with the Socialist councillor's blessing, took it over and started cleaning it up. Within days there was an uproar from Christian Democrat members of the council, who accused Fo of being an 'enemy of the regime' and tried to revoke the permission. La Comune decided to occupy the building, and local volunteers began helping to make it habitable. The council replied by erecting a fence round the building, and La Comune produced a series of leaflets ('The rats thank the DC'), demonstrations, rallies of up to 10,000 people, and various fund-raising activities which included a performance of *Mistero buffo* in the gardens to 15,000 people. 'Occupying the Palazzina Liberty is one of the most important theatrical events we have ever staged'[1] Fo commented at the time. La Comune obtained permission via a court order brought against them by the council to remain temporarily in the building, and they set about turning it into a local community centre. Plans were developed which included a library, day-nursery, conference centre, and theatre and audiovisual workshops, and La Comune hung a red flag from the roof – a gesture which would have been inconceivable at Arnold Wesker's Centre 42 or Joan Littlewood's Theatre Workshop. La Comune's first theatrical offering at their new home, however, *Porta e Belli contro il potere* (*Porta and Belli against the Authorities*), a series of polemical poetry readings, was deemed inappropriate for the theatre's new popular audience, and taken off after a week.

During the summer of 1974, Fo worked on a play about a series of events which had occurred in Marghera, Turin and the south of Italy, and became known as *autoriduzione* or 'appropriation', within a movement of 'civil disobedience'. Fo was subsequently accused of using the play to foment a similar popular movement in Milan, since it predicted the spread of the phenomenon. People had refused to pay the rising prices in supermarkets, public transport, gas and electricity bills, insisting on paying what they considered to be a 'fair price'. Italy was going through a severe economic crisis – there was a large deficit in the balance of payments, exports had diminished, and workers were being laid off all over the country. The clout of the trade unions, who had achieved a number of improvements for workers during the 'hot autumn' of 1969, was beginning to pale as employers fought back through the Confederation of Industry, claiming that the 'cost of work' was too high. In Italy, employers are responsible for paying health and social security contributions for their workers, as well as a proportion of their sickness benefit and a 'thirteenth month' salary in December, and consequently many of them were tightening their belts and putting workers into *cassa integrazione*, a system under which laid-off workers receive 80 per cent of their wages from the state until they are either re-employed or made definitively redundant. During this time of rising prices and falling employment, the PCI was busy pursuing a policy of collaboration with the Christian Democrats at governmental level – the famous 'historic compromise'. They had also interpreted events in Chile in terms of a need to declare war against radical, extremist elements, and pursue a moderate line of reformism which was neither anti-USA nor anti-USSR. 'Civil disobedience' and *autoriduzione* was a grass-roots movements which was a better substitute for striking – as Antonia explained in Fo's new play, *Non si paga! Non si paga!* (*Can't Pay? Won't Pay!*):

Some workers who'd appeared from a nearby factory started shouting . . . 'It's your right to pay the right prices . . . It's just like a strike, but it's even better than a strike, since we workers always get our pay docked when we go on strike. In this type of strike, at last it's the bosses who have to pay for it! . . . Don't pay! Don't pay! And that goes for all the money you've cheated us out of over the years we've been shopping here.[2]

Can't Pay? Won't Pay! is probably Fo's most well-known play – it is certainly the one which has received most productions outside Italy. It is his most comic and entertaining work in terms of its plot complications and reversals of situation, smoothly incorporating political points into the farcical mechanism, and keeping the sometimes 'preachy' long speeches of some of his other plays to a minimum. Like most of his plays since 1968, it was written as a response to a political need and dealt with a specific political situation. Fo and La Comune discussed the text of the piece with groups of workers before presenting it in public, in order to ensure it dealt accurately with what was a particularly working-class predicament (and several changes were made as a result of these discussions). As Fo explained in his preface to the play, even the farcical form (for which he was criticised from some quarters for returning to the theatrical mechanism of his 'bourgeois' plays) is connected with a basic need:

As in old Neapolitan and Venetian popular farces . . . here the starting point, the fundamental impetus, is hunger. The initial, instinctive solution in which everyone takes care of himself in resolving the atavistic problem of appetite develops into a need to work collectively, to get organised and fight together – not just for survival, but to live in a world where there are less brightly-lit shop windows, less motorways, and no government corruption, no thieves – the real thieves, the big fish, that is – and where there is justice, justice for all.[3]

This basic revolutionary message of the play, also inherent in its plot situation, is sometimes obscured in foreign productions which obviously lack the specific, collective social background of the original (including the squatting of the Palazzina Liberty). In terms of Fo's work, the play lies closest to 'Zanni's Monologue' in *Mistero buffo*, in which a starving peasant tries to eat himself, and to the gallows humour of *Accidental Death*. In terms of English farce, there is a danger of reducing it to the slick, middle-class boulevard comedy of Alan Ayckbourn rather than to the sick, outrageous, but basically working-class humour of Joe Orton's *Loot* (with which it shares a coffin as a repository for criminal deeds), a play which is also in its way about 'justice'.

Can't Pay? Won't Pay! is set in a 'modest working-class flat' to which Antonia returns from the local supermarket after indulging in some *autoriduzione* with her fellow-housewives, which has got so chaotic and out-of-hand that it has turned into outright looting, curbed only by the arrival of the police. The play is Fo's first feminist comedy insofar as it deals directly with the problems working-class women have in running a household in times of economic crisis. Also, most of the far-fetched and farcical explanations used to disguise the real reasons behind the play's bizarre events have a social and political origin. After Antonia off-loads her stolen goods on to her neighbour Margherita, for example, she explains the latter's consequent 'pregnancy' by explaining that since Margherita is a catholic, she can't take the pill, and has hitherto had to tape up her stomach to avoid being sacked by her employer on grounds of maternity. Her subterfuge is a result of her husband Giovanni's legalitarian, line-toeing PCI view of *autoriduzione*:

> This miserable flotsam of society, breaking the law and being provocative. They're playing right into the bosses' hands – now they'll be able to go round saying workers are thieves and the dregs of society and should be thrown into prison . . .[4]

He states that if he caught his wife doing such a thing he would kill her, and then take advantage of the newly-passed Italian divorce law. Ironically, when the police arrive, searching the area (which contains more than a thousand working-class families), Giovanni opens the door to a Constable who could almost have stepped out of a play by Howard Brenton, in that he is a Maoist with a degree, and in full sympathy with *autoriduzione*. Giovanni is taken aback, since his tolerance for the police extends only as far as the PCI MP Amendola's view of them as necessary 'sons of the people', to which the Constable retorts:

> We're no sons of the people . . . we're slaves . . . the slaves and thugs of the bosses. We're the ones who have to apply their laws, and protect their racketeering and their bombs![5]

This leads Giovanni to the paranoid conclusion that the Constable is an *agent provocateur*. He is subsequently convinced of the economic justifications for *autoriduzione*, however, when Margherita's husband Luigi reveals that the factory where they both work is being closed down and they are being put on *cassa integrazione*. When the two men encounter the Maoist Constable who is assisting at a collision between two lorries carrying illegal bags of sugar and flour, they are persuaded to steal some of the goods and 'save them from destruction'. Borrowing a stratagem from the Vietcong, they hide their stolen sacks in a coffin. Meanwhile their wives have been caught with their bellies full by the *carabiniere*, trying to stash their stolen goods, and Antonia has to concoct a story about the fictitious feast of 'Saint Eulalia', an old woman whom God made pregnant and whose disbelieving husband was struck blind. This covering story is almost immediately substantiated by a power cut, and the *carabiniere* is struck unconscious while trying to find the door in the dark. The men hide the coffin in the same closet where the women have hidden the *carabiniere*, believing him to be dead. The situation is resolved neatly – unusually for Fo – with Giovanni confessing his own appropriation to his wife, and the *carabiniere* emerging from the closet believing he has become pregnant. The two couples then witness a battle in the streets below between the police and the local women, which ends with the police withdrawing. They then discuss the political consequences of the revolutionary course of events, which Giovanni sees – at least in the original version of the play – in the Utopian contexts of 'a world where you can even see the sky and the plants producing flowers, and where there's spring, and girls laughing and singing.[6]

Despite the fact that *Can't Pay? Won't Pay!* became Fo's most popular play abroad, critical response to it in Italy was surprisingly tepid. Many critics saw a conflict between the superbly crafted farcical plot and the play's political statements and Marxist analyses, although this is far less evident than in many of Fo's other plays. (At this point it must be said that the English version directed by Robert Walker in London was exemplary in pruning the play's occasional verbal excesses and tightening up the situation in a way that is at times even better than the original.) Lanfranco Binni, normally one of Fo's most sympathetic critics, saw the play as a ponderously didactic attempt to incorporate topical political arguments into a farce in which there was a considerable imbalance between Fo's protagonist and the other characters, and which was ambiguous in its treatment of 'appropriation'.

Substituting another actor for Fo possibly corrects this imbalance, although the character of Antonia is sufficiently fully drawn, while the play's plot is sufficiently ingenious to carry the political weight of the situation. To see the play as an incitement to theft would be to ignore the deliberate comic and satirical exaggeration which Fo employs in virtually all his farces, particularly in the comic resolution of *Can't Pay? Won't Pay!*, which stands traditional farce on its head.

Largely as a result of the play's popularity abroad – it was in the repertoire of the Berliner Ensemble for a number of years as well as running for almost two years in London's West End – Fo produced a revised, updated version of the piece at the Palazzina Liberty in September 1980. At the time, 24,000 Fiat workers had been put on *cassa integrazione*, and Giovanni and Luigi became Fiat workers, while Fo added references to the political situation in Poland (where workers were literally 'on their knees') and Afghanistan, while making jokes about Pope Wojtyla. Responses to this new version of the play were again far from favourable, and not helped by the lack of the political background of the original version. The new edition of the play appeared at a time when the enthusiasm and positivism of left wing politics in Italy had eroded, whereas it had previously nourished and sustained Fo's work in a way which had given it a topical popularity and made him a major spokesman for the Italian left. By 1980, the extra-parliamentary left had become dissipated, due to the increase in terrorism and the widespread arrests of left-wing groups accused of sympathising with terrorism – the case of Toni Negri being a prime example.* As *La Repubblica*'s theatre critic Ugo Volli commented, Fo's political rallying calls ran the risk of coming across as empty rhetoric:

> We listened to the same old arguments the other evening at the Palazzina Liberty, among the usual above-capacity crowd, with growing embarrassment and irritation. There was something, or rather a number of things, which made them tired and empty, the fruit of pure rhetoric without an object. The crowd was huge, yes, but different. Not the younger brothers and sisters of the audience of six years ago, nor even the same people six years on. Rather it was almost a normal audience, left wing but not militant, mixed in with theatregoers . . . Then, obviously, there was the historical context. Mass illegality, *autoriduzioni* and the like are not only all over and done with, but forgotten issues after years of bloodshed. Ideas like socialism and revolution and the working class have become much more complex (if not confused), and seeking an impetus for action has now become somewhat difficult.[7]

Volli's comments are symptomatic of what had happened to the Italian left since the mid 1970s, and further proof of the 'throwaway' nature of most of Fo's plays, which made the re-working of *Can't Pay? Won't Pay!* something of an exercise in nostalgia. It was thus ironic that Fo, an exponent of journalistic, topical, documentary political theatre, was proposed as a candidate for the Nobel Prize for Literature in February 1975, by members of the Pen Club, including Simone de Beauvoir and Alberto Moravia – sure proof of the durability of his plays and their place in theatre history.

Political pamphlets

Fo's next play was another 'throwaway' piece written as a response to the Italian parliamentary elections of June 1975. Parts of it were even used in an election TV transmission by the left-wing party Pdup,† who were at the time connected to the *Manifesto* group but also attached to the PCI. In it, Fo elaborated his dwarf trick of *La Signora è da buttare* in a caricature of the Christian Democrat government minister – and sometime Prime Minister – Amintore Fanfani. In

---

Toni Negri: a writer and lecturer in Political Science at the University of Padua and the Sorbonne, and the leading figure of the ultra-left *Autonomia* movement in Italy. He was arrested and imprisoned – charged with 'subversion of the state' – during the wave of arrests of the *Autonomi* on 7 April, 1979. In 1983, while still in prison, he was elected a member of parliament representing the Italian Radical Party (PRI), and released from prison. After a motion was passed in parliament (from which the Radical Party abstained) to have him re-imprisoned, he fled to France. In April 1984, he was sentenced to life imprisonment plus thirty years, under a number of charges including that of 'inspiring' various acts of terrorism.
†Pdup: *Partito Democratico per Unità Proletaria*, a splinter party from the PCI.

Fanfani rapito (*Fanfani Kidnapped*), Fo achieved a theatrical *tour de force* in performance terms, his hands in a pair of shoes, while the mime Arturo Corso performed physical gestures behind him, enabling him to fly through the air and even walk on walls. The play is an election pamphlet, exaggerating the already somewhat comic, buffoonesque antics of Fanfani in a plot in which he is kidnapped, not by the Red Brigades, but as part of a scheme by the then Prime Minister Giulio Andreotti to gain public sympathy and support for the Christian Democrats. As Fo stated at the time, 'The play isn't intended to demonstrate that Fanfani is a villain and the DC his victim. It explains that Christian Democracy as a whole has represented a moral outrage for thirty years in its arrogance, its contempt for the people, and its embezzlements.'[8] Subjected to an interrogation by his tame captors, Fanfani offers a confession of all the 'crimes' of 30 years of Christian Democracy, and accuses his colleagues of various kinds of corruption. His kidnappers, faced with a suspicious mass media, are forced to send Fanfani's ear (J. Paul Getty style) to the Italian public to prove the kidnapping is genuine. As a result, they have to move their hideout, and Fanfani is transported, in drag, to an abortion clinic run by nuns. An attack of nerves causes his stomach to swell up with intestinal gas and he is given a Ceasarian operation which produces a blackshirt fascist puppet. He then ascends to heaven, which, is worse than earth, and undergoes a trial at the hands of a guerilla-Madonna (Franca Rame) and a revolutionary Christ, and is kicked out for his political crimes. The Madonna predicts the defeat of the Christian Democrats and the victory of the working class, while Fanfani wakes up in his office to discover that the entire proceedings have been a bad dream. At this point, a group of real kidnappers break in and drag him away, acting on Andreotti's orders. Although the Madonna's predictions did not come true, the left gained a considerable number of votes in the elections.

Since the kidnapping and murder of Aldo Moro in 1978 (about which Fo was to attempt another play), *Fanfani Rapito* might appear in bad taste, which indicates the tendency of many of Fo's plays not to outlive the dramatic political situations they comment on, although *Fanfani Rapito* is a more extreme example than most of a play written for a specific occasion. It is worth noting that the play opened simultaneously with Giorgio Strehler's production of Goldoni's *Campiello* (later done at the National Theatre in London) at the Piccolo Teatro. The contrast between Fo's makeshift political satire and the glossy, carnivalesque Venice of Strehler's stylish, lush but rather empty production could not have been more extreme, and illustrates how far Fo had diverged from his earlier work with the Piccolo, which he now saw as an example of:

> cultural colonialism. It's centralism – they put on plays for the centre, then move around with a colonialist mentality, putting on three, four or five plays, all of them equally centrist, not done for *that particular place*, not creating plays which people need. *The Three Sisters* has nothing to offer the people of Quarto Oggiaro, but they are interested in what we have to say about appropriation and class struggle . . . (The Piccolo) does Brecht with tinsel . . . There's a very intelligent lighting operator at the Piccolo . . . who used to say, 'well, tonight I'm off to light *The Caucasian Chalk Cherry Orchard*. He'd got the message.[9]

Meanwhile, Carmelo Bene, the king of Italian avant-garde theatre, was gaining a reputation in Europe with his semi-pornographic *S.A.D.E.*, an exercise in theatrical megalomania which was to lead to a series of unintentionally comic 'adaptations' of Shakespeare's tragedies. The Palazzina Liberty, on the other hand, had become a community theatre which attracted non-theatregoers on a scale at least ten times that of the Half Moon Theatre in the East End of London, and where workers, students and local people came for the political content of Fo's plays as much as for their author's creative genius, rather than for strictly theatregoing reasons.

In June 1975, Fo, Rame and other members of La Comune went to China, an experience which Fo was enthusiastic about, particularly for the examples of popular theatre he saw. He recalled a Shanghai storyteller's representation of a tram journey through the city:

> A bit like me in *Mistero buffo*, he reconstructed people's comments, even if they were banal at times, and expressed their concerns – their discussions about work, wages and struggles against Lin Piao. He portrayed a character who thought Confucius was a party director, and another one who hadn't got the gist of the latest party directives. All this was done in a grotesque vein, accompanied by drum rolls which set the beat of the occasion.[10]

In a discussion with the Artistic Company of Jinan, a group of dancers, acrobats and actors ten times the size of La Comune, who performed in factories, shipyards, mines and army barracks, pursuing a Maoist cultural line, Fo found many points in common with the work of La Comune. On his return to Italy, he took issue with Michelangelo Antonioni, accusing the film director of reflecting only a dignified, surface view of Chinese reality in his controversial documentary *Cina – Chung Kuo* (*China – The Centre of the World*, 1974), and of presenting an unduly pessimistic, Western intellectual's view of the Chinese way of life. Fo's response to China was essentially optimistic, seeing the vestiges of the cultural revolution in terms of an ironic, satirical, anti-official popular culture which he related to his own situation in Italy. He attempted to write a play about his experiences in China, but was unable to find a suitable theatrical form, and it was not until two years later that he was to use the theatrical material he picked up in China in his monologue *The Story of the Tigress*. In the meantime, Fo continued his research into the *giullari*, writing and directing a series of mediaeval and popular Sicilian sketches and ballads performed by Cicciu Busacca and his two daughters in the style of the Sicilian *cantastorie*, under the title of *La Giullarata*. This piece included 'The Origin of the *Giullari*' from *Mistero buffo*, and is closer to the various editions of *Ci ragiono e canto* and Fo's experiments in popular musical forms than to his political plays.

In 1976 Fo returned to the political arena of the Palazzina Liberty to confront the drug problem, which, arriving later in Italy than in most other European countries, was rapidly becoming a bigger problem than elsewhere due to Mafia involvement in drug manufacturing and racketeering and the putative use of drugs indirectly by state authorities to erode the forces of the revolutionary left. Some militant left groups, like Ananguardia Operaia and the Movimento Lavoratori per il Socialismo, had even gone to the extent of setting up vigilante groups who went around Italian cities beating up drug dealers and mounting anti-drug campaigns. Fo saw drugs as 'a class problem: rich people consume and use drugs, while poor people are used and consumed by drugs.'[11]

In the play, *La marjuana della mamma è la più bella* (*Mother's Marijuana is the Best*), Fo again uses a farcical format, in which Grandpa (Fo), and a classic, fat, southern Italian *mamma* (Rame), pretend to be drug addicts and dealers in order to teach their son Luigi a lesson, since they have discovered that he has been smoking marijuana. Fo set out to attack the Italian press and government's 'censorship' of the drug problem, and to discuss it in social, cultural and political as well as medical and scientific terms, but later considered the play as not having taken a sufficiently solid stand on the problem. The play's main concern is to expose the complete failure of the Italian authorities to deal with the problem in medical and scientific terms, preferring to criminalise it, while thousands of housewives continue to resort to 'mother's little helpers'. In his preface to the play, Fo stated that he had

> tried to involve people by entertaining them, making them laugh until they get gooseflesh if possible. We think that the intelligence that operates through satire and mockery, along with the rationality of irony, is, when all's said and done, the best and healthiest of all drugs, particularly when obtuse authorities are continually trying to repress every citizen who has ideas about freedom.[12]

In fact the play succeeds best as comic entertainment, using devices of disguise and deception similar to those of *Can't Pay? Won't Pay!* The somewhat parochial political context of the play, however, renders it of less interest than its predecessor, even though both plays deal with relatively universal problems. In 1980 the Belt and Braces Roadshow, after their London success with *Accidental Death of an Anarchist*, commissioned from me a translation of *Mother's Marijuana is the Best*, but this English version was never performed, due partly to the transfer of *Anarchist* to the West End, and partly to the difficulty of making the play relevant to English audiences. It is a long-winded piece, which at one point refers directly to its own 'preaching',[13] while borrowing a lot of its slapstick stage business from Fo's earlier farces.

One of the play's most hilarious sequences, however, would appear to derive from the Shanghai storyteller Fo enthused about. Grandpa relates how he took LSD by mistake (for aspirin), and hallucinated a farcical tram journey in his wardrobe, which ends up in the Milan police station where he meets Pinelli in mid-air. This is Fo at his imaginative, improvisional, self-quoting best, and the speech generates an ingenious train-journey metaphor which runs throughout the play. Another notable feature of the play is that the PCI Grandpa is given some convincing and sympathetic lines which describe the current situation in the Italian revolutionary left at a time when, according to the statistics the play quotes, 65 per cent of people under 24 had been unable to find their first job.[14]

> Wonderfully united, you new left groups, aren't you? And then you complain we don't give you any credibility in the PCI! You're riddled with sectarianism – beating the shit out of one another over a load of shit![15]

The play was criticised for being too ponderously didactic and for neglecting the political symptoms which were to lead to a renewal of the revolutionary spirit of. the Italian left in 1977, when there were often violent clashes between students and police, and the Autonomia movement, of which Toni Negri was a prominent figure, began to make its presence felt at a conference of 30,000 left-wing militants in Bologna.

Return to TV and *Female Parts*

After a 14 year absence, 1977 was the year of Fo's triumphant return to Italian television – the result of a change in the administration of RAI brought about by the left's gains in the elections of the previous year. Two 'cycles' of Fo's plays were shown on the non-religious, socialist-inclined second channel of RAI, and they represented a valuable retrospective of Fo's work, although his more politically contentious plays like *Accidental Death of an Anarchist, Can't Pay? Won't Pay!* and *Fanfani Rapito* were not included in the transmissions. These plays were subsequently filmed by La Commune in order to have a permanent record of them. The two different versions of *Mistero buffo* which went out on TV nevertheless managed to cause considerable controversy, as we have seen in Chapter One. Two editions of *Ci ragiono e canto* were also screened, together with *Settimo: ruba un po' meno, Isabella . . .*, and a new, updated version of *La signora è da buttare*, adding references to Johnson, Nixon and Ford, and a sequence in which Fo plays a dwarf representing Saint George fighting against the dragon, as well as a virtuoso number in which he plays a trombone. Fo and Rame also put together a new play for the TV series, where for the first time they directly confronted women's problems, *Parliamo di donne (Let's Talk about Women)*. This was an attempt to give Franca Rame a series of roles which were not the usual 'support' roles which she had played in most of Fo's work prior to the 1970s, and to deal with the condition of women. Although Rame denies being a militant feminist (and the show was criticised for simply presenting female roles rather than exploring female problems), *Parliamo di donne* was a kind of women's version of *Il dito nell'occhio*, being a collection of sketches and songs (including *Mamma Togni* and *Michele Lu Lanzone* which were lifted from two previous Fo plays) dealing with situations like abortion, the absence of actresses in the Elizabethan theatre, the holy family and the like. One piece stood out in particular – entitled *Il risveglio (Waking Up)*, it was a monologue dealing with a working-class mother who wakes up and goes through her morning chores with her baby before going off to work, only to discover that she has lost her key. She reconstructs her actions throughout the previous day and evening, including the argument she has had with her husband (who is asleep in bed), until she finally discovers where the key is. Finally she realises that it is Sunday and that her entire rigmarole of actions has been unnecessary. The play presents a realistic, inside view of the predicament of many working-class mothers in Italian cities:

> We slave away like pack-horses and never even get a moment to ourselves. Is this what marriage is all about? Has it ever entered your head that I might have problems too? Do you ever ask me if I'm tired, or if I'd like a hand? Who cooks your dinner? I do. Who does the dishes afterwards? I do. Who does the shopping? I do. Who does all the financial somersaults to survive until the end of the month? And then I have to hold down a job on top of all that![16]

The fact that this tirade avoids being rhetorical by coming in the context of the woman's reconstruction of her argument with her husband – an argument which is at least partially resolved, indicates the near-naturalism of the piece, which is also not without its comic aspects.

Later in 1977, the Fos collaborated on a series of five monologues performed by Franca Rame under the title *Tutta casa, letto e chiesa (All House, Bed and*

Church), which indicted the classic traditional Italian male view of women. Over the next six years these plays were re-elaborated, transformed and reconstructed until they were unrecognisable, in the context of a one-woman show which Franca Rame toured all over Italy and Europe, achieving an acclaim which almost paralleled that of Fo's *Mistero buffo*. In constructing the play, which resulted from a series of discussions with women in factories and research into women's 'testimonies' throughout Italy, and was then tried out in front of a women's collective, Franca Rame played a more prominent role than usual as a writer, sketching out situations which were then put into dramatic form by Fo. The plays were a reversal of the second-order role Rame had always played in La Comune, and through which she was able to identify with the female characters – who extend across different class boundaries – she performs:

> I've understood completely what the condition of women and wives involves, especially that of the wife of a famous actor like Fo. It means always being put in second place in relation to a man, and being judged as incapable of any autonomous choice.[17]

Since she began performing *Tutta casa, letto e chiesa*, Rame has become independent of her previous collaboration with Fo. She has performed in only two of Fo's plays since 1977, and the couple often tour separately (Fo with various editions of *Mistero buffo*). It is significant that it was Rame, rather than Fo, who was the first to perform in London, at the Riverside Studios in 1982.

The first production of *Tutta casa, letto e chiesa* at the Palazzina Liberty in December 1977 consisted of the five monologues, which lasted 2½ hours, being performed on a virtually bare stage (as in *Mistero buffo*) with only the minimum props and settings required. The sparsity emphasised the 'breaking down of the fourth wall' which Fo had advocated in all his plays since 1968, as well as the 'epic acting' involved in directly presenting (rather than representing) a character, complete with comments and asides to the audience, and avoiding any attempt at a naturalistic portrayal. In *Waking Up*, as we have seen, the pretext for a monologue is the woman's conversation with her baby (which the audience can clearly see is a doll). In the second piece, *Una donna tutta sola* (*A Woman on her Own*), the character presented, a lower-middle-class housewife whose husband locks her in the house to prevent the sexual misdemeanours she is prone to, converses with a new, unseen neighbour. In the longest and most comic of the monologues, the 'woman on her own', who has already survived a couple of suicide attempts, has to contend with the advances of her husband's crippled brother (who watches pornographic films in the next room), a peeping Tom with a telescope, an obscene phone-caller whom she continually confuses with her husband, who is being pursued by a creditor, and her ex-English teacher who is in love with her and tries to break into the house. While she irons to the blaring sound of a radio, record player and cassette recorder, and her brother-in-law hoots the horn on his wheelchair for her attention, her baby cries and the phone rings, she confides frankly in her new neighbour, discussing her sexual problems in a disarmingly comic way:

> Well, I can tell you everything's far from OK as far as me and my husband are concerned – I just can't manage to . . . You know . . . I just don't feel anything. How can I put it . . . That's it – yes – that's a word I can never bring myself to say; I really have to force it out – orgasm. It sounds like the

name of some hideous animal, some sort of squat little monkey halfway
between a mandrill and an orangutang. I get the feeling I've read about one
somewhere in the newspaper: 'a fully grown orgasm has escaped from the
American circus . . . The orgasm was recaptured after a furious struggle with
firemen.' And when people start talking about 'reaching orgasm', it sounds a
bit like catching the tram after you've had to run like hell . . .'[18]

For her projected performance of the show at the Public Theatre in New
York in September 1983, Rame changed the English title to *Adult Orgasm
Escapes from the Zoo*, in acknowledgement that the ingenuous, open and
basically cheerful character of this monologue, who finally slams the door on her
English teacher's hand, shoots the peeping Tom, pushes her brother-in-law
down the stairs in his wheelchair, and sits waiting calmly, rifle in hand, for her
husband to return home, is one of her finest and funniest farcical creations.

The third monologue, *La mamma fricchettona* (*Freak Mother*), was eventually
discarded as it dealt with a typical Italian mother who pursues her son, who has
left home and joined a group of 'Metropolitan Indians'. This libertarian hippie
movement, which flourished briefly in Italy in the mid-1970s (the hippie
phenomenon was late arriving in Italy) soon became outmoded. The play is set
in a confessional in a church where the Mother takes refuge after she has
abandoned her family to become a 'witch mother' to the hippie movement and
discovered drugs and free love, and been denounced to the police by her family
as a result. The play's situation vaguely parallels the generation-reversal of
Mother's Marijuana – as the mother becomes increasingly 'liberated', her son
becomes increasingly conservative. This was followed by a direct confrontation
of women's sexual problems in *The Same Old Story*, which shows that sexism
and male domination are just as prominent in left-wing circles as they are in
other environments:

> Of course I want to make love, but not like a pinball machine, where all you
> have to do is put your money in the slot and my lights light up and you bash
> your balls around ping ping pong pong. Go on then, knock me about as much
> as you like. No, right, if you knock me about I go into tilt. You get the
> picture?[19]

The play begins as a one-sided conversation between a woman and her lover
(who is unseen), and confronts the problems of contraception, abortion,
'phallocracy' and unwanted children. The monologue is mainly taken up by a
rather absurd, scatological 'fairy tale' about a little girl with a doll who uses
swearwords, which is used to prove in a roundabout way that women of all
social classes have 'the same story' as far as male sexism is concerned. The
original version of the show concluded with *Medea*, which was based not on
Euripides but on a popular Italian version of the Medea story which originated
in Magna Grecia. It was performed in the dialect of that region, with Rame
performing different 'choral' roles as well as the tragic protagonist who becomes
a symbol of a 'new woman' who kills her children not out of jealousy but out of
a desire for liberation from the shackles of domestic servitude. In the course of
more than 500 performances of the plays, various other monologues have been
added, including a Roman *Lysistrata*, *Ulrike Meinhof*, and a monologue about
Irmgard Moeller, *Tomorrow's News*. The Fos organised a petition for Moeller
after the Stammheim 'suicides' in 1978, and it was signed by a number of

prominent Italian writers and directors, which led to accusations against Fo of supporting terrorism in an article in the Italian magazine *Panorama* by the PCI MP (and sometime poet) Antonello Trombadori.

Accusations of supporting terrorism were to dog the Fos from this period onwards, largely because of Franca Rame's involvement in Soccorso Rosso Militante (Militant Red Aid), which tried to help political prisoners (frequently suspected terrorists) both in Italy and abroad – one example being the Fos' involvement in a campaign to release Petra Krause, a Swiss-Italian woman who was accused and charged of a series of terrorist-related offences in Milan and Switzerland in 1975, and whose temporary release from prison Soccorso Rosso managed to secure in 1977. However, the Fos have never been charged with or even accused of terrorist-related activities in Italy, apart from unfounded accusations in the right-wing Italian press and an abortive inquiry into Franca Rame's political activities in 1973 by an Italian magistrate, Mario Sossi, which yielded nothing incriminating. The following year Sossi was kidnapped by members of the Brigate Rosse, but set free after a series of interrogations which revealed, among other things, the Red Brigades' contempt for and total variance from the political line pursued by the Fos.

From her involvement in Soccorso Rosso Militante, in which she wrote letters and organised legal aid to some 800 Italian prisoners, Rame wrote a monologue, *La madre (The Mother)*, which she added to her one-woman show in 1982. Based on accounts by women who were relatives of terrorist suspects being detained in Italy's special prisons, the play is an indictment of the Italian government's treatment of prisoners awaiting trial, who can be held in prison for up to five years and four months before their cases first come to court, and ten years and eight months before their final trial. The protagonist of the piece is a mother who sees a photo of her son on the TV news, and learns that he has been arrested and charged with being a terrorist involved in a political assassination. The play takes the form of a direct address to the audience, focusing on the mother's reactions to this fact. The play emphasises the human issues behind terrorism in a way which, far from being imputable as support for terrorism, comes across as a strong condemnation of it, by highlighting the repressive and inhumane laws which operate in Italy as a result of terrorism.

The mother describes in detail the indignities and humiliations of visiting her son in a high-security prison in Sardinia, where she is forced to undergo anal and vaginal searches before being allowed to see her son, whom she is horrified to discover has a swollen face and broken hands as a result of being beaten up by police. The play is a chilling indictment of strip-searching, and Rame's performance of it in London in 1983 served to complement a campaign against similar practices in Armagh Jail in Northern Ireland – another example of the universality of many of the political issues the Fos' plays confront in an Italian context. Rame's left-wing, liberal, tolerant Mother (but the play stresses it could happen to anyone) is outraged by 'being treated like . . . like an animal', and thinks of denouncing the strip-searching to the newspapers:

'As soon as I get out of here, I'll report it. I'll write to the papers. Oh yes I will.' But then I just felt like laughing: write to the papers? But what newspaper is going to publish anything on what I am going through now? I . . . I am only the mother of a terrorist. 65 per cent of people are in favour of capital punishment . . . I . . . I opened my legs and let her get on with the job.[20]

Like the woman who is raped in *I Cant Move, I Can't Scream, My Voice is Gone*, who decides to put off reporting the rape until the next day, as she can't bear the thought of describing her experience to the police, and Ulrike Meinhof trapped in her fish tank-like cell in Stammheim, the Mother is a representative of female rage at female impotence in a male-dominated system of repression. The plays themselves are a powerful medium for the voice of oppressed women to be heard publically, and all three are direct cries from the heart unmediated by any paraphernalia of dramatic representation.

In 1981, a second edition of *Tutta casa, letto e chiesa* opened at the Teatro Odeon in Milan, a theatre which the Fos had not set foot in for 16 years, and whose plush red velvet still housed a predominantly bourgeois audience. The reasons for this return to the bourgeois theatre were partly the eviction of La Comune from the Palazzina Liberty (although they subsequently used a converted cinema, the Cristallo, as their base) and partly a desire to demonstrate that the women's problems the plays confronted were of an 'inter-class' concern, and addressed themselves to all types of women. As Franca Rame explained:

> I realised that in turning our backs on the so-called bourgeois theatre, we were refusing a portion of spectators who would never have come to a stadium or under a tent, but still has the right to be entertained, to laugh, and at the same time to see certain problems dealt with.[21]

Dario Fo had already made something of a return to the bourgeois theatre in 1978, after touring *La storia della tigre* around Italy. He was approached by the prestigious Teatro alla Scala, which was celebrating its bicentenary, and asked to become a director, in what at first seemed an acknowledgement of his importance, albeit controversial, as a theatrical figure both in Italy and abroad, an importance which had been consolidated by his success on Italian TV. At the time of his appointment, Fo justified his entry into one of the bastions of the Italian and European cultural establishment in the following terms:

> There's little to be scandalised about. La Scala is hardly the stamping ground of the conformist bourgeoisie, or monumental productions, or the academy. It's a great theatre with a history which often included satire against the authorities and periods of great political tension . . . It also put on the first theatrical representation of class struggle, in *William Tell*, whose protagonist is a highlander supported by a crowd of peasants who fight for their rights against the bosses.[22]

Plans for a collaboration between Fo and La Scala were to include co-writing and directing a new opera by the Communist composer Luigi Nono, and some little-known Verdi operas, but his first task, and in the event, the only one which got off the ground, was a production of Stravinsky's *The Soldier's Tale*, which Strehler had also directed at La Scala in 1957. Fo set about almost completely rewriting Ramuz' libretto, politicising it and adding *Grammelot*, as well as expanding it to include Stravinsky's *Octet*, which caused music critics to be disgruntled. Fo turned the work into 'a kind of accusation against capitalism, which speculates on the concept of patriotism and uses the peasant, the poor devil who is eradicated from his land, and entices him with traffic, business and bogus dreams, taking away his fields and his culture.'[23] The soldier-protagonist became a type of Zanni, in a 'choral' production which used a cast of 32 (as opposed to 4 in the original) students from La Scala, and Fo shredded Stravinsky's opera in mounting a visually spectacular 'image track' to the music. The production, which Fo wrote, designed and directed but did not act in, is a rare example of his capacities as a director of a large-scale work, consisting of 14 'stage pictures', including the city, the stock exchange, war, a market and a 'ship of fools'. There was an ingenious use of basically simple stage props, like sticks and newspapers, to create stunning visual effects, and Fo used a giant cane puppet and a Brechtian inventiveness which would seem to illustrate the words of the Devil: 'Create the revolution with imagination'. In changing the work from a chamber opera to a 'piazza opera', Fo's *Soldier's Tale* fitted the bill for La Scala's 'decentralisation' programme, opening in Cremona and playing in a circus tent in Rome. This was ideal for Fo's own work, but in the context of La Scala represented a type of ghettoisation, and after disagreements with the La Scala administration, Fo terminated his collaboration with them.

Confronting terrorism and *Trumpets and Raspberries*

In 1979 Fo wrote and performed a series of television sketches which were transmitted by the second channel of RAI under the titles *Buona sera con Dario Fo* and *Buona sera con Franca Rame*, provoking little in the way of controversy, perhaps due to the fact that they were broadcast in a safe, early evening slot. Meanwhile Fo was working on a play about the kidnap and murder of Aldo Moro, an event which had put Italian terrorism into the international news headlines. *The Tragedy of Aldo Moro*, as Fo called the play, was based on the letters Moro wrote to his Christian Democrat colleagues while in a 'people's prison', pleading with his colleagues to negotiate with his captors. Fo saw a resemblance between the tone of the letters and that of Greek tragedy, and the situation of *Philoctetes* in particular, seeing the DC government's refusal to negotiate as using Moro as a scapegoat and sacrificial victim for their own self-preservation. Fo cast the play in the form of a Greek tragedy, with Satyrs, Bacchanals, a Court Jester Narrator, and eight Christian Democrats, as well as Moro (who was to be played by Fo). This gave it a static, wordy form, which got too bogged-down in the particular details of the event – quoting extensively from Moro's letters, Fo tried out the first act of the play once as a public reading in support of the campaign for the release of Toni Negri and the other victims of the wave of arrests carried out against members of the *Autonomia* and other Italian far-left groups on 7 April, 1979. He then discarded it, although the text of this first act (the second act was never completed) was published in *Panorama* and *Lotta Continua*. Fo found himself unable to clarify in dramatic form the confusing course of events surrounding the 'Moro tragedy' which he wanted to relate to the context of Italian terrorism as a whole, and jettisoned the project. Terrorism had become the most predominant political problem in Italy, and had been used to pour discredit on the left, so successfully that most of the extraparliamentary groups were being forced to keep a low profile, if not go underground to avoid being criminalised. Discussing terrorism from a leftist point of view became increasingly delicate in a situation in which Moro, whose overtures to the PCI had made him something of a controversial figure in the

DC, and despite his otherwise highly conservative views, had become mythologised into a kind of heroic martyr figure of Italian democracy. In the play, one of Moro's colleagues comments on the DC's refusal to negotiate with terrorists:

> What exactly are you trying to get at, Aldo? Are you trying to claim that the tragic increase in violence is all the fault of our policy of refusing to go to the negotiating table? So we're to blame for the fact that the *brigatisti* have become so ruthless, are we? Are you trying to say that if we agreed to empty the prisons and release their so-called 'comrades', we'd now be in an idyllic state of peace? I suppose the Red Brigades would just be showering flowers and confetti around the place, and helping old ladies across the street, and instead of exploding bombs, they'd be letting off fancy fireworks to thrill the kiddies?[24]

Faced with the bewildering complexities of the extreme DC-BR dialectics of the Moro situation at a time when there was little impetus left in the grass-roots Italian left, and no opportunity to deal with events in his usual comic-satirical way, Fo was well advised to abandon this abortive attempt to deal with terrorism, although he clearly felt an obligation to go ahead with it. In fact, no Italian writer or film director (discounting Bertolucci's dismally inadequate *Tragedy of a Ridiculous Man*, about a terrorist kidnapping, and Leonardo Sciascia's documentary book on Moro's letters, *L'Affaire Moro*) was able to deal with a situation which Fo described as

> a state of affairs in Italy where there is no longer any talk of reform, where the logic of the lesser of two evils has been discarded, where trade unionists have been forced on to their knees, and class struggle has been thwarted at every turn . . . What is needed is the courage to assess contradictions, and to strive to understand at all costs.[25]

The difficulty of maintaining an objective viewpoint, together with the problems of sorting out the morass of information and contradictory events in a complex issue where (unlike the relatively clear-cut Pinelli affair) there was no defendable party, required more distance than Fo was in a position to have. It is interesting to note that in 1983 the Spanish writer Jorge Semprun, who has written a number of screenplays for Costa Gavras' films, completed a play about the Moro kidnapping, which indicates that perhaps it takes a non-Italian to assess the issue from a distance. Fo was also to return to the issue, confronting it in a more imaginative, fictional form, two years later.

Ironically, despite Fo's continued anti-terrorist stance, he and his wife were refused a visa to enter the United States in 1980, where they were to perform *Mistero buffo* and *Tutta casa letto e chiesa* in the Festival of Italian Theatre at the New York Town Hall. The reasons given for this refusal by the American embassy in Rome were the activities of Soccorso Rosso in helping political prisoners in Italy, which was seen as a support of terrorist violence. In fact Franca Rame had visited some of the leaders of the Red Brigades, including Renato Curcio, in prison, at the time of the Moro kidnapping, in an attempt to persuade them to speak out publically and advocate Moro's release, but had been unable to achieve any results. Consequently, in New York in May 1980, amid accusations of McCarthyism, 'An Evening without Dario Fo and Franca Rame' was held, attended by Richard Foreman, Martin Scorcese, Arthur Miller,

Bernard Malamud, Sol Yurick, Ellen Stewart and others, at which students of
New York University presented an English version of the first act of *Can't Pay?
Won't Pay!* Piero Sciotto read a letter from the Fos deploring the situation and
explaining the problem caused by the new law of 'repentant terrorists' in Italy,
which often led to the arrest of innocent people. This event probably brought
the Fos more publicity than they would have received if they had been granted a
visa. As one New York critic pointed out, the Fos were in select company –
Brecht, Charlie Chaplin and Gabriel Garcia Márquez had also been refused
entry to the US. In their annual conference, the American Critics' Association
protested about the situation, sending a letter to the Secretary of State Edmund
Muskie. Nevertheless, in September 1983, when the Fos were scheduled to
perform *Mistero buffo* and *Tutta casa, letto e chiesa* at Joseph Papp's Public
Theatre in New York, and to run theatre workshops in the theatre departments
of the Universities of Boston, Los Angeles and Washington, the American
Department of State once again refused them an entry visa to the USA,
accusing them of 'belonging to organisations supporting terrorist groups'[26] and
citing Soccorso Rosso. This despite the fact that Fo has no involvement with the
prison aid group, and that in 1983 he was the foreign author whose plays had
received the most productions in the American (and world) theatre. *Tutta casa,
letto e chiesa* was at the time being performed throughout America by 18
different American theatre companies, including a production of the play by film
director Arthur Penn with the actress Estelle Parsons. Papp promptly sent a
telegram to President Reagan, appealing to him as a theatrical 'colleague', while
the Fos began a law suit against the US State Department for damages which
they intend to donate to sacked workers, occupied factories, anti-drug
organisations, handicapped people, squats, and prisoners and their families. In a
press conference in Milan, Fo outlined the gravity and illegality of the charge
made against him and his wife by the US State Department:

> We are Italian citizens who are supposed to have committed the crime of
> aiding and abetting terrorists in Italy. The Italian judicial authorities,
> however, have never charged us or even made inquiries into the activities
> carried out by Soccorso Rosso, nor have they accused us of any support of
> terrorism: in any case our position on the subject is well-known. Now the
> Americans arrive on the scene and decide that we support terrorists, which
> means either that the Italian judicial authorities aren't doing their job or that
> they are in complicity with us.[27]

With *Clacson, trombette e pernacchi* (literally 'Car Horns, Trumpets and
Raspberries', a 'Carnival' title which was rendered in an American production
of the play in 1983 as *About Face,*) which opened at the Cinema Cristallo in
Milan in January 1981, Fo overcame his block about confronting issues related
to terrorism, in what was his first play for five years (since *Mother's Marijuana*).
The play's farcical form resembled that of its predecessor, and showed clearly
that Fo's sympathies were categorically against terrorism and any violent form of
political action. It incorporates Moro's letters and Fo's comments on current
Italian political events, while using comic devices which closely resemble Fo's
farces of the 1950s and 1960s, particularly the mistaken identity situation of
Aveva due pistole . . . , while borrowing some of its trappings from Plautus'
Menaechmi. The basic situation is that of a 'comedy of errors' (or 'comedy of
terror'), in which Antonio, a Fiat worker in *cassa integrazione*, who begins

where Giovanni in *Can't Pay? Won't Pay!* leaves off, saves the life of Fiat boss Giovanni Agnelli – one of Italy's most prominent international businessmen and the owner of the Juventus football team – after a road accident which occurs while terrorists are trying to kidnap Agnelli. The Fiat boss is disfigured in the accident, and after Antonio flees, leaving his jacket over Agnelli, the latter is mistaken for Antonio and undergoes plastic surgery which gives him the face of the worker. This leads to a double identity situation (both Antonio and Agnelli are played by Fo) when Antonio's wife Rosa (Franca Rame) takes Agnelli for her prodigal husband after an encounter with Antonio's mistress Lucia, who is unable to reveal the 'exchange' of identities to Rosa. The real Antonio is forced to go into hiding for fear that he will be implicated in the terrorist kidnapping since his car (a Fiat, naturally) in which he rescued Agnelli, has been spotted:

ANTONIO: I'm done for. A wanted terrorist! They probably think I'm the brains behind the whole plot! And what's more, I've saved my own boss – the face that sacked 40 thousand workers. I'm really stuffed.

LUCIA: Oh, come on, don't be so pessimistic. OK, the guy's an arsehole, but as soon as he comes to and lets on he's Agnelli and you saved him, you're in line for a big reward.

ANTONIO: Oh yeah? You think he'd admit to having his face saved by one of his scumbag workers?[28]

Agnelli (who is referred to throughout the play as 'The Double') has lost the power of speech as well as memory, which occasions some variations of *Grammelot* as the Doctors try to restore his power of speech so that the police can interrogate him. The situation is a farcical 'about face' in which Agnelli comes under accusation of terrorism. In the confusion of identities, both characters succeed in hoodwinking the police while stretching the credibility of the situation to breaking point, calling for theories of schizophrenia as well as amnesia to cover up the difference between Antonio and the Double. The farcical situation reaches its peak when Rosa uses a mincing machine and feeding apparatus to feed Antonio, strapping him to a chair (since the Double can only be fed through the nose) and forcing him to play his clarinet to keep him from crying out. The police leap on the feeding apparatus and use it as a torture device (since it is more sophisticated than their own methods) and force a false confession of terrorist activities out of Antonio. In the final scene of the play, agents from rival sections of the Italian secret political police – Digos, Sisde, Sismi and Ucigos, take up hiding places behind various articles of furniture in the room to await the outcome of the situation – a satire on the efforts of the various factions of the Italian police to cover themselves in glory by capturing terrorists. It is then revealed that Agnelli has plagiarised Moro's letters to government ministers, who have responded differently this time, calling for an amnesty on political prisoners in exchange for Agnelli. This proves the latter's claim that he is more important than Italian politicians:

I represent the real centre of power . . . Don't you see that? Haven't you read your Karl Marx? Yes, I know. Nowadays it's only we top level industrial management people who bother to read *Das Kapital*, especially the bit where it says that 'the true source of power is economic and financial, public holdings, the stock exchange, banks and mechandising – in short, capital. . . .' I am the state! The capital I represent is the state! You've got no choice but to save my dignity, even if you die in the process![29]

This speech, which is delivered while Agnelli is standing aloft on all the previously mobile furniture which has now been arranged into a kind of staircase, exemplifies one of the play's defects – a tendency to make lengthy political statements which come across as lectures, as in the Double's previous three-page potted history of recent Italian political events which accuses the Italian government of using terrorism as a pretext to avoid problems like unemployment, inflation, education, hospital reform and the Mafia.

Trumpets and Raspberries seemed to take a backward step in its treatment of the women characters. There is a virtual cat-fight between Rosa and the radical-chic Lucia in the hospital, and the deception of Rosa, who, unlike Antonia in *Can't Pay? Won't Pay!*, is presented as a repressed, working-class housewife, blissful about being able to do her husband's washing and ironing again, comes across as needlessly cruel, despite her unwitting 'revenge' on Antonio via the feeding device. Not surprisingly, Franca Rame was dissatisfied with the role of Rosa, which was definitely retrogressive in comparison with the characters she was portraying in *Tutta casa, letto e chiesa*, and despite playing to 50,000 spectators in 34 performances in Milan, the play toured only sporadically over the course of the next year, and was then dropped. It opened at a time when another terrorist kidnapping, that of the judge D'Urso, was in a dramatic phase, and this gave the play considerable topicality, although its opening night was marred by inaccurate press reports of an incident which led to further accusations against Fo of supporting terrorism. In an extra-theatrical practice by now customary in performances of Fo's plays, relatives of prisoners in Trani, in Apulia, where there had been prison riots, read the text of a report they had filed against the prison director, mentioning violent incidents against prisoners after the revolt. The fact that many of the prisoners in Trani were terrorist suspects was misconstrued as support on Fo and Rame's part for not only the prison revolt but also terrorism. The episode highlights the 'bad press' Fo had been getting in the Italian media. In the context of continuing smear campaigns against the Italian left, Fo had spoken out on a problem which was becoming increasingly difficult to put into perspective. As Chiara Valentini commented:

> Enormous courage is needed to speak about current events at the present time, and no one up to now has been up to it. Dario Fo has tried, without pussyfooting around, choosing the path of political theatre, taking equal risks on both aesthetic and legal fronts. The tabloid press has realised this, and when it hasn't ignored him, it has attacked him hypocritically, without having the courage to get down to the point. Young and theatreless audiences have also realised this, and queued for hours at the Cristallo box office in Milan, hoping that at last here was someone talking about ourselves and our history.[30]

Although in Valentini's view, *Trumpets and Raspberries* was less accomplished than even *Grande Pantomina . . .* and *Dito nell'occhio*, the fact was that Fo had confronted Italian political issues of the 1980s alone. The play, despite its longueurs, was a unique example of contemporary political theatre, which made its points forcefully in suggesting that the connections between high finance and terrorism may not be as far-fetched as they would seem. Productions of the play were immediately planned in 15 different countries.

Adapting Brecht

In 1981 Fo became the most widely produced Italian playwright in the world. Productions of his work had been put on in Japan, India, Australasia, and even (despite his pro-PLO stance) Israel. He was invited by the Berliner Ensemble to do an 'updated' adaptation of Brecht's *Threepenny Opera*, but after completely re-writing the play, and adding his usual satire on domestic consumer products (in the wedding scene between Polly and MacHeath scores of electrical appliance wedding gifts arrive on a *tapis roulant*), Fo's version was rejected by Brecht's daughter Barbara and it was never done at the Berliner Ensemble. Fo claimed to be following Brecht's own example in showing a healthy disrespect for the classics, which also kicked against the embalment of Brecht's plays as classics in the European bourgeois theatre. He also claimed to base his version more on John Gay's *Beggar's Opera* than on Brecht's rewrite of Gay, and cut all of Brecht's and Kurt Weill's songs, using the somewhat dubious and risky form of a rock opera, with 24 pastiches of songs, re-written by Fiorenzo Carpi, by the likes of David Bowie, Patti Smith, Frank Zappa, Janis Joplin and Jimi Hendrix (suggested by Fo's son Jacopo) which became totally unrecognisable in their 'Italianisation'. In December 1981 Fo's adaptation was taken up by the Teatro Stabile di Torino and the Teatro Il Fabbricone of Prato, and with the title of *L'opera dello sghignazzo* (which literally means 'The Opera of the Sneering Laugh', and expresses a concept Fo had used frequently in his previous plays, that of pouring scorn and contempt on the authorities), it opened at the latter theatre. Il Fabbricone had developed a highly aesthetic, refined and lush house style from the productions of Luca Ronconi, a director who had made his name in the 1960s with a highly 'rough', knockabout version of Ariosto's *Orlando furioso*, and since became a formal, conceptual, stylish director of workshop productions similar in concept to those of Peter Brook, but resulting in visually impressive, somewhat 'deadly' classical revivals. In this context, Fo stated that, in choosing the 1980s (although it is in fact more 1960s, as the musical models suggest) form of a rock opera, he was

> respecting historical progression. Gay's *Beggar's Opera* used popular music of the 1700s, the irreverent, scurrilous music of inns and festivals, the pop of the time, in other words. . . . *The Threepenny Opera* also used the popular music of its period: waltzes, tangos, ragtime, variety and German cabaret. For the 1980s, rock was inevitable, and we've recreated everything, without making any reference to Weill's music.[31]

What this meant was that *Mack the Knife* was substituted by an instantly forgettable rock song about 'plastic cosmetic culture' (if Brecht's and Weill's songs were at first described by critics as 'forgettable', Fo's are far more so), and *Pirate Jenny* became a 'futuristic' electronic number about a *Blue Metal Starship*. As he had done in his adaptation of Michel's *The Sunday Walk*, Fo had a rock band on stage, but the outdated, hybrid rock form detracted from a play in which not a single line of Brecht's or Gay's versions was retained. In using an impressively visual, modular set capable of accommodating any number of scenic actions, Fo was following Piscator's idea for staging *The Threepenny Opera*, but the result was more a Ronconi-like glossy veneer which, together with the fact that Fo used professional actors from the establishment theatre (having by now disbanded La Commune as an acting company), caused the play to steer dangerously close to the 'plastic, cosmetic culture' it was satirising. Fo's role was originally that of adaptor, director and designer (as in the more fortunate *Soldier's Tale*), but after poor critical reception, which found other things to criticise in the play apart from the rather dubious charge of sacrilege against Brecht, Fo took over the role of Peachum in a salvage operation at the Teatro Nazionale in Milan in April 1982. This new version added topical references to the Falklands War, and the case of the Mafia boss Cutolo, who became a model for MacHeath, which meant that the play became another political performance vehicle for Fo's comic improvisations in an example of epic acting which outdid Brecht. It also meant that when Fo was not on stage, the play became very lacklustre. Peachum became a crooked lawyer who organises a racket of fake drug addicts whom he uses to 'fiddle' the state system, and the role reflected Fo's constant battle against the theatricality of Italian political reality. As Peachum states in Fo's version:

> This job is a theatrical job . . . and the theatre is fiction. Only great fiction manages to outdo reality . . . If you have a duodenal ulcer and describe it in real terms, you achieve a nauseating, repellant effect. As Diderot said – and also Bertolt Brecht, who stole it from him: 'The worst stage drunk is the actor who drinks for real.'[32]

A more alarming symptom reflected by Fo's *Opera dello sghignazzo* is the widespread tendency of contemporary Italian directors to adapt existing texts to their own frequently self-indulgent concerns – as in Ronconi's stifling of Ibsen's *Ghosts* at Spoleto in 1982. Although Fo normally is exemplary in his use of secondary material to tease out points of political importance and impact, his *Threepenny Opera* was unable to improve on Brecht's or Gay's plays, and he was possibly foolhardy to try. Eduardo de Filippo commented on the phenomenon of adaptation in a lecture to students at Rome University in 1982:

> I will curse down to the seventh generation anyone who changes a single line or word of a play of mine. I've had enough of adaptors, revisers and re-elaborators . . . I would like to incriminate anyone who uses the preposition 'from' – as in 'from Shakespeare' – for theatrical fraud.[33]

The problem of adaptation – ironically compounded by the fact that Eduardo himself later accepted a commission to write a 'Neapolitan version' of Shakespeare's *Tempest* – is one which also applies to foreign versions of Fo's own plays, which require extensive adaptation at times due to their detailed, topical references to Italian political issues which non-Italian audiences cannot be expected to understand. This is a subject I shall return to in the following chapter.

In 1982, Fo continued to demonstrate his consummate skill as an adaptor and performer of Mediaeval texts in *Il fabulazzo osceno*, an example of his exhumation of little-known popular texts which he uses as vehicles for his dazzling improvisatory abilities as a sole performer, and his scathing political sallies at figures of authority. The following year, he returned to the format of the clown-show revue-sketch in *Patapumfete*, which he wrote and directed for the clown duo I Colombaioni, confronting contemporary social problems such as drugs, violence, video games, factory production lines and TV quizzes in an essentially physical, slapstick way to highlight the dehumanising, brain-damaging

high-tech trappings of an increasingly epileptic contemporary culture.
Patampufete also included a two-handed version of 'The Morality of the Blind
Man and the Cripple' from *Mistero buffo*, which proved only how much more
imaginative, suggestive and consummately theatrical Fo's own solo performance
of the piece is. While Fo would appear to be experiencing something of a crisis
as a playwright in the 1980s, at a time when there is a widespread crisis of
creativity in the Italian cinema and theatre at large, he remains unique as a
practitioner of political theatre in Italy, while his genius as an actor and mime
continues to make itself felt increasingly outside Italy. The same is true of
Franca Rame, who continues to perform *Tutta casa, letto e chiesa* throughout
the world to considerable acclaim.

In the 1980s, Fo and Rame have had increasing difficulty organising their
schedules to accommodate what they see as a fundamental commitment to
touring their work in Italy with the ever-increasing pressures of invitations to
tour abroad. While Fo alternated performances of *Il fabulazzo osceno* in
northern Italy with *Mistero buffo* and *La storia della tigre* in Sweden and
Germany, Rame took her latest edition of *Tutta casa, letto e chiesa* to Montreal,
Sweden and Germany, and both had to turn down offers from as far afield as
Australia and Majorca. At the end of 1983, the couple were considering going
to Cuba – a fitting choice after being refused entry to the US – and Fo had
definite commitments in Germany. The consistently lower profile they have been
given in the Italian press since their success abroad coincides ironically with a
riflusso or decline in the optimism and militancy of the Italian left, for reasons
outlined elsewhere, which has led to a downward curve in the Fos' popularity at
home. In November of 1983 they began work on a new play, *Coppia aperta,
quasi spalancata* (*Open Couple – Wide Open, Even*), a two-hander in which Fo
directed his wife and an actor who had worked with them several times
previously, Nicola de Buono. The play tackles a theme which at first sight seems
more the domain of a farceur like Alan Ayckbourn – the ironies and
contradictions of a couple who have agreed to pursue an 'open relationship', live
separately, but continue to discuss their extra-marital affairs. But *Open Couple*
is no made-to-measure farce, and nor does it necessarily reflect the Fos' own
private predicament as performers who are frequently cities or even countries
apart. 'It's not a thesis play', Fo stated. 'Almost every line is taken from
conversations we've had with our friends. It's an autobiography of the
intellectuals we know, with an added surrealistic charge.' He points out that the
apparently private concern of the piece is no new departure for him, as many of
his plays, including *Female Parts* and the Agnelli play, have had marital
relations at their core. 'The problem exists for everyone, including the working
class – it's universal. The woman's role in the family situation is always one of
subjugation, like the proletariat, while the man plays the role of the
bourgeoisie.'[34]

Any suspicion that the Fos have even temporarily retired from political
theatre are put paid to by the Brechtian form of *Open Couple*, which consists of
a series of flashbacks of a couple's disastrous attempts to live separate lives.
They frequently step out of character to comment on events, criticise each
other's inconsistencies, and wryly observe each other's semi-serious suicide
attempts which express the emotional torment of their situation. 'The play
shows a private situation which becomes public and political', de Buono
commented. The idea of the 'open couple' is shown to be a fallacy because, as

Fo explains the sexual politics of the situation, 'it works from the husband's point of view as long as he has other relationships, but when his wife does likewise, he breaks down and wants to go back to the conventional couple situation.' In the final scene the husband appears to commit suicide in the bath with a hairdryer (an idea adapted from *Goldfinger*) when his wife's lover, a whizz-kid nuclear scientist cum rock musician whom he believes she has invented, makes an appearance. Such a complicated interplay of deception and play-acting has been built up between the couple that we are unsure whether his suicide is real or simulated. In rehearsals, Fo insists on the tragic vein of the play, constantly calling for more dramatic tension. 'The wife really does want to kill herself, and her husband actually shoots her in the foot during a scuffle at one point – if you don't play the tragedy it'll turn into a light comedy, a *pochade*, which it isn't. There's a tragic basis to the play which turns into comedy through the situation.' One of Fo's consistent criticisms of foreign productions of his work is that they try to force the comedy. 'They take the farce to an extent where the story isn't convincing any more, and as a result people end up laughing less.' It becomes clear why he is not playing the part of the husband himself when he steps in to demonstrate a gag which in his hands is so hilarious it topples the serious balance of the play. The husband and wife are playing cards when she drops a clanger about her new relationship with the nuclear physicist. Fo showers the pack of cards into the air to underline the fit of self-recrimination in which the husband storms across the stage. 'Snow effect' comments Rame laconically, and the line is added to the play. After a week's rehearsal, they are already well into a second version of the original text, and lines are being added, cut and re-discussed continuously.

Open Couple contains a number of echoes of *Accidental Death of an Anarchist*, like its fourth floor setting, and the wife's attempts to throw herself out of the window, which, along with other running gags which re-surface from previous Fo plays, emphasise its undiminished political charge. But they also stress what has changed in Italian left-wing politics over the past decade. 'In *Accidental Death* I talked about the 'liberating belch' caused by scandal, where people's imagination creates a catharsis which distracts attention from the real political problems. In this play there's a line saying that now there's not even that belch left any more – there's no more indignation. A lot of the political militants of the '60s and '70s have drifted into the orange people, or got into macrobiotic food, or played about with the 'open couple' idea. In the face of the failure of revolutionary ideals, the basic problem is how people relate to one another.' At one point in the play, the wife describes how she and her new lover decide to go to Comiso, the Greenham Common of Sicily. The husband paints the scene scathingly as a desire to join up with a bunch of clapped-out hippies, Communist Party tenderfoots, geriatric ex-partisans and arthritic left-wing MPs. In fact the couple only got as far as Parma, as it became more important for them to consummate their sexual relationship. 'I deal only indirectly with the nuclear problem in the play because it's riddled with speculation', says Fo. 'The Socialist Party and the government are involved in all sorts of dirty double-dealing with the USA and the USSR. It's not a question of making the masses aware of the nuclear threat. I think people are sufficiently aware. What is needed is an autonomous popular movement.'

By a coincidence, while the Fos are rehearsing in the cold, dingy Teatro Cristallo, an ex-music hall and converted cinema which they have made their occasional base in Milan since losing the Palazzina Liberty, the Piccolo Teatro is housing a lush, lavish production by Giorgio Strehler – Fo's one-time collaborator and now arch-rival – of Lessing's *Minna von Barnhelm*. This light, romantic comedy, which Strehler sees as 'a search for the real couple in which the maternal code forms a dialectic, based on love, with the paternal code' could not contrast more in its frivolous conventionality with Fo's concerns in *Open Couple*. With military-style music provided by Fo's old collaborator, Fiorenzo Carpi, and lighting and set design in a sepia black and white which is dazzling, it is all style, and poles apart from the functional utilitarianism of Fo's approach to stagecraft. 'I've written more than forty plays' Fo affirms, 'and all of them are about things taken from reality. Like the total alienation of the woman in *Homecoming*.'

Homecoming (*Rientro a casa*) is a monologue written in collaboration with Franca Rame who performed it in tandem with *Open Couple* in a double-bill which opened in Trieste in December 1983 and Milan in February 1984. Using back-projected slides to set the scene, the play deals with a mother returning to a squalid, grimy, misty and anonymous apartment block in South East Milan after a day of protest and misadventure. Having left her husband in disgust at his using her as a sexual convenience, taking twenty-one seconds to complete the sexual act, she has ended up spending the day in a hotel room with a colleague from her office who has been in love with her for years. In the evening, drunk, bewildered and exhausted, she arrives home, and is reconciled with her husband in the darkness of the bedroom. The following morning she discovers she has got the wrong apartment and the wrong family – a story-line which brings home the universality of the sexual problems Fo is dealing with. A similar sexual misunderstanding and confusion of identities lies at the basis of *Il candelaio* (*The Candle Maker*), an as-yet unperformed monologue written for Franca Rame in 1983. This play reflects the renewed interest Fo has taken in the English Elizabethan theatre since coming to London. Its basic situation reflects the sexual substitution of Shakespeare's *Measure for Measure*, although it is in fact based on a play by the sixteenth century Neapolitan playwright Giordano Bruno. In Fo's version, a costumist announces to the audience that the actress about to perform the piece is indisposed, and ends up performing it herself in a theatrical image of the art of disguise and dissemblance. The Candle Maker has grown tired of his wife and begun to frequent a prostitute, whom the wife approaches to learn the art of sexual attraction so she can win back her husband. The prostitute obliges, and trains the wife in her art, and the husband is taken in. The wife concludes 'he's rediscovered me as a whore, and I've rediscovered him as a whorer. We've thrown convenience and respect to the winds, and perhaps now some real respect has grown between us.'[35]

Fo stresses that all his plays, whatever theme they deal with, show the cultural and economic basis of social problems. 'However,' he adds, 'I'm not a politician and I don't make political speeches.' Despite this disclaimer, he is frequently treated as a politician, as his arrest in Sardinia and the refusal of his visa to enter the US indicates. What he is, and continues to be, is a thorn in the side of Italian state authorities and repressive regimes the world over. His position is akin to that of the wife in *Open Couple*, who eschews officially sanctioned forms of protest within the accepted channels:

You can't just pile on the fine-sounding Sunday strolls organised by the regime and led by the fanfares of the authorities. You have to have the guts to weather people's indifference and scorn.[36]

This is a battle Fo, as a militant, committed artist working in a consciously popular medium, has continued to fight, and the widespread recognition he has obtained is a measure of his success.

5: FO IN THE UK

Our own work has always managed to survive, at least up to now, because of the fact that we have always taken situations of struggle as our point of reference. (Dario Fo interviewed in London, May 1983.)

Dario Fo's plays were beginning to be produced in translation outside Italy as early as 1960, but it was not until 1978, with Robert Walker's production of *We Can't Pay? We Won't Pay!* at the Half Moon Theatre in London, that his work began to become known in the UK. By this time Fo was already the most widely performed playwright in world theatre, and European directors and theatre groups, like the Belgian theatre collective NewsScene, which dedicated itself exclusively to producing Fo's plays over a period of four years, had already performed translated versions of most of Fo's adaptable plays. One reason for this state of affairs was possibly the relative proximity both geographically and culturally of France, Germany, Belgium and Spain to Italy (although Fo's work was also very popular in Scandinavia), and the fact that he toured these countries, while the traditionally provincial, parochial English are more isolated, and slower to respond to cultural events – particularly those of a highly 'unofficial' nature – in the rest of Europe.

The most immediate difficulty, however, which held up the arrival of Fo's work in the UK (and the USA, and the rest of the English-speaking world), was the specific nature of his plays which, being largely written as a direct response to particular Italian political situations, made their reference points difficult to translate into an English context even when their implications were universal (as in the case of price increases in *Can't Pay? Won't Pay!*). Understanding *Accidental Death of an Anarchist* without any knowledge of the Pinelli affair and the 'Strategy of tension' is difficult, to say the least. The problems of how to cope with specific topical and cultural references in Fo's plays, such as his repeated criticisms of the Italian Communist Party, which the majority of English audiences could not be expected to grasp, were apparent. Frequently these reference points could not simply be cut without disrupting the entire logic and development of the plays. This is not, however, tantamount to saying that there was any lack of a comparable tradition of working-class and popular culture in the British theatre, which made appreciation of these factors in Fo's work difficult. Fo's own comments on this subject, as reported in an interview with Catherine Itzin in London in 1980, reflect that there may have been a reciprocal lack of understanding:

Left intellectuals in Britain seemed to have created a strange cult of the working class, glorifying the people and worshipping their lack of culture. Left theatre people here, he thought, didn't really know much about working-class culture and even seemed proud of the fact.[1]

This is to give the lie to the work of, to name a few, 7:84, Belt and Braces, and a play like Trevor Griffiths' *Comedians*, all of which drew heavily on working-class culture, or Arden's use of popular ballad forms and Mediaeval popular theatre. Rather than lacking any equivalent cultural context for Fo's plays (with the exception of the Catholic church), what British adaptors and directors had to confront was the need to find an English equivalent for the specifically Italian cultural and political references they contained, which then had to be placed in the context of English working-class and popular culture. This often involved a need for extensive re-writing and adaptation, which ran the risk of losing sight of the author's original intentions and political aims. In changing the reference points of Fo's plays, there was a danger of obscuring their conclusions.

Adapting Fo – *We Can't Pay? We Won't Pay!*

In the context of the above, the English version of *We Can't Pay? We Won't Pay!* (to maintain its first title, and that of the published English version), translated by Lino Pertile, adapted by Bill Colvill and Robert Walker, and directed by the latter at the Half Moon Theatre in London in May 1978 (subsequently transferring to the West End in July 1981 in a revised edition) remains the most accurate and plausible version of a Dario Fo play in the UK. The spirit of the original is maintained, and the relatively few cuts and alterations which occur in placing the play in an English working-class context could even be said to improve on the original, making it less prolix, pruning a number of Fo's indulgences and generally tightening the farcical situation of the play. It is no coincidence that *We Can't Pay? We Won't Pay!* opened at the Half Moon, a small, 100-seat theatre in the East End of London, which had gained a reputation for being one of the few alternative Fringe theatres in London to put on politically relevant plays, many of which were directly concerned with the problems of the local working-class community, to audiences who included as many local, non-theatregoers as regular theatre frequenters. One of the theatre workers who was involved at the outset with the development of the Half Moon in the mid-1970s was the socialist writer Steve Gooch, three of whose plays were produced there – *Female Transport*, about women prisoners, *Will Wat?*, about Wat Tyler and the 'first English revolution', and *The Motor Show*, about industrial strife at the Ford car factory in Dagenham – all subjects which could be said to parallel the concerns of Fo's work. In a recent interview, Gooch recalled that

> The early days at the Half Moon represented to me a way to work as a playwright which was not totally circumscribed by the conventional relationship of the playwright to the theatre; what I was interested in was a way of communicating more directly to an audience which had a more intimate relationship to the theatre I was working with. The early days at the Half Moon were very like that in the sense that it was people who were living in that area and working in the area, who got the place started . . . I believe that in working-class life there is a culture and there are values which are not adequately celebrated in established theatre. I was looking for that kind of

context in which to write, looking for the places where people were actually getting to grips with the problems of trying to reach a working-class audience in the theatre.[2]

The similarities between Gooch's concerns and those of the Palazzina Liberty do not need to be underlined, except to stress the vast difference between the 'intimate' social structure which the Half Moon enjoyed, a factor which also affected its house style, and the audiences of often more than 3,000 people which Fo played to, necessitating a far more out-flung, public style of theatre which had to rely on communicating to a crowd. The difference in theatrical mode is akin to that between an orderly meeting and a mass rally.

It was apt that it was Robert Walker who 'discovered' and pioneered Fo's work in the UK. Walker, a tireless experimenter on the London Fringe, had in the early 1970s introduced the radically new theatre of the Austrian playwright Peter Handke to English audiences, and later did a number of productions of Brecht at the Half Moon, where he also directed the world premiere of *Mayakovsky*, a highly political play about the Russian poet who had influenced Fo so much, by the East German playwright Stefan Schütz. Together with the working-class socialist playwright Bill Colvill, Walker transformed Fo's play into a genuinely down-to-earth, working-class colloquial and slangy idiom which fixed the play firmly in an appropriate English context while maintaining the Italian names and references essential to the play's plot and situation. One example of the successful Anglicisation of their version is one of the few speeches they interpolate into the play, in which the Maoist police sergeant (whose character is indexed more obviously by having him quote from Mao's *Little Red Book*) encourages Luigi and Giovanni to take the contraband goods they are helping him to load up:

Do you want to know what'll happen from here? I shall write a full report, a model of brevity and procedure, the result of which charges will be laid. A brief item on *News at Ten* will allude to a brilliant police operation where contraband has been seized and men are sought. Duly alerted by the said item the industrialists will take a quick fortuitous trip over the border. Having laid my evidence before the judge, he will, with a pained expression, because it's a bit like welching on your own kind, sentence them to four months. The industrialists will hear about this whilst sunning themselves on the beaches of St Tropez and will immediately appeal to the President who will commute the sentence to a stiff fine.[3]

This crisply cynical parody of official police language is directly in the vein of a number of contemporary British playwrights who write political satire, while being appropriate to Fo's own mode of debunking judicial procedures in plays like *Accidental Death of an Anarchist*. It is also indicative of Walker's and Colvill's terse, economical but witty transposition of the original. Despite the relevance of the play's themes – fighting price increases – to English audiences, however, the Half Moon production passed relatively unnoticed in London. No national newspaper sent a first-string critic along to review it, and *The Guardian*, normally sympathetic to left-wing theatre, dispensed with play and production in three paragraphs, which, although reasonably favourable, managed to omit Fo's surname from the review. Although *Can't Pay? Won't Pay!* had already proved to be Fo's most popular and successful play throughout

Europe, this first venture to secure the author long-overdue recognition in the UK was insufficient – through no fault of the production – and it was to be almost another two years before Fo's work was to reappear in the London theatre.

Adapting Fo II – *Accidental Death of an Anarchist*

The Half Moon Theatre was also the venue of the second of Fo's plays to be seen in London – Belt and Braces' version of *Accidental Death of an Anarchist*, adapted and directed by Gavin Richards from an English translation by Gillian Hanna – which opened in October 1979, although the first performance of the play was at Dartington College in January of that year, and it had toured Liverpool and other places in the north of England before coming to London. Belt and Braces has described itself as 'a touring theatre company, founded in 1973. Its primary aim is to entertain, but with material and forms which are articulate, progressive and created from the viewpoint of working and oppressed people.'[4] – aims which are in keeping with those of La Comune. Like the difference in scale between the Half Moon and the Palazzina Liberty, however, the difference in scale between Belt and Braces and La Comune is enormous – a fact illustrated by Belt and Braces, threatened with cuts in their Arts Council subsidy, asking audiences at the end of their performances of *Accidental Death* to donate money to help the company survive. La Comune, who have only in recent years had any state subsidy at all from the Italian government, and then only the minimum one, have been able to raise thousands of pounds from their audiences for extra-theatrical causes such as occupied factories, laid-off workers and political detainees – an indication of the relative health of self-managing political theatre in the two countries. Belt and Braces' appeal was commented on acidly by Sheridan Morley, the theatre critic of *Punch*:

> True, the threatened Arts Council cutbacks . . . are appalling; but it ill behoves a company having achieved such an anarchically good box-office hit to turn around and demand public money for it. Belt and Braces does after all indicate some form of self-support.[5]

In fact the company went on to achieve enormous commercial success with the play, which transferred to the West End, and became a 'hit' for almost two years.

The Belt and Braces adaptation of *Accidental Death of an Anarchist* had the potential to be a reasonably accurate transposition of Fo's play to an English music hall, popular theatrical vein, while maintaining its incisive and excoriating political perspective. Richards, formerly a member of John McGrath's 7:84, for whom he had directed one of Arden's most politically overt plays, *The Ballygombeen Bequest*, about land expropriation in Northern Ireland, which had to be taken off after an estate agent took legal action against it, was a writer, director and actor whose work had mixed popular forms with abrasive political content; Gillian Hanna, a member of the feminist theatre group Monstrous Regiment, had previously translated and adapted Dacia Maraini's *Conversation between a Prostitute and a Client*, and Alfred Molina, a London-born actor of Italian extraction, who played the part of the Maniac which Fo had created for himself, subsequently received *Plays and Players'* Most Promising New Actor award for his performance. Richards' adaptation and the style of his direction of the piece, however, severely distorted the meaning and intention of the original, cutting it extensively and adding speeches and stage business which often went completely against the grain of Fo's play, despite using a highly-non-naturalistic, agit-prop form of staging in keeping with Fo's generally minimal use of sets and props. Since this version became the most successful English production of any of Fo's plays (and recently received the final accolade of being transmitted in a version for television by Channel Four in September 1983), it is worth going into detail about some of its faults, while stressing that as popular, music-hall-derived comedy in a particularly English vein, it had considerable merit and entertainment value. Richards has indicated his approach to the play as a presentational, open-form mode of popular theatre as follows:

> The most important point about the play is that it is what popular theatre is about, not only in Italy but also in this country. What we haven't really succeeded in doing is adapting a popular form successfully for a larger audience without writing something which either condescends to sexism or racism, or which falls back on the easy jokes, the extremely vicious anti-people edges of humour. Fo is an important lesson for us (in left-wing political theatre) because, effortlessly, he destroys the invisible fourth wall and creates live theatre again.[6]

But in using his idea of Fo's theatre as a presentational, rather than representational, framework within which to incorporate English forms of popular theatre like pantomime and corny jokes, Richards' approach to the play, where direct address, asides, and exaggeratedly slapstick stage business are at a premium, results in putting Fo's play across almost in inverted commas, imposing a self-reflecting superstructure which often reduces the characters to caricature. Whereas Robert Walker's production of *Can't Pay? Won't Pay!* could perhaps be faulted for being too naturalistic, Richards' version of *Accidental Death* goes to the opposite extreme, reducing the police characters to almost racist Italian stereotypes, breaking into snatches of doggerel Italian, and even calling one of them 'Inspector Pissani', an unfortunate creation who at one point is made to resort to rosary beads. Fo's essential point about the police characters in the play is missed – despite being bumbling, incompetent buffoons, they are always capable of maintaining an aggressive, threatening front, and are dangerous both for their right-wing political convictions and in their capacity to perpetrate the not infrequent 'accidents' in which innocent people lose their lives. Richards, trying to update and broaden the political perspective of Fo's piece, has the Maniac state glibly:

> These four were there torturing students at the CBS HQ in Paris in May 1968, in the USA at Attica, at Kent State. (*Gives details of examples of political murder and state repression in Britain*.) All this in the name of 'justice' and 'democracy'.[7]

While being the type of solemn rhetoric which Fo never descends to even in his most discursive, long-winded speeches – which are nevertheless always argued through rather than blandly stated – this speech attempts to turn the bungling, ineffectual clowns we have seen into compendium, all-purpose political villains. This is not to suggest that Fo expended undue sympathy on the police characters, but they were at least three-dimensional comic figures who were also

seen to be capable of being menacing. As Franca Rame commented on the
West End production of the play:

> I think the image of Italy as seen from abroad is often ridiculous – in the
> London production of *Anarchist* the characters looked like nineteenth century
> Mafioso types, with long sideburns. It was a very glossy production, with
> stock characters who were like dummies – they reduced the play to a simple
> farce.[8]

Fo's original, in reducing police violence to harmless fisticuffs among themselves
(whereas Richards adds a scene in which the Superintendent enters with a
blackjack from beating up a suspect), concentrates on their stubborn illogicality,
making them all the more insidious, and the anarchist's death (which Richards
has the police admitting to outright) all the more of a painful outrage. In order
to cope with the complicated political background detail of the play, which Fo
could rely on his audience's knowledge of, and which reduces any likelihood of
crass simplifications of the police characters' behaviour, Belt and Braces
produced an admirably-researched, lengthy programme in the form of a
newspaper, relating the play's situation to events in Northern Ireland and the
recent death of the teacher Blair Peach at the hands of London police in an
anti-fascist demonstration. This painstaking explanation of the play's political
relevance both in Italy in the UK relegated Fo's arguments to an extra-theatrical
context. The English version also mangled some of Fo's most effectively political
comic business, in cutting the police agents who appear in the audience at the
Superintendent's command (this despite Belt and Braces' assertion that they
feared police interruption of the performance at Wyndham's Theatre), and all
but cutting the hilarious sequence in which the Maniac puts forward the 'three
shoes' theory. In his introductory comments to the published edition of Belt and
Braces' *Accidental Death*, Fo was restrained in his comments about its loss of his
intentions:

> I am aware . . . that certain moments in the play which were of obvious
> theatrical and political importance at the time had necessarily to be replaced
> because of their limited reference – that is to say, because an English
> audience would be unaware of their background and, above all, because it is
> impossible to restate them in a theatrical context with sufficient pithiness and
> immediacy.
>   So I have the impression – more than an impression – that some passages
> which have been skipped in Gavin Richards' version may have produced some
> erosion at a satirical level, that is to say in the relationship of the tragic to the
> grotesque, which was the foundation of the original work, in favour of
> solutions which are exclusively comic.[9]

But it is not only the removal of the play's tragic background – and the entire
logical mechanism of the play still depends on Pinelli's 'defenestration',
whatever its social context – that cause many of Richards's 'comic solutions' to
ring false. Some of them work against the comic tension which Fo builds up in
terms of pure stagecraft, as in having the Superintendent grabbing the Inspector
after the latter has actually jumped out the window, which destroys the
delicately wrought farcical intrigue with which the Maniac has driven both
characters to the point of almost willingly jumping from the window, only to be
surprised on the window ledge by the Constable. Likewise, passing guitars in to

accompany the Maniac and the Police singing the anarchist song at the end of
Act One is an excessive and unnecessary 'breaking of the fourth wall' which
undermines what in Fo's play is a comic *tour de force*. Likewise, having the
Maniac carry his costume changes in a plastic bag reduces the element of
surprise in having him change his disguises off-stage, while destroying the
plausibility of his duping of the police. Other comic expedients in the Belt and
Braces version, like revealing the Maniac's identity as that of a Jewish
sportswriter for *Lotta Continua*, in order to identify him as a member of the
'lunatic fringe', are examples of the 'easy joke' which Richards claimed to
eschew. Such jokey approximations of Fo's intentions, which the Belt and
Braces' version suffers from all too frequently, indicate the way in which they
held the play at arms length, as it were, using it for their own comic purposes.
One extended joke at Fo's expense (which was enjoyed by Franca Rame)
attempts to justify the liberties they have taken:

PISSANI: This is unheard of distortion of the author's meaning!
MANIAC: He'll get his royalties. Who's moaning?
PISSANI: Get back to the script!
SUPERINTENDENT: This is an insult to Dario Fo!
FELETTI: Good. I've got a bone to pick with him. Why is there only one
        woman's part in his blasted play. I feel marooned!
MANIAC: The author's sexist?
FELETTI: He's pre-historic!
BERTOZZO: Then why are we bothering?
MANIAC: He's a pre-historic genius! On with the dance![10]

This exchange indicates the detachment with which Richards' version regards
Fo's play, with its equation of upholders of the original text with the point of
view of the police characters. Most English audiences and critics, however,
could not be expected to share this detached perspective, or hold the play at
arm's length as the adaptor does. Reviewers of the play tended to take the
additions, alterations and distortions as Fo's own words, leading to a confusion
and misunderstanding which reached a serious extreme in the case of the blatant
misrepresentation of the final scene. Catherine Itzin, reviewing the play in
Tribune, described and commented on Richards' version on the play's ending as
follows:

The cops are handcuffed, and a bomb is ticking away. Does the journalist
escape with her story (yes, it's a woman) leaving the corrupt cops to be blown
to the fate their immorality deserves, or does she let liberal humanitarian
principles prevail and let them go? The play presents both alternative endings,
so perfectly dramatised as to leave the conclusion inescapable that, with the
time bomb of fascism ticking away, the fascists will take advantage of liberal
dithering and blood will be shed.
    In the aftermath of the terrorist murder of Airey Neave, it is profoundly
unnerving to have the terrorist argument put so persuasively.[11]

The two different endings which Fo used for the play, which were never
presented as alternatives, but correspond to two different versions of the play
performed at different times, tell a different story, which make it clear that Fo
never had any intention of presenting 'the terrorist argument'. In the first
ending, the Maniac appears to blow himself up offstage, in an ironic replay of

the police version of the anarchist's death, only to reappear as the 'real' examining magistrate, beginning the play again from the beginning. In the later version, he merely uses the bomb as a threat so that he can escape with his tape recording of his interview with the police. Richards' own comments on his ending indicate that Itzin's response was justified:

> Actually we were right – she should have let the policemen blow up. If you're down to a choice and you're down to thirty seconds, you let them blow up.[12]

Neither of Fo's endings put forward any argument for blowing up the police. The central argument of *Accidental Death of an Anarchist* was that the police should be exposed publically both in their responsiblity for the death of Pinelli and in their collusion with the fascist group responsible for the Piazza Fontana bombing, and brought to justice. In the light of subsequent, wrongful accusations against Fo of support of terrorism, Richards' final addition to this play does him a double injustice, and illustrates the dangerous extremes to which misrepresentation of his plays can lead.

The marketing of Fo in the UK

Belt and Braces' production of *Accidental Death of an Anarchist* became an unprecedented success in both left-wing English circles and in the London establishment theatre. Tariq Ali, reviewing the Half Moon production in *Socialist Challenge*, described the play as:

> the best that I have seen in this country for the last 15 years (and for two of these I had to see five plays a week as the theatre critic of a bourgeois magazine) . . . Fo, close to the bone in Italy, would saw through it in Callaghan's Britain. Don't just go and see the play. Take all your friends as well.[13]

Ali's advice was clearly heeded. The Half Moon was packed out for two separate runs of the play. As a result, the West End producer Ian Alberry, who faced with declining audiences and profits in the West End, had been pursuing a policy of importing productions from London Fringe theatres and the Royal Shakespeare Company directly into the West End rather than trying to mount costly new productions, invited Belt and Braces to transfer *Accidental Death* to Wyndhams Theatre. Alberry stated his policy in the following terms: 'If one factory can make shoes so cheaply, I'd be crazy to put up another at twice the cost.'[14] Hedging his bets on this politically explosive commodity, he transferred it in tandem with another Fringe production, the Richmond Orange Tree's production of a relatively innocuous American comedy, Israel Horowitz's *The Primary English Class*, under the umbrella title *Two Farces*. This led Belt and Braces into a political dilemma: whether to risk accusations of a political sell-out into what they described as 'the minefields of commercialism' or, alternatively, following the example invoked by Richards of Francis Ford Coppola's film *Apocalypse Now*, of using the commercial channels of consumerist entertainment to attack the political values they are founded on, and reaching for a mass audience. The second option was clearly more attractive, and the company regarded themselves as 'the left Fringe company that has kept its integrity best over the last five years and gone into the West End'.[15] Consequently, Richards took over the part of the Maniac from Alfred Molina, who was booked to appear at another West End theatre. Molina received the *Plays and Players* 'Best Actor' award and Richards was subsequently nominated for the Society of West End Theatre award. Albery's 'cheap shoes' policy paid off for *Accidental Death*, but not for *The Primary English Class*, which was eventually taken off, leaving Richards and Belt and Braces to continue their production for almost two years. Massive concessions on ticket prices were made to the unemployed, and in the early months of the run up to a third of the audience may have consisted of people who could otherwise never have afforded to go to a West End theatre. This phenomenon was commented on rather snobbishly by a theatre critic of *The Observer*:

> the ultimate in absurdist West End first nights: a mob of be-parka'd, dungaree'd supporters and usherettes touting the *Socialist Worker* and *Socialist Challenge* along with the programmes and icecreams. With the aid of several excellent players, Gavin Richards, the adaptor, director and lead clown of this essay in Italian agit-prop, turned the auditorium into a fair simulacrum of left-wing pub theatre – with all its good humour and camaraderie, but also with its complacent conviction of being right in being Left.[17]

In many respects the production paralleled Fo's own achievement in bringing his political satire to vast audiences in Italy and throughout Europe, and creating a sense of community with his spectators; it was thus unfortunate that so many of his intentions in *Accidental Death* were misrepresented in the London production. Fo himself, when he saw it, not understanding English, confined his criticisms to the fact that it was overplayed and excessively crude and slapstick, 'overloaded, verging terribly on the grotesque . . . with the excessive buffoonery they introduced into it. For us this buffoonery is "anti-style" . . . not "style" in some vague sense, but "style" in the sense of a satirical form of theatre that seeks to wound, to disturb people, to hit them where it hurts.'[18] For a time, because of the liberties it took with the play's content, he sought to forbid any further productions of Richards' version, which was being requested in a number of British provincial theatres, as well as in Australasia and South Africa, while the Broadway producer Alexander Cohen bought an option on it, due to the West End success. But Fo later relented, saying that 'if nothing else it enabled people to see a style, theatrical language and technique, a conception of theatre, which otherwise they might never have seen. And not only the *technique*, but also the *content*, the politics of it.[18]

Encouraged by the commercial success of *Accidental Death*, Albery and his production company, Omega, invited Robert Walker to re-mount his Half Moon production of *We Can't Pay? We Won't Pay!* at the Criterion Theatre in the West End, where it opened in July 1981 under the title *Can't Pay? Won't Pay!* and likewise ran for almost two years. Hampered by a pastel pink and blue set which was apparently modelled on the idea of Neapolitan icecream, and in no way corresponded to any notion of a working-class apartment in Milan, this production nevertheless remains the most accurate and incisive version of Fo's work seen in London. With Alfred Molina playing Giovanni as a Fiat worker (incorporating Fo's 1980 updating of the play), and the comic actress Maggie Steed playing Margherita, it managed to put across a distinctly Italian spirit

without the demeaning stereotyping of *Accidental Death*. In my view the
production pruned a lot of the play's political jokes along with the title, and
added a few innocuous gags like a 'Where did you get that hat?' routine, a
police sergeant swinging on a drainpipe, and a cuckoo clock collapsing. It also
added a song at the end – 'Sebben che siamo donne' (Though we're women),
originally sung by farmworkers at the turn of the century, but here travestied in
an English version irrelevant to the original. It is also worth pointing out that
Fo's play ended with the local women and the police fighting it out in the
street – a battle which the women win. Both English versions substitute a hastily
patched-up marital quarrel between Antonia and Giovanni. Another curious
innacuracy is Antonia's offer to sell some of her supermarket goods to
Margherita at the beginning of the play – a mistake which is symbolic in
suggesting that Italian generosity, sharing and community feelings do not
transpose well to an English context. The universal nature of the play's theme,
together with its smooth proficiency as an almost well-made farce, made it easier
for West End audiences to enjoy the comedy without pondering unduly on its
radical political message of appropriation, which may have been relegated too
much to a remote Italian setting. This is confirmed by the comments of the
notoriously right-wing *Daily Telegraph*, which were used as publicity for the play
in the West End:

> It is rare to find a farce original enough to forget bedroom antics and find
> jokes in rising prices and quips in unpaid bills and redundancy notices. This
> Dario Fo does with ease, thanks to an ever-bubbling onrush of comic ideas
> and a natural liking for anyone in a desperate fix. He makes you glad to be
> alive.[20]

This mild digestion of Fo's comedy into the reactionary framework of bourgeois
farce suggests that the play's political statements were perhaps couched too
cosily within the traditionalist format of the production. Despite the fact that Fo
regards farce as an essentially popular form, and in this case the point of origin
is hunger and exploitation (the contrary of being 'glad to be alive'), the
conservative, status quo-endorsing connotations of Whitehall farce in Britain
could have been responsible for incorporating *Can't Pay* into a traditional,
boulevard frame of reference – a danger for which the play was criticised by
many left-wing sources in Italy. This exposes a general problem inherent in
assimilating Fo's plays into the commercial, establishment structure of the West
End; one which was pinpointed by Trott as follows in the conclusion of his
article:

> the danger is that once West End theatre managements have sucked the sugar
> off Fo's plays. they will quickly spit out the pill. As long as our alternative
> companies make their main aim transfers to the West End, we are unlikely to
> see the commitment to mounting Fo for his own sake, in a way that it can
> reach large audiences.[21]

But given the generally diminutive size of Britain's Fringe theatres and
alternative theatre groups, and their predominantly precarious financial
predicament under a Conservative government, it is difficult to envisage a
non-West End production of Fo's work reaching the audiences it deserves in the
UK. A relatively non-commercial outlet exists in theatres like the National and
the Royal Shakespeare Company, state-subsidised venues similar to those in

Itaiy which Fo has begun to perform in the 1980s, but with their hierarchical structures and subscription audiences they do not appear to offer a solution.

Adapting Fo III – *Female Parts*

After the success of *Accidental Death of an Anarchist*, the National Theatre, in line with its policy of putting on occasional plays by European writers, decided that Fo's work was a culturally marketable proposition, and opted for an English version of *Tutta casa, letto e chiesa*. This was accurately translated by Margaret Kunzle, a constant collaborator with the Fos and an interpreter for them in Milan, and adapted by Olwen Wymark, a prolifically experimental Fringe and radio playwright whose work had begun to espouse feminist themes. Perhaps uncertain of the monologues' viability in one of their large auditoriums, after they had successfully destroyed the reputation of the Austrian playwright Thomas Bernhardt in the UK with a disastrous production of his play *The Force of Habit* in the mid-1970s, the National chose their smallest, most 'intimate' theatre, the Cottesloe, to mount the pieces. There being no colloquial equivalent in English to the German *Kinder, Küche und Kirche*, the plays' overall title was changed to *Female Parts*, but the National Theatre, fearing this sexually explicit title might offend their patrons, changed it to *One Woman Plays*. This led to the usual confusion by critics between the adaptor's additions and alterations and the authors' text, as in the case of *The Times* critic Irving Wardle:

> The authors have found the right title for these four pieces, but they could not be called 'one character plays'. . . . It is some small comfort that Fo and Rame are writing about Italy which gave the word *machismo* to a grateful world . . .[22]

Cultural misunderstandings such as this (*machismo*, of course, is a Spanish word) indicate the readiness of critics (and no doubt audiences) to regard Fo's plays as taking place in a remote, socially and culturally inferior country – an argument for a total Anglicisation of the plays, as Franca Rame has suggested. In the case of the final piece in *Female Parts*, the authors were totally misrepresented. Stuart Hood, who in 1982 wrote and presented *Throwaway Theatre*, a considered assessment of Fo's work and the problems involved in presenting it in the UK, for BBC Radio 4, which concluded that 'Part of the success of Fo's work in the West End must be attributed to the fact that it can be enjoyed on a non-political level',[23] was responsible for the translation. In transferring the Magna Grecia dialect of the original into a bland and stilted modern English, and omitting Fo and Rame's essential introduction to the piece, he allowed it to be interpreted, as Wardle did, as 'a feminist justification for child slaughter'. One of the principal problems of the adaptation of *Female Parts* is its failure to find a suitable English idiom for each of the four characters, particularly the protagonist of *Waking Up* who, unlike the earthy, gutsy female characters of Walker's *Can't Pay? Won't Pay!*, speaks a tame, middle-class approximation of a working-class idiom, as in the following passage:

> Your dirty socks . . . who washes them eh? How many times have you washed my socks? We should talk to each other, Luigi! We never talk. I

mean it's okay with me that your problems are my problems but why can't my problems be your problems too instead of yours being ours and mine being only mine. I want us to live together . . . not just in the same place. We should talk to each other![24]

This speech, appearing as it does, in the context of a blazing domestic row (even if it is being recalled), seems woefully – though deliberately – convoluted and weak. Likewise, the character of *A Woman Alone* is repeatedly tripped up by a lack of guts in the language. This means that added impetus was thrown on the actress playing the parts, and the South African-born Yvonne Bryceland coped admirably in the National Theatre production, making up in tone and emphasis for what she lacked in lines. Michael Bogdanov's production at the National, apart from being questionable in resorting to a male director, used a detailed, naturalist setting for *Waking Up* and *A Woman Alone*, whereas in Franca Rame's own performance the first piece was frequently done without a set or props, and the second with only the minimum props necessary on a virtually bare stage, which in itself indicates how the National Theatre processed the plays into its predominantly sterile, machine-like house style. As a result, the improvisatory, farcical aspects of the pieces tended to become more sober, which helps to explain Franca Rame's reservations about the production:

> The English actress was very good and the direction was very accurate. However, it got a lot fewer laughs than it did in Italy, and less applause. This I think is because it was a different type of theatre from ours – it was a more naturalistic type of acting and direction. We always try to eliminate the superstructure, the excess, because the most important thing is the content. This is a theatrical choice which is epic rather than naturalistic.[25]

This 'non-epic' aspect of the National production, which imposed its own middle-class superstructure on the plays, together with its more forbidding social ambience (where 'be-parka'd and dungareed' spectators made less frequent incursions) tended to reduce the political impact of the pieces, although Lloyd Trott suggests otherwise:

> Such is the thrust of the direction here, combined with a virtuoso performance from Yvonne Bryceland in all four pieces, that the audience cannot leave the theatre without coming to some new or re-assessment of what they think woman's lot to be.[26]

Although these comments appear somewhat prescriptive and grandiose for a production which all but stifled the spontaneity of the original pieces, *Female Parts* remained in the National Theatre's repertoire for two years, in no small way assisted by Yvonne Bryceland's incisive performance, which later successfully toured South Africa, while Olwen Wymark's adaptation has been produced throughout the UK and Australasia. London audiences were able to assess Franca Rame's own performance of the pieces when the actress performed them herself in Italian with English subtitles at the Riverside Studios in May 1982, although perhaps the most predominant aspect of her performance to strike English audiences and critics was her glamour.

In March 1983 an English version of four of the lesser-performed monologues from the first published edition of *Tutta casa, letto e chiesa* were performed at the Drill Hall in London by the feminist group Monstrous Regiment in a translation by Gillian Hanna. This production, entitled *The Fourth Wall*, was directed by Penny Cherns, designed by Hildegaard Bechtler, and performed by Paola Dionisotti in tandem with Maggie Nicols. It opened with *Ulrike Meinhof*, and included *Tomorrow's News*, one of the Fos' most abrasive political monologues based around Red Army Fraction member Gudrun Ensslin, the sole survivor of the Stammheim prison 'suicides', for whom the Fos campaigned extensively in the late 1970s. The Monstrous Regiment production also included two other pieces which were discarded by Franca Rame soon after she first began touring *Tutta casa, letto e chiesa*. The English group's rendition of these was described by Rosalind Carne in *The Guardian* as follows:

> *Alice in Wonderless Land* is a heavy-handed attempt to overeach (sic) the original by turning the White Rabbit into a sex-exploitation movie mogul. *The Whore in the Madhouse* presents a questionable analysis of the ethics of prostitution, making the offensive assumption that the prostitutes have lost their self-respect.[27]

The retrieval of these pieces for an English production was clearly worthwhile, and the monologues were adapted into duologues with cabaret elements and musical accompaniment. Despite attracting little attention from press and public and having only a short run, the Fringe context of the production and the care and dedication exerted on it make it one of the few English productions of the Fos' work which does some justice to its originals both politically and theatrically.

Mistero buffo in London

Dario Fo's performance of *Mistero buffo* in London in May 1983, together with Franca Rame's second edition of *Tutta casa, letto e chiesa*, and the theatre workshops which both ran with English actors and actresses – which were religiously recorded, transcribed and later published – brought about a belated recognition of Fo and Rame as the world's most important contemporary exponents of popular political theatre. Billed in London as a 'classic', 14 years after it had first been performed, *Mistero buffo* won over the English audiences and critics who managed to get seats in the small Riverside Studios to the warmth, humour and comedy of Fo's performance. Fo's appearance in London was largely due to the efforts of David Gotthard, the artistic director of the Riverside Studios, which had housed Franca Rame's performance of *Tutta casa, letto e chiesa* the previous year, and to which, when threatened with closure due to a reduction in its grant from Hamersmith Council, Fo had given a long-term 'loan' of £7,000 – a rare case of Italy helping Britain out economically. Despite Gotthard's entrepreneurial foresight, however – attempts were made to lure Fo into a West End theatre after his three week run at the Riverside – he was unceremoniously sacked by the GLC-backed Riverside board in 1985.

Whereas French critics in 1974 had immediately found points of comparison between Fo and Chaplin and Jacques Tati, British reviewers pulled out the stops in invoking Anglo-Saxon cultural reference-points in which to encapsulate the spontaneous, chameleon-like ease of Fo's performance range, and it is worth listing some of these as an indication of the polymath which English critics received him as. Steve Grant of *Time Out*, after meeting the Fos in Milan, wrote 'As a couple they have the status, charisma and attendant problems of a

cross between Miller and Monroe, John and Yoko, John Arden and Margaretta
D'Arcy, and Richard Briars and Felicity Kendall. . . . He's rather like a
souped-up Gypsy Dave Frost cum Tommy Cooper with a bit of Ken Campbell
rolled in.' Jim Hiley in *The Observer*, after meeting Fo and seeing *Il fabulazzo
osceno*, wrote 'It's as if Terry Wogan had suddenly acquired the technique of
Marcel Marceau, the charisma of Richard Pryor, the intellectualism of Jonathan
Miller and the politics of Ken Livingstone'. Michael Billington in *The Guardian*
invites us to 'Imagine, if you can, Dick Gregory crossed with Billy Dainty and
Jacques Tati . . . Like many soloists (such as Ruth Draper), Fo can also evoke a
crowd.' To Michael Coveney of *The Financial Times*, 'The whole event is like a
Ken Dodd special scuppered by a cheerfully left-wing blasphemer . . . Fo
himself is a physical blend of Barry Humphries and Jacques Tati', while Brian
Glanville, reporting on Fo's workshops in *The Sunday Times* makes the
inevitable comparison with John Cleese's silly walks, adding that 'Like Max
Wall or Tommy Trinder, he'll make use of a latecomer. . . . Like Roy Hudd, he
may crack a "difficult" joke, and pretend that one part of the audience has got
it, the other hasn't . . .' John Barber in *The Daily Telegraph* described Fo as
possessing 'an impertinent Lombard nose and John Betjeman's mouth', while
Giles Gordon in *The Spectator* saw him as 'a kind, gentle man, as if Alan
Ayckbourn took to writing political texts . . . with teeth which, when he grins,
which he does a lot, recall Cardew Robinson'. These excursions into cultural
anthropology indicate that Fo can represent all things to all people, of all
political persuasions. Apart from the first two, they are all based on seeing
performances of *Zanni's Grammelot, The Raising of Lazarus, Boniface VIII,
The American Technocrat, Scapino's Teaching Lesson* and (in the workshops)
The Morality of the Blind Man and the Cripple, together with Fo's improvised,
topical sketches introducing the pieces, which represents a minute fraction of
Fo's solo performance repertoire. But given this, the general conclusion of
many British critics seems to be that Fo is a likeable and brilliant
performer in his own right, and that his tendency to revolutionary politics is a
by-product which can be taken with a pinch of salt. A fair proportion of the
comparisons made are to music hall and TV comedians who propagate a cosy,
reactionary form of popular English humour, including smut – a narrow
reduction of the abrasive, grotesque, frequently scatological and mocking nature
of Fo's political satire. In suggesting that the English could never produce a
clown like Fo because in *Mistero buffo* he relies on a historical background of
papacy and religious repression, Michael Stewart in *Tribune* attempts to
pigeonhole Fo's satirical targets into a cultural category remote from British
concerns – forgetting that the visit of Pope John-Paul II – a constant source of
Fo's topical lampoons – to the UK caused the Falklands war to recede into the
background of the British public conscience, and neglecting Fo's constant
barrage of scorn directed at a vast range of Italian political contradictions. That
Fo's influence has begun to be felt on political theatre in Britain is indicated by
the Dario Fo/Franca Rame Theatre Project which was held at the Riverside
Studios in London in January 1984. Conceived as a British response to Fo's and
Rame's performances at the Riverside the previous spring, this event consisted
of a rehearsed reading of *Hooters, Trumpets and Raspberries* (*Clacson, trombette
e pernacchi*, and performances of the three monologues *I Don't Move
. . ., The Mother* and *Michèle Spear-Head*, which received their English
premieres along with responding monologues by English women playwrights,

including Pam Gems and Michelene Wandor, the 1982 Theatre Company's ensemble English version of *Mistero buffo*, and a discussion forum on the subject 'Is political theatre alive and well in Britain?' This cross-fertilisation of Fo with English theatre seems an admirable way of approaching the Fos' work both politically and theatrically, while no doubt clearing up a number of Anglo-Saxon misconceptions about it. These continue to proliferate in press reports about Fo, however, if Irving Wardle's assumption in *The Times* that Agnelli's kidnapping in *Clacson* is based on an actual event is any indication. Most of the play's comedy for an Italian audience derives from the fact that its central situation is a colossal political joke, for which Fo deliberately chose Agnelli rather than Moro. Wardle does describe Fo's visit to London in retrospect as 'a revelation comparable to London's first sight of the Berliner Ensemble'[28] – high praise indeed, and evidence that Fo's importance is beginning to filter through into Anglo-Saxon theatre. As a reviewer summing up the Riverside forum on English political theatre concluded in *City Limits*:

> If alternative theatre (in Britain) is to lose many of its sources of funding, then Fo's Italian experience stands as a salutary reminder. Audiences are the key to survival. Ideology may be the first rule according to Fo (if somewhat sardonically in his eyes), but the second is surely that political theatre need not be divorced from either humour or entertainment values.[29]

Audiences are important for Fo's plays also, and it is to be hoped that a good deal more of them, starting with a full-scale production of *Clacson*, and including *La storia della tigre* and *Il fabulazzo osceno* as well as some of his earlier work like *Archangels Don't Play Pinball*, will be seen in the UK and elsewhere in the near future. If this happens, a fuller picture of the extraordinary theatrical breadth and political impact of this unique actor, playwright and director will begin to emerge.

6: AT HOME AND ABROAD 1984-85

I've been told that (the London) productions have unearthed a sort of current which has affected writers as well as performers. They've been forced to use quite different techniques from what they normally use. The same thing happened in France. It took years to find a company who could perform our plays, and there were terrible gaps. The point isn't that we aren't performed well, but that the plays are experienced in a different way. (Fo in *Sipario*, September 1983.)

Some attempt to provide a fuller picture of Fo's work to English audiences was made in Dennis Marks' 50 minute BBC Arena television programme, *The Theatre of Dario Fo*, which was transmitted on BBC2 on 28 February, 1984. The programme was seen mainly by a tiny, educated section of the British viewing public – a far cry from the popular audiences Fo's work reaches in Italy. TV and video are ideal media for Fo and Rame's solo work, which relies predominantly on body movement and facial expression, and largely abandons costume, makeup, props and settings. Marks' programme included large chunks of *Boniface VIII*, one of the more straightforward and theatrically less interesting pieces from *Mistero buffo*, but little of this performance, filmed in a circus tent during the 1983 Venice carnival, was shot from close up enough for television audiences to gain its full benefits. *Boniface VIII* was described as 'the most popular' of the numerous pieces that make up *Mistero buffo* (a contestable assumption, since it is rarely among the audience requests Fo receives), leading some of the newspaper previews of the programme to assume that *Mistero buffo* was entirely about Boniface VIII.[1] The programme did include an uncredited extract from *The Resurrection of Lazarus*, but further confused the issue by stating that Fo had been performing *Mistero buffo* for 20 years, inspiring the preview of the programme in *The Times* to inform us that Fo 'became a television star, performing for 20 years in his own show that consistently topped the ratings with viewing figures of around 20 million'![2] A long and irrelevant sequence of the Neapolitan performer Beppe Barra in the guise of the 'sad eyed' commedia dell' arte character Pulcinella was intended to illustrate the influence of the commedia on Fo. No examples at all were given of Franca Rame's work – indeed she made only one, brief and unannounced, appearance in the entire programme, in which she came across as little more than an appendage to her husband, repeating her oft-told story about La Comune's benefit performance for an occupied factory in Bologna, when audiences bought more than 10,000 glasses made by the workers. There were a number of inaccurate claims, like the suggestion that La Compagnia Fo-Rame's work in the 1960s was 'couched in a theatrical mask of fun and spectacle', and that in plays like *Isabella, Three*

Sailing Ships and a Con Man, 'the satire was comfortably cushioned by the sixteenth century setting and costumes'. The fact that the play was charged with offence against the Italian armed forces, and the censorship problems it ran into, suggest that this was far from the case. Fo and Rame's work outside of *Boniface VIII* was dealt with only in a rapid and confusing montage of their TV cycle, including some rare footage of *Ci ragiono e canto*, with an uncredited appearance by Cicciu Busacca, and Gavin Richards' adaptation of *Accidental Death of an Anarchist*. What emerged from the programme was a misleading, incomplete approximation of Fo's work which did nothing to expand his already known performance repertoire and provided little background information to his (or indeed Rame's) work. It might be argued that such a task was beyond a 50 minute TV profile, but comparison with Birgitta Bergmark and Carlo Barsotti's 1977 Swedish TV programme, *Gott folk, här kommer gycklaren: Dario Fo e Franca Rame* (*Good People, Here Come the Jesters . . .*) does not bear this out. This clear, imaginatively filmed programme provided extracts from *Zanni's Grammelot, The Same Old Story, Waking Up* and *The Child Jesus' First Miracle*, as well as improvised pieces by Fo about the Italian police and Pope Pius VI, interspersed with cogent interviews with Fo and Rame about their early work, popular theatre, the Italian Communist Party, farce, Rame's solo performances, and Soccorso Rosso. It also included illuminating footage of the couple rehearsing *The Same Old Story*, and a powerful sequence of one of Rame's performances of *Waking Up* at an occupied factory, followed by a discussion with the audience of workers. All the salient theatrical and political information about Fo and Rame's work up to 1977 is adequately covered, while the comedy and the political force of their work is captured with an impact which Marks' programme does not even begin to achieve.

Teaching praxis

Some of the restrictions of the BBC Arena programme could be attributed to the fact that it was made at a time when Fo and Rame were peripatetic, and had to make the most of the Venice carnival as a somewhat spurious example of elements of popular culture and commedia dell'arte reflected in Fo's work. It also dealt briefly with the summer school where Fo and Rame teach theatre in Santa Cristina di Gubbio. This school, known as the 'Free University of Alcatraz', and run by Jacopo Fo, has become an international alternative study centre in theatre, music, literature, journalism, pottery, aerobics, Italian for foreigners and numerous other subjects, involving figures like Dacia Maraini, Lucio Dalla, Enzo Jannacci and the Colombaioni brothers. In the Arena programme, we see part of one of the demonstration-lessons Fo holds on the commedia dell'arte, using masks made by Donata Sartori. Fo's role as a teacher of commedia forms differs greatly from his role as a performer. The commedia half-masks restrict vastly the rich range of facial expressions which are his stock-in-trade, and the stylised, stereotyped movements of commedia characters like il Dottore differ greatly from the fluid, supple and unrestricted movements Fo employs in fleshing out the multitude of characters he plays in his own solo pieces. A case in point is his portrayal of Zanni, a prototype of Harlequin. The *lazzo* (improvised business) in which Zanni chases, catches and eats a fly is one of the best-known of the commedia dell'arte, and a prominent feature of *Mistero buffo*. In the Arena progamme we see Fo doing the piece in a mask, obscuring the facial expressions ranging from mock irritation to delight which are precisely the most comically appealing aspects of Fo's performance of the piece. Fo's use of commedia dell'arte, then, might be compared to the way a musician uses scales.

In April 1984, Fo and Donato Sartori held a seminar on commedia masks at the Projektgruppen Sartoris Masker in Copenhagen, and Fo brought the resulting teaching-demonstration, 'The History of Masks', to the Riverside Studios in London a few months later. This 'master class', translated by Stuart Hood, consisted of a demonstration of the various commedia masks and the voices and movements traditionally associated with them, and culminated in a performance of *'The Wedding Feast of Canaan'* from *Mistero buffo*. Robert Page, writing in *The Times*, was unstinting in his praise of the workshop:

> Dario Fo, impresario of the left, maestro of comic communism, is fast becoming the kind of cult star in England that he is in his native Italy. Perhaps he cannot quite fill a football stadium here – yet – but he can draw sell-out audiences at the Riverside.

This suggestion that Fo is becoming a 'cult star' in the UK is somewhat alarming. The West End productions of his plays have surely reached audiences wider than mere cult-followers, while according him a similar status in Italy, where he is virtually a household name on a par with a popular comedian like Ken Dodd, is quite mistaken. Far from operating as a 'cult star', Fo uses work like 'The History of Masks' to an educational purpose, the effect of which is, hopefully, to dispel the kind of misconceptions about his work which English critics seem very prone to.

After 'The History of Masks', Fo and Rame performed *Mistero buffo* and *Tutta casa, letto e chiesa* at the 1984 Edinburgh Festival, where they were billed in the Fringe section, while the visiting Berliner Ensemble appeared in the main festival drama programme – an apt positioning of the two groups *vis-a-vis* official culture. It is interesting to note that *Mistero buffo* created resonances for at least one Edinburgh reviewer with the sixteenth century Scottish satirist Lindsay, whose work has exerted considerable influence on the discomforting political plays of John Arden. Allen Wright, reviewing *Mistero buffo* in *The Scotsman*, suggested that Fo:

> trades in satire of classic quality – the mediaeval Italian equivalent of the comical passages in Sir David Lindsay's satire of the Thrie Estites. Both *The Resurrection of Lazarus* and *Boniface VIII* bear some resemblance to the Scots satire's remarks on the sale of indulgences and vanity and corruption of the clergy.[3]

While English reviewers have sought equivalents for Fo's works in contemporary TV comedians, and then questioned the relevance to Britain of his satire of church authorities, Wright's comments suggest that the traditional roots of *Mistero buffo* might have stronger resonances in English Renaissance and mediaeval theatre.

Fo expanded his teaching performances at the beginning of the 1984–85 Italian theatre season, after he was invited to open a special all-Italian project at the prestigious mainstream Teatro di Roma, under the title 'From the commedia dell'arte to Variety'. Fo outlined his didactic aims for the project in an interview in the newspaper *La Repubblica*:

I'll explain and demonstrate, along with extracts from *Mistero buffo*, how the allusive power of gesture is faster than that of writing. It is the audience who influences the mould, the weave, the charge and the physiognomy of a performance, by the way in which they react. Certain things won't work if they're only written in advance, which is why I regard myself as an adherent to texts that are compiled in a pentagram including rhythm and sound.[4]

These comments indicate the gap which exists between Fo's plays in their written form, and his own performances of the plays – a gap which is widened considerably further in translations of the texts into another language. At the Teatro di Roma Fo performed a series of extracts from *Mistero buffo, La storia della tigre* and *Il fabulazzo osceno*, frequently freezing and de-constructing them on the spot, explaining his movements and mimic techniques. The results, a fascinating self-analysis of his own performance, were televised in 6 one-hour parts on the 3rd channel of the RAI in February and March 1985, under the title 'The Tricks of the Trade'. He demonstrates how, for example, he changes from one character to another in *The Resurrection of Lazarus* in the course of representing an entire crowd of people, or how, in *The Story of the Tigress*, the performer can create different angles of perspective similar to close-ups, tracking shots, pans or cross-fades in the cinema. Fo's minimalism of means in his solo performances creates curious resonances in a mass-media society. Eugenio Barba, for whose International School of Theatre Anthropology Fo has done a number of performance-seminars, has reported how the Japanese sculptor Wakafuji was struck by the similarity between some of Fo's movements in *The Story of The Tigress* and the karate gesture known as *neko hashi daci*, or 'standing on cats' feet'. Barba himself has compared a 'synthesis' of Fo's movements in the same piece to those of a Schultz comic strip.[5] Barba's observations show how Fo's performances cover a wide range of visual techniques which stimulate an audience's imagination; that they are very much 'theatre of the eye', to use the title of an exhibition devoted to Fo's theatre work in Rome. This exhibition, '*Dario Fo: Il Teatro dell'occhio*', opened at the Palazzo Braschi at the same time as Fo's lecture-demonstrations at the Teatro di Roma. This acclaim for his work by the 'higher' Italian cultural institutions suggests that his success and popularity outside Italy is beginning to be acknowledged.

Another interesting feature revealed by the TV programmes 'The Tricks of the Trade' is the way in which Fo has embellished his pieces in the course of their repeated public exposure. In *The Story of the Tigress*, for example, the roaring lessons which the tigress and her cub give to the Chinese villagers to help them intimidate the Japanese invaders have expanded from a couple of simple roars in the early performances of the piece to a fully orchestrated sequence of demonstrations, imitations and reactions involving extraordinary vocal modulations and timing. Fo has explained how one piece from *Il fabulazzo osceno*, 'The Butterfly Mouse', has similarly expanded from its original format of a 15 minute sketch to a performance vehicle lasting 40 minutes, largely through 'the accumulation of pauses, digressions, interpolations and stage business'.[6]

Accidental Death of an Anarchist on Broadway

In November 1984, the world-renowned Neapolitan actor-playwright Eduardo de

Filippo died, and Fo, as the only other Italian actor-playwright of comparable stature, was asked to speak at his funeral – a speech which, however, Fo claims was censored by the Italian national TV networks.[7] The news of de Filippo's death broke shortly before the news that Fo and Rame had finally been granted an entry visa to the USA for the occasion of the Broadway opening of *Accidental Death of an Anarchist* at the Belasco Theatre. The play, brought to Broadway, 14 years after its first performance in Italy, by producer Alexander Cohen, was in fact a transfer of a production of the play by the Washington Arena Stage, adapted by Richard Nelson from a translation by Suzanne Cowan, and directed by Douglas Wager, at the Kreeger Theatre in Washington nine months earlier. For Broadway, the production was almost completely recast, and the English actor Jonathan Pryce took over the main role (here called 'the Fool', alias 'Antonio A. Antonio') from Richard Bauer. Nelson's adaptation transposes the play from Milan to Rome (for no clearly apparent reason), and includes a good many topical American references, in accordance with a note by Fo published in the Washington Arena programme:

> The American public, seeing this play in its present adaptation, obviously cannot feel the real, tragic, tangible atmosphere which the Italian public brought with them when they came to the performance. It can share this only by the act of imagination or – better still – by substituting for the violence practised by the powers in Italy (the police, the judiciary, the economy of banks and multinationals) equally tragic or brutal facts from the recent history of America.[8]

But it is debatable whether the adaptor found suitably 'tragic or brutal facts' with which to localise the play, if references (mentioned in reviews of the production) to a fiasco at a Beach Boys concert, government cheese giveaways, Jimmy Carter's debate briefing book, and lines like the Fool's 'Jesus! – no, I was him last week', or his summation of the past 20 years of American political history as non-stop spectacular entertainment are any indication. Also questionable is the substitution of the anarchist song *Nostra patria è il mondo intero* by *Look for the Union Label*, which the Fool induces the police characters to perform wearing women's wigs. Such transpositions suggest a complete lack of a necessary tragic, violent and dangerous political context for the humour, which is necessary to give the play the grotesque, farcical impact it achieved in its original form. Mel Gussow, writing in the *New York Times*, summed up the Washington Arena production in this way:

> The Arena version of the play is not as funny as the one anglicised and performed by Gavin Richards in London . . . In this less zany version, the second act briefly slows down and then winds towards a confusing conclusion. America would still seem to be in need of a true 'Anarchist' adaptation.[9]

A previous adaptation of the play by John Lahr had been performed with little success in Los Angeles, and it appeared from the Washington production that the play needed substantial reworking. The casting of Pryce was clearly an attempt to emulate Richards' West End version of the play, and reviews of the Broadway production, which closed after only a few months, suggested that Pryce's high-powered performance almost turned the play into a one-man show. The timing of the production, with its references to Reagan's electoral campaign coming after the president's comfortable re-election, was also unfortunate, and critical concensus appeared to indicate that the play's satirical force was too soft. This concensus is borne out by Fo's own brief comments on the production in an article he wrote for the Italian popular weekly magazine *Oggi* after his and Rame's trip to New York:

> Jonathan Pryce is excellent. His timing is good, he gets the most out of the gags, and he's very likeable. But Franca and I couldn't help noticing how some of the more aggressive passages in the play had been softened, and some of the more brutal political jokes had been replaced with euphemistically innocuous stuff.[10]

But Fo and Rame nonetheless rose to the occasion of their first visit to the USA, and clearly enjoyed all the publicity and red-carpet celebrity status they were given, while expressing a resolve to return there as soon as they could to perform. Fo turned his speech of thanks to the first-night audience at the Belasco theatre into a performance vehicle:

> Our most sincere thanks go to your president, Ronald Reagan, for the magnificent publicity campaign he organised for our Broadway debut. Yes, only now can I reveal to you that it was our friend Ronald's idea to refuse us entry visas twice. He did it in cahoots with us, so we could get to be famous in the USA. He rang us up in person in Italy: 'Hello? This is Ronald. Listen, I've had an idea. I won't let you have a visa just yet. That way there'll be one hell of an outcry, and people will start asking 'Who are these two actors?' What are their plays like? How come they're so dangerous?' Public interest will mount up, and then to cap it all, the day before I'm sworn in for another term – kerpow! I'll give you a visa. That way people will think I'm being real democratic. Even though I am a Republican. And you'll get yourselves standing ovations!' Well, that's exactly what happened. Reagan's never forgotten his youth, when he was an actor. He just wanted to make a show of solidarity with two of his colleagues.[10]

Adapting Fo IV – *Trumpets and Raspberries*

The September 1983 issue of the Italian theatre magazine *Sipario* profiles Fo and Rame's success in London, stating that 'after Shakespeare, Dario Fo competes with Andrew Lloyd Webber as the most frequently performed playwright in England'.[11] In an interview in the same article, Franca Rame talks about the London productions of *One Woman Plays* and *Can't Pay? Won't Pay!*:

> 'The motivations for putting on these plays are different from ours. When we did *Non si paga! Non si paga!* we started from a real situation, just as the work we did on women was very precise, both theatrically and ideologically. Here *Non si paga!* is taken just as a play, without any real starting point. In my show, because I've worked on it, and especially because I've worked on it with audiences, I get a thousand or so laughs. Here it's a couple of hundred, because they've cut the translation, chucked out what they don't understand, and distorted the overtly political aspects.'[12]

While this helps to illuminate the difficulties involved in dealing with Fo and Rame's work, which is essentially a process which never ceases developing in front of an audience, in terms of imported products, Rame's comments apply equally to the West End's next Dario Fo production. *Trumpets and Raspberries*, the pruned-down title given to Fo's play about Fiat boss Gianni Agnelli, *Clacson, Trombette e Pernacchi*, opened at the Phoenix Theatre in the same week as the Broadway production of *Accidental Death of an Anarchist*. Directed by Roger Smith from a translation by Roger McAvoy and Anna-Maria Giugni, with Griff Rhys Jones in the double role of Agnelli and Antonio Berardi created by Fo, this production was also a transfer, having originated at the Watford Playhouse.

The subject of *Trumpets and Raspberries*, which depends a great deal on the key role of Agnelli, whom few English spectators can be expected to have heard of, poses problems in transferring the play to an English context, and the adaptors wisely chose to retain the Italian setting of the play as much as possible. In a very useful programme note to the play, Stuart Hood explains the most important facts about Agnelli, but omits any mention of the fact that he is honorary president of the Juventus football teams, and the text of the play likewise omits all Fo's references to Juventus. Leaving aside the fact that the club was later to hit international headlines due to the massacre of some of its supporters in a European Cup final at Brussels by Liverpool supporters in May 1985, it seems a curious omission, since football fanaticism is a strong cultural attribute (although not, perhaps, to middle-class theatre audiences) that Italy and the UK have in common. More so, at least, than a knowledge of Italian politicians like Spadolini, Rognoni and Valiani, who are retained in the English version along with a number of Italian places and events, requiring 14 footnotes in the Pluto Press edition of the text. Attempts to contextualise Agnelli seem to have proved difficult. Hood's programme note compares him with Michael Edwardes of British Leyland, a comparison which is changed to Ian MacGregor of the National Coal Board in the published version of the text. In the publicity leaflet about the production, Antonio's rescue of Agnelli is described as being 'like Arthur Scargill rescuing Ian MacGregor', and these references to the miners' strike are apt, if skin deep (Antonio in no way corresponds to a union leader like Scargill). But Michael Billington, in his *Guardian* review of the opening night performance at the Phoenix, reports how Agnelli was described as 'a cross between John de Lorean and the Duke of Kent'[13] which seems rather more innocuous, as well as far-fetched.

McAvoy and Giugni's version of the play claims to have been edited by Franca Rame, and a number of cuts (including the 3-page resumé of recent Italian political history in Fo's text of the play) certainly improve the flow of the play, while other alterations are less justifiable. One major restructuring of the original text which Fo and Rame made in performance was the transposition of the first scene, set in a car wrecker's yard, to half way through the second scene, set in a hospital. This was done for practical reasons, in order to avoid a separate set for the car-wrecker's yard, occasioning a rather awkward explanatory note about this back-tracking in which Fo enters and 'steps into' his role of Antonio. The resultant breaking of the fourth wall, which Fo easily builds into his performance style in the play, is transferred holus-bolus into the British version:

> *At this point, enter from backstage the actor who plays the part of* ANTONIO.
> ANTONIO: Excuse me . . . Excuse me . . . I'm going to have to interrupt at
> this point, because a misunderstanding is being created.

The actors on stage freeze. ANTONIO *moves to the front of the stage and addresses the audience directly.*
The lights go down in the operating theatre. The actors exit.
ANTONIO *remains front-stage, and behind him, a platform is wheeled on. On it are two car seats and assorted scrap parts of motor cars. We are in a breaker's yard.*

In this play, I take the part of Antonio, Rosa's husband. But I am not the donar kebab you see here on the operating table. That's someone else. So who is it? Well, in order to explain this, I'm going to have to put things in order, and go back 24 hours, to yesterday evening. So, last night, or rather at about two o'clock this morning, I, Antonio Berardi, Fiat worker, was parked in my car in a secluded spot on the outskirts of Turin . . . . [14]

Since the car wrecker's yard is now represented by a complete set, the point of the original restructuring is now completely destroyed, and we are left with a clumsy piece of direct address and a 'flashback' for no apparent reason. The essential expository information contained in the car-wrecker's yard scene, which included Antonio's description of his rescue of Agnelli, would surely be more smoothly put across by reverting to the play's original chronological order. One beneficial side-effect of the re-allocation of the scene is that it establishes a Brechtian stepping out of character. Although it appears that this was established right from the beginning of the play in the West End production, by the actor explaining who Agnelli is to the audience, it is used effectively, if somewhat cutely, later in the play by Antonio's wife Rosa:

ROSA: Ladies and gentlemen. Three days have passed since the last scene. Well if he can do it so can I. Here, do you know who he is? It's only Gianni Agnelli, living in Rosa's house . . . [15]

Like Gavin Richards' adaptation of *Accidental Death of an Anarchist*, *Trumpets and Raspberries* transposes Fo and Rame's relaxed, open style of direct, and frequently improvised, address to audiences as themselves rather than the characters they are playing, into the somewhat more stilted and self-conscious devices of English music hall. These uses of direct address rely on spontaneity and ad-libbing for them to work, as in the moment in the play when the Doctor is trying to inject Agnelli/Antonio with a sedative:

At this point, the actors pretend to make a slip-up on stage. The DOCTOR *pretends to trip, and loses his hypodermic syringe. The* ACTRESS *playing* ROSA *looks disconcerted as she picks up the syringe. The* ACTORS *burst out laughing, the* ACTOR *playing the* DOCTOR *feigns embarrassment and consternation. The* ACTOR *playing the part of* ANTONIO *speaks.*

ACTOR PLAYING THE PART OF ANTONIO: Well, there you are, it could have happened to anybody . . . particularly to real doctors! But anyway, it's my fault, because I spun him round too fast. It's my fault. Doctors, as we know are never responsible, either in civil or in criminal law. OK, let's start again where we left off . . . [16]

Scripted in this way, such a piece of stage business seems clumsy and long-winded. A *lazzo* similar to the farcical antics of the police in the second act of *Accidental Death of an Anarchist*, it relies on improvisation by the cast performing the play, and shows signs of originating from an 'accident' in Fo's original performance of the play.

Many of the additions in McAvoy and Giugni's adaptation of *Trumpets and Raspberries* contrast sharply with the spirit of the original, like the following exchange:

DOCTOR: Maybe he was knocked down by a car . . . Some hit and run driver. In fact the person who handed him over to the Red Cross promptly – poof – disappeared!

ROSA: Poof was he aye? May God strike him down! . . .[17]

The banal anti-homosexual joke is incidental to say the least, while Rosa's speech is given Catholic attributes which are nowhere present in the original. Most of Fo's work satirises the Catholic church in one way or another, but *Trumpets and Raspberries*, interestingly, does not. Other interpolated gags like having the Doctor break into German (whereas Antonio's speech inflexions faintly suggest an Irish brogue) seem equally inappropriate, as does a jokey reference to a game called 'terrorist bingo' and Rosa's resort to witchcraft on her rival Lucia. The effect of such gags not only cheapens and softens the impact of the play's grotesque extended joke, which incorporates force-feeding and police brutality, but trivialises the serious political points the play is making. It is worth comparing an extract from Fo's original text with the transformation it has undergone in McAvoy and Giugni's adaptation. In the third scene of Act One, Agnelli (the Double) is recovering from a series of operations, including plastic surgery which has made his face resemble Antonio's, and is suffering from amnesia and speech deficiencies. A Police Inspector and a Magistrate, under the Doctor's supervision, are trying to induce him to remember his past, with a view to getting him to confess he was responsible for the terrorist kidnapping of Agnelli:

MAGISTRATE: Tell me, Antonio – do you remember any details from your childhood?

DOUBLE: When I was little . . . I used to like cars . . . Right from when I was a toddler!

MAGISTRATE: Well, all small children like cars.

DOUBLE: I liked them more than anyone! I lived in a bi-i-ig building.

DOCTOR: Everything seems big to a child.

DOUBLE: And I had a brother and a sister and we all used to dress up in sailor suits.

POLICEMAN: Shall I write that down about the sailor suits, sir?

INSPECTOR: No, we don't want any of that nonsense!

MAGISTRATE: Interesting! Do go on.

DOUBLE: I liked football. I supported Juventus.

INSPECTOR: Juventus supporter, eh? Interesting.

DOUBLE: I supported the whole team. Then I got fed up with them and handed it all over to my brother.

MAGISTRATE *(laughing)*: Peculiar way of expressing himself. What do you remember about your mother and father?

DOUBLE: Mother? Can't remember a thing. No mummy. Daddy, daddy – yes! He used to take me to see all the cars . . .

INSPECTOR: Oh yes. Did he work at Fiat too?

DOUBLE: Work? Don't remember . . . Fiat? Yes, I think so . . . Ah vra ma tra . . . (*Uncoordinated gestures.*) He was a strange, cold bloke my father. Used to wear a black shirt and call Mussolini an arsehole – ha ha! Hey! I can laugh!

MAGISTRATE: Well, I suppose if he was a worker he would've worn a black shirt.

DOUBLE: He used to say things . . . Tell funny stories. If I can just force . . .

DOCTOR: No – don't strain yourself, please!

DOUBLE: Now I remember! He used to say 'Everything's up for sale in this world. It's all a question of the market prices. You can even buy off the pope if you have to! And the peelers, the peepers, the creepers, the nippers, the stinkers, the crappers and the shitholes. It's just a question of how much you're prepared to pay'.

INSPECTOR: What exactly did he mean by that?

DOUBLE: Quite simple really. Old underworld nonesense slang. You've got the pope, the chief of police – that's the peeler . . . and the creepers are the police inspectors . . .

INSPECTOR: I see!

DOUBLE: The nippers are the police superintendents, the peepers are the magistrates, and the judges are the stinkers. Councillors are crappers and the Minister of Justice is the shithole.

MAGISTRATE: His father sounds a bit much if you ask me.

DOUBLE: He was a bloody great slob. Rabid catholic too. He used to say, 'Never judge a man by appearances. Judge him by his good deeds. Property deeds.' He was a stickler about the law, too. 'Render unto Caesar what is Caesar's', he'd say. '32 stab wounds!' This talking's doing me good. I feel much better already.[18]

McAvoy and Giugni's version runs as follows:

EXAMINING MAGISTRATE: You're right. Listen, Mr Berardi, do you remember any particular details of your childhood?

DOUBLE: My childhood! Yes . . . When I was a child . . . I liked motor cars, when I was a child . . .

EXAMINING MAGISTRATE: But all little boys like motor cars . . .

DOUBLE: But I liked them mooore! I lived in a greeeat big maaansion . . .

DOCTOR: In childhood memories, everything is always big.

DOUBLE: Yes. And when you're big it can be fucking enormous if you play your cards right. I remember when I was fourteen I was given a cowboy outfit.

EXAMINING MAGISTRATE: Cowboy outfit?

DOUBLE: Yes, and I've been running it ever since. Does that mean anything to you?

POLICEMAN (*with typewriter*): . . . Cowboy outfit.

INSPECTOR: Scrub that out. Cowboy outfits.

EXAMINING MAGISTRATE: What do you recall about your mother and
                your father?

DOUBLE: My mother . . . I don't remember . . . No . . . Nothing . . .
                Mummy, no . . . At this moment, have no recollection of
                mother . . .

EXAMINING MAGISTRATE: You don't remember?

DOUBLE: I'm trying to remember . . . my mummy . . .

INSPECTOR: But don't strain yourself . . .

DOUBLE: Wait a minute, I want to remember . . .

EXAMINING MAGISTRATE: But you don't have to . . .

DOUBLE: I want to remember! I loved my mummy. I don't remember
                my mummy . . . I haven't got a mummy! (*He cries,
                heartbroken.*) I've looked everywhere in my memory, but I
                haven't got a mummy! (*He rests his head on the
                INSPECTOR's shoulder.*)

INSPECTOR: What are you doing?

DOUBLE: Won't you give me a little cuddly-wuddly . . .

INSPECTOR: Cuddly-wuddly!

DOUBLE: Just a little one . . .

INSPECTOR: Please, pull yourself together!

DOUBLE: Please. Peezy, weezy, weezy.

INSPECTOR: Get off me. Stuff your mummy.

DOUBLE: He said he wants to stuff my mummy! You better start
                praying that my memory doesn't come back, because if my
                memory does come back and I remember who I am and who
                I was . . . then . . . Whiiish, roar, roar! (*He becomes like
                King Kong.*) I do remember my father, though . . . He
                always used to take me to see the cars . . .

INSPECTOR: Did he work at Fiat too?

DOUBLE: Eh? Work? (*He slyly rests his head on the* INSPECTOR's
                shoulder.)

INSPECTOR: Pull yourself together . . .!

DOUBLE: Oh look – I can laugh! Ah, it does me good to talk. I feel as
                if I'm getting better already.

Apart from the discrepancy in length, other considerable differences can be seen
between the two versions. The addition of the Reagan joke with the cowboy
outfit reference succeeded in giving a topical slant to the original, and this gag
was cited by Michael Billington in his *Guardian* review of the play as one of the
'good verbal gags' it contained.[13] All of the ensuing interrogation sequence,
however, culminating in the puerile, sexist joke 'he said he wants to stuff my
mummy', is entirely the adaptors' invention. As such, it betrays a caricatured,
almost racist stereotyping of received Italian characteristics like 'mammismo'
seen from a British point of view; the type of caricaturing Franca Rame objected
to in Richards' *Accidental Death of an Anarchist*. Certainly, the sniggeringly
homophobic humour arising from the Double cuddling the Inspector seems to
owe more to Jerry Lewis than political satire. An interesting feature of the
adaptation is its reliance on American references (here Reagan and King Kong,
elsewhere Starsky and Hutch and Sam Peckinpah) for gags, where British
equivalents would surely have been more relevant and hard-hitting. I have

already commented on the omission of references to Juventus, while Mussolini is surely sufficiently well-known to English audiences to warrant retention. The extended comic sequence of grammelot-like word-play which follows in Fo's version serves to satirise Agnelli senior's cynical lessons in corruption and financial crime, while stretching the scene's key mechanism of mistaken identity by building the Double's speech deficiencies into a comic tour de force in Fo's performance of the play. As such, discarding it may be justifiable, but the overall impression one is left of the scene in its British version is quite at variance with the original, both in content and in spirit.

Although McAvoy and Giugni's adaptation gives at times a surprisingly literal rendition of Fo's text, at others it travesties it by drawing on the most banal, clichéd aspects of Italian culture in a misguided attempt to relocate the play in an Italian context comprehensible to non-Italians. Even a re-enactment of Michelangelo's *Creation* (already well-known from English advertisements for giving blood) is dragged in to literalise a theory expounded by one of the secret police agents (whose radio signal is given as 'Fellini 8½'!) that Agnelli is responsible for the police manhunt in the play. Such an intrusion of Italian 'high' culture is surely quite remote from Fo's commitment to popular culture. The inadequacies of the English version are perhaps summed up in the sub-titling of *Trumpets and Raspberries* as 'a new comedy by Dario Fo'. While the play opened in the West End nearly four years after Fo's first performance of it in Italy, the use of the term 'comedy' is curious in the light of Fo's notes to the director of the Washington production of *Accidental Death of an Anarchist:*

> 'Don't call my play a comedy. There is a misunderstanding of the word. I call it farce. In current language, farce is understood as vulgar, trivial, facile, very simple. In truth, this is a cliché of Official Culture. What they call comedy today has lost the rebellious strain of ancient times. What is provocative and rebellious is farce. The establishment goes for comedy, the people for farce.[8]

This distinction between comedy and farce, and the lack of political abrasiveness in *Trumpets and Raspberries*, are pinpointed in Irving Wardle's assessment of the West End production in *The Times*:

> What is lacking from Roger Smith's production is a sense of the cruel reality behind the gags. This is very much an entertainment for people who know nothing about Italian justice and care less. Griff Rhys Jones makes a beaming first entry to explain Agnelli's identity in words of one syllable, and thereafter farcical business takes over to the exclusion of any line of thought.[20]

The casting of Griff Rhys Jones is in itself a reflection of the 'official' and 'Establishment' nature of the whole enterprise. Jones, unlike his predecessors in the West End in roles created by Fo, Alfred Molina and Gavin Richards, who both have backgrounds in politically militant theatre, belongs to a politically innocuous English comic tradition, as indicated by the title of a film script he wrote, *Morons from Outer Space*. Graduating from radio light entertainment, he rose to prominence in politically escapist, 'alternative' comedy shows like *Not the 9 O'Clock News* and *Alas Smith and Jones*. His commitment to a new series of the latter programme caused *Trumpets and Raspberries* to close in May 1985, after a run only slightly longer than the Broadway *Anarchist*.

Fo and Shakespeare, Rame and *Elisabetta*

Before the closure of *Trumpets and Raspberries*, Jones and the playwright John McGrath, whose work with 7:84 in both Scotland and England is, at least in the 1980s, the closest political and theatrical equivalent to Fo's in the UK, recorded a programme about Fo for Channel Four. In it they commented on videotapes of performances of *Mistero buffo*. McGrath has commented on the differences between Fo's *giullarate* and the popular working-class forms of theatre used by 7:84 in a way which throws light on some of the problems of transposing Fo's plays to an Anglo-Saxon context:

> I was very struck by the fact that the root of Fo's comedy is peasant, and essentially all the stuff about the body and eating and gluttony, and the wonderful outrage he gets, is a peasant thing. I was also very struck by the fact that our comedy, and our kind of radical entertainment, is industrial, and goes back through variety and vaudeville to industrial roots. But I think there is a way in which we can in a sense 'call up' the peasant, which is through the mystery plays, and Shakespeare, who encompassed that sort of peasant tradition within his rather more urban comedies. I don't think we've lost it completely, but we don't have that kind of through-line contact with mediaeval buffoonery and peasants that Dario Fo certainly has. But I'm not particularly worried by that, because we're dealing most of the time with people who are in an industrial society.[21]

McGrath's comparison of Fo's cultural roots with Shakespeare is particularly apt, in the light of the play which Fo and Rame began performing almost as soon as they returned to Italy from New York, at the end of 1984. *Quasi per caso una donna: Elisabetta* (*A Woman Almost by Chance: Elisabeth*), in which Rame played Queen Elisabeth I of England, and Fo her transvestite cosmetic adviser, is full of references to Shakespeare's plays, and shows evidence that Fo's exposure to English culture has had an influence on his work. Fo described the new play in an interview with the critic Ugo Volli:

> The action takes place in 1601, but its theme is very topical. It's about the commitment of the intellectual, and the need to participate in world events and take a position. It's worth stressing that it's a political play, but it's also moral, and makes a statement about the function of theatre . . . The theatre shouldn't be regarded in an idealistic way, as if it dealt with stories that have no relation to reality.[22]

Fo begins the play in his normal way with a prologue, without his costume, giving a quasi-history lesson explaining the play's setting and historical background, incorporating his English *grammelot* from *Mistero buffo*, 'The English Lawyer'. He then reappears in long skirts, ruffles and a maid's cap as 'La Donnazza, a sort of Celestina, a villainess who dabbles in intrigues and plots, and comments on the action. She is a figure of the people, a plebeian figure even, lowly and full of ingenuity. A bit like a Shakespearian fool.'[22] The plot of the play involves a *coup d'état* which the Duke of Essex, an ex-lover of the Queen, has plotted against her, with the assistance of Shakespeare's impresario, Southampton. There is thus a good deal of talk about Shakespeare in the play, although he does not appear as a character, and Elisabeth begins reading his plays, finding strong resemblances between herself and Richard II, Cleopatra and Hamlet. This occasions a reworked reprise of one of Fo's earliest comic routines from *Poer nano* in the early 1950s, an elaboration of the plot of Hamlet. Rame portrays Queen Elisabeth as

a terrible woman, who speaks Greek and French at court, and then proceeds to crack dirty jokes. She has her skin stretched in an extremely painful sort of facelift, and has applications of insects similar to leeches, who eat up her fat. She also has her breasts stung by bees to give them an uplift . . . Hers is the first modern state. She invented the secret service and modern politics. There's even a sort of Moro affair, when three lords are kidnapped and held to ransom by rebels. She, naturally, doesn't give in to this, and maintains a hard line.[22]

Although the play would no doubt raise a few eyebrows among Shakespearian scholars, Rame's dramatic role as Elisabeth was compared by some Italian critics to her role as the Spanish Queen Isabella in *Isabella, Three Sailing Ships and a Con Man* more than 20 years previously. There were also aspects of the theme of *Elisabetta*, notably the role of the intellectual in power politics, which linked it with the earlier play. One critic who made this comparison was the playwright Carlo Maria Pensa, who described *Elisabetta* as follows:

The idea . . . is wonderful. In the English court at the turn of the 17th century, the sluggish and sluttish sovereign battles against conspiracies, disguises, amorous intrigues, betrayals, hard line revolutionaries, and cellulitis. She is aided and abetted by the radical cosmetic remedies of La Donnazza, a sort of court jester in petticoats. This clumsy character, who speaks in a reinvented Padano dialect, is brought to irresistible comic life by Dario Fo.[23]

The idea, however, Pensa concludes, is not sustained by the play's dramatic structure, which is fragmentary, disconnected and unbalanced, and too reliant on Fo and Rame's seemingly unrelated solo performances, which spill over any attempt at dramatic shape. What this suggests is that they may have 'outgrown' the conventional dramatic structures of the pre-written play through their extensive work in a solo, *canovaccio* (improvised) tradition.

The text of *Elisabetta* was published at the end of 1984 in a special Dario Fo issue of the Italian theatre magazine *Ridotto*, which included translations of a number of British press reviews of *Mistero buffo*, *The History of Masks* and *Tutta casa, letto e chiesa* (*Female Parts*). This indicates that Fo and Rame's critical reception in the UK has been taken very seriously indeed in Italy, and been a major factor in giving them a more respectable profile at home. As the editorial note to *Ridotto* put it:

We are proud to dedicate this issue to Dario Fo. Since the universal validity of his theatre has gained recognition, we have set out to provide a suitable mark of acknowledgement of his work by means of a sample of the interest his plays have aroused among audiences and critics throughout the world.[24]

Only three of these 'samples' are not British. Similarly, the subject matter of *Elisabetta* reflects the results of Fo's acclaim in the UK. In his spoken introduction to the play, he suggests that there is a political motive for choosing its particularly English and historical subject:

You could say that life as we know it and our conception of the state originated (in the 1600s). Remember Thomas More and that other great statesman and philosopher, Bacon? These people determined our present notions of the state and politics, for better or for worse. I mean in the sense of employing openly the most scandalous laws, corruption, hypocrisy, alliances and opportunism, not to mention the most obscene compromise.[25]

Fo refers to the birth of the secret police and the institution by Edward VII of the possibility of 'supergrassing' and going Queen's evidence as political features of Elizabethan England which have particular relevance to our time. This relevance, however, tends to be stated rather than demonstrated in the play. *Elisabetta* is set in 1601, after the execution of Mary Stuart (whose decapitated head Elizabeth has nightmares about) and could be seen as a sequel to Schiller's *Mary Stuart* – a play which has had considerable impact on recent Italian theatre. In 1983 it was revived in a particularly lush, glossy and saccharine production by Franco Zeffirelli, in an attempt to rekindle a fashion for romantic drama. Earlier, the feminist playwright Dacia Maraini had written a modern, all-women adaptation of Schiller's play, reducing it to a ritualistic encounter between Elizabeth and Mary, backed up by the queens' respective ladies-in-waiting, with all of the play's four roles actable by two women. Similar in concept to Jean Genet's play *The Maids*, Maraini's *Maria Stuarda* created considerable interest outside Italy, most notably in a Dutch production set in a boxing ring. Her version of the play was also an attempt to make its subject matter accessible and relevant to contemporary women, and in doing so used simple, direct and unelaborate language. As Maraini has stated:

> What language can we put in the mouths of people on stage who are representing reality, even if it is imagined? We are too used to the hybrid Italian of translations, which is so poor. I think the language of normal Italian today is completely lacking in sensuality. It's grey, uniform and pretty monotonous and abstract. So when you write, you have to bear in mind the way people speak, and use a language which is close to them and comprehensible.[26]

In Fo's work this need for a direct, accessible but also colourful language is expressed through dialect. In *Elisabetta* his invented transvestite character Donnazza speaks in Veneto dialect, mixed with what is described as 'a ragbag of argots and dialects'[27]. Franca Rame's Elisabetta uses a gutsy, earthy form of speech more appropriate to a prostitute than a queen, but also more appropriate to Elizabethan parlance than Schiller's elegant verse. At one point in Fo's play, Elizabeth's lady-in-waiting, Martha, reprimands Donnazza for her vulgar speech. 'I pick up my way of talking from being in the company of queens'[28] is the response.

The action of *Elisabetta* also has an earthiness and vulgarity which links it firmly to popular theatre and satirises the historical pageantry and gentility normally associated with the play's subject. Fo borrows the situation of his earlier monologue, *The Candlemaker*, in casting himself in the role of Elizabeth's beautician, who is employed to make her look more sexually attractive to her ex-lover, Essex, as part of her attempt to thwart his coup against her. Apart from giving her leeches to lose weight, and high-heeled clogs to improve her walking, the Donnazza administers bee stings to the queen's nipples to make them more prominent. In a grotesque climax to this 'treatment', the queen ends up literally pissing herself. This beautification is linked to one of the play's main themes, expressed in its subtitle, of transvestitism and dressing up to play a part in power politics and history. In what is probably a cheeky reference to an incident which happened at Buckingham Palace in 1983, when a young Irishman found his way into the Queen's chamber, Fo's play has a hired killer discovered climbing the walls of the palace. In the ensuing alarm, Elisabetta has to get rid of her young semi-naked lover, Thomas, who turns out to be the intruder's son. The queen dresses him up in her gown and ceremonial wig:

DONNAZZA (*to actor*): That's classy. Very tasteful indeed. Real theatrical.

ELIZABETH (*Rame*): If you he-men were forced to wear dresses like that in battle instead of armour, there'd be no more wars, I warrant you. How does it feel?

BOY: Like being squashed inside a cage in hell. Oh, the shame. Don't breathe a word to a soul. I beg of you.

DONNAZZA: Why don't you try on these high-heeled clogs for size?

ELIZABETH: Good idea. Come on, jump to it! See if you can walk in them. Come on, chin up – quick march! Mind you don't topple over – you look like a paralytic duck. Clumsy clod.

BOY: It's hard with high heels . . .

ELIZABETH: Come on, chin up. Kidneys in – wiggle your hips – that's it. Splendid. Isn't he a treat, Martha? Lovely! You haven't played little girls' parts before, have you? You know I'm the patron of a boys' theatre company.

BOY: Yes marm. The Queen's Boys.

ELIZABETH: Not one of them makes a convincing girl. You do though.

BOY: You're making fun of me again.

ELIZABETH: Oh no I'm not. I was just about to let you in on a secret, Thomas. I'm too embarrassed now.

MARTHA: Come now. Don't you think it's time you turned your attention to more serious matters?

ELIZABETH: Oh get off my back Martha. See, Thomas, she doesn't want me to talk about it.

BOY: You can be perfectly frank with me, marm.

ELIZABETH: You won't go blabbing about it?

DONNAZZA: Spit it out, marm. Drop your clanger!

ELIZABETH: Right. I'm not a woman. In the complete sense.

BOY: What? Not a woman?

DONNAZZA: What a sob story!

ELIZABETH: Oh come on. I bet you've heard all the gossip already. It's a big topic of conversation at court. That blabbermouth Ben Jonson was even going to write a play about it until someone burned his theatre down and he had second thoughts.

MARTHA: I should think so.

DONNAZZA: Oh yes, I know him, the bastard. He was going to put that play on in his theatre. What was it called again?

ELIZABETH: *Perforce a virgin.*

DONNAZZA: That's the one . . .

ELIZABETH: The virgin perforce was me.

DONNAZZA: The queen played by a transvestite!

BOY: How vulgar!
ELIZABETH: Vulgar? What do you mean? Don't be so impressionable,
            Thomas! What would you say if I told you I was born a boy
            and my mother passed me off as a girl so my father wouldn't
            strangle me in my cradle?
BOY: You've got to be joking.
DONNAZZA: It's no joke. It's all true. All because her mother Anne
            Boleyn was in her husband Henry the Red's bad books. He
            roared at her – 'Anna, you slut!' Oops, sorry marm. 'If you
            bear me a son, I'll beat you black and blue, and the bastard
            bairn'll never get to be the King of England.' Right?
ELIZABETH: Exactly. And when I was born a boy –
BOY: A boy? You?
ELIZABETH: That's right. My mother hollered out 'It's a girl!'
DONNAZZA: And hid his little willy!
MARTHA: Stop it Elizabeth. You're driving me mad.
ELIZABETH: Shut up! Why should I hide it? I'll tell him straight from the
            horse's mouth – yes, that's right, I'm a male homosexual! They
            raped my brain day after day and inverted my nature. I'm a
            man-woman. Go on, laugh. Queen Elizabeth – what a hoot![29]

Like Maraini's *Maria Stuarda*, Fo's play deals with the dilemma of a woman
assuming what is traditionally a male role in power politics. *Elisabetta*, however,
treats this theme in terms of grotesque farce and burlesque, and although it has
some fine farcical moments, as a text it frequently seems over-written and
convoluted. Fo's Donnazza parts are often little more than one-line repetitions
of what has already been said by other characters, and she seems little more
than a comic choral figure at times. Fo's claims for the play's contemporary
political relevance are difficult to substantiate in the text – the implied parallel
between the kidnapping of four of Elisabeth's Lords by Essex, who offers them
in exchange for the release of twenty-four political prisoners, and the Aldo
Moro kidnapping, is a subject which Fo dealt with far more comprehensively in
Car Horns, Trumpets and Raspberries. But Fo and Rame's work does show signs
of continuing to deal in a unique and unparalleled way with contemporary
Italian political issues, if their announcement of a new play about the potentially
explosive subject of the Mafia[30] is any indication. In the meantime, there is still a
considerable number of Fo's texts from the 1950s, 60s and 70s – including
Isabella and *7th Commandment: Thou Shalt Steal a bit Less* – to be discovered
by English speaking theatres.
    The issue of *Ridotto* in which the text of *Elisabetta* appeared also stated that,
by the end of 1984, 39 of Fo's plays had been performed in 45 different
countries since 1960. *Accidental Death of an Anarchist* had been performed in 37
countries, *Tutta casa, letto e chiesa* (*Female Parts*) in 31, *Non si paga! Non si
paga!* (*Can't Pay? Won't Pay!*) in 30, and *7th Commandment* and *Mistero buffo*
in 18 each.[31] The UK, then, still has considerable ground to make up. For
despite a good deal of positive critical acclaim for Fo and Rame's work in the
UK, there is still considerable uncomprehending, provincial response which
parallels initial English responses to the work of Brecht. A case in point is
Desmond Christy's review in *The Guardian* of Michael Batz's Yorick Theatre
Company production in Latchmere in April 1985 of David Hirst's translation of

The Worker Knows 300 Words, The Boss Knows 1,000 – That's Why he's the Boss. This play is one of Fo's most polemical, agit-prop pieces, dating from the late 1960s, and lacking a part written by Fo for himself. But it is both ideologically and formally one of his most powerful pieces, requiring considerable courage and commitment to put it to the test of time. Christy dismissed the play rhetorically in the first paragraph of his review:

> Dario Fo is not only a brilliant satirist; he is also a thinker. He thinks that 'the people' have a vast culture which has been almost obliterated by their oppressors – the church, the state, and capitalism. It's the work of his popular theatre to rediscover it. But is there anything to rediscover?[32]

In Thatcher's Britain the retrieval of forms of popular culture and entertainment in the theatre has become increasingly precarious, as the recent cancellation of 7:84 England's Arts Council Grant indicates. Nonetheless, Christy's question could be answered by indicating Ken Loach's film about songs invented as a result of the miner's strike, *Which Side Are You On?* To suggest that the rediscovery of popular culture, and the rediscovery of Fo's early plays, is of little or no value, is to seriously call into question the value of theatre as anything more than a rootless and useless form of leisure. Fo and Rame's work has already resisted attempts to reduce it to innocuous West End entertainment, and their achievements in Italy and elsewhere are living proof of vitality and value.

NOTES

All translations of quotations are by the author, unless otherwise indicated.

Introduction
1. Dario Fo and Franca Rame, *Theatre Workshops at Riverside Studios, London April 28, May 5, 12, 13 and 19, 1983*, London, Red Notes, 1983, pp. 40–41.
2. Steve Grant and Tony Mitchell, 'An Interview with Dario Fo and Franca Rame', *Theater*, Vol. 14, No. 3, Summer/Fall, 1983, p. 46.
3. Dario Fo, 'Dialogue with an Audience', *Theatre Quarterly*, Vol. IX, No. 35, Autumn, 1979, p. 15.

Chapter One
1. Dario Fo, *Mistero buffo*, Bertani, Verona, 1977, p. xix.
2. *Ibid.*, p. 9.
3. *Ibid.*, p. 9.
4. Lanfranco Binni, *Dario Fo*, Il Castoro, 1977, p. 52.
5. *Mistero buffo, op. cit.*, pp. 4–5.
6. In Chiara Valentini, *La storia di Dario Fo*, Feltrinelli, 1977, p. 125.
7. Dario Fo, *Pum, pum! Chi e? La polizia*, Bertani, Verona, 1974, pp. 234–5.
8. *Il teatro politico di Dario Fo*, Mazzotta, 1977, p. 6.
9. *Ibid.*, p. 60.
10. In Valentini, *op. cit.*, p. 128.
11. Ugo Volli, in *La Repubblica*, 3 March, 1979.
12. In Erminia Artese, *Dario Fo parla di Dario Fo*, Lerici, 1977, pp. 53–5.
13. Michele Straniero, *Giullari e Fo*, Lato Side, 1978.
14. In *Panorama*, 21 November, 1978.
15. Artese, *op. cit.*, pp. 84–5.
16. *Mistero buffo*, p. vii.
17. Artese, p. 19.
18. *Mistero buffo*, p. xx.
19. *Il teatro politico di Dario Fo, op. cit.*, p. 72.
20. Artese, pp. 51, 68.
21. *Ibid.*, p. 140.
22. *Mistero buffo*, p. 100.
23. Artese, pp. 139–140.
24. Paolo Puppa, *Il teatro di Dario Fo*, Marsilio, 1978, pp. 113–4.
25. *Mistero buffo*, p. 215.
26. *Ibid.*, p. 213.
27. *Ibid.*, p. 217.
28. *Ibid.*, p. 184.
29. *Artese.*, p. 137.
30. In *Il Messaggero*, March 30, 1980.
31. Dario Fo, *La storia della tigre*, La Comune, 1980, p. 3.
32. *Ibid.*, pp. 8–9.
33. In *Il Messaggero*, March 30, 1980.
34. In *The International Daily News*, April 1, 1980.

35. In *Il Messaggero*, March 30, 1980.
36. *Theater*, Vol. 13, No. 4, Winter 1982, p. 88.
37. Dario fo, *Il fabulazzo osceno*, La Comune, 1982, p. 1.
38. In *La Repubblica*, 30 May, 1981.

Chapter Two

1. Bianca Fo Rambois, *Io, da grande mi sposo un partigiano*, Torini, Einaudi, 1976, pp. 10–11.
2. Artese, *op. cit.*, pp. 8–9.
3. Valentini, *op. cit.*, p. 21.
4. *Ibid.*, p. 25.
5. Caludio Meldolesi, *Su un comico in rivolta: Dario Fo il bufalo il bambino*, Roma, Bulzoni, 1978, pp. 25–26.
6. Dario Fo & Jacopo Fo, *Poer nano*, Milano/Ottaviano, 1976, p. 5.
7. Luigi Ballerini & Giuseppe Risso, 'Dario Fo Explains' (translated by Lauren Hallquist and Fiorenza Weinpple), *The Drama Review* 77, Vol. 22, No. 1, March 1978, p. 36.
8. Valentini, *op. cit.*, pp. 39–40.
9. *Ibid.*, p. 35.
10. Lanfranco Binni (ed.) in Dario Fo, *Ballate e canzoni*, Roma/Newton Compton, 1977, p. 26.
11. Meldolesi, *op. cit.*, p. 42.
12. Valentini, *op. cit.*, p. 53.
13. *Ibid.*, p. 55.
14. *La Repubblica*, October 25, 1980.
15. Valentini, *op. cit.*, p. 58.
16. *Ibid.*, p. 64.
17. *Le commedie di Dario Fo* Vol. 1, Torino/Einaudi, 1966, p. 26.
18. Puppa, *op. cit.*, p. 37.
19. Ballerini & Risso, *op. cit.*, p. 46.
20. *The Scotsman*, 29.8.83.
21. *La Repubblica*, 24–5 April, 1977.
22. Valentini, *op. cit.*, p. 85.
23. *Le commedie di Dario Fo*, Vol. 2, Torino/Einaudi, 1966, p. 44
24. *Ibid.*, p. 86.
25. *La Repubblica*, February 1979.
26. *Le commedie di Dario Fo*, Vol. 2, *op. cit.*, p. 172.
27. Artese, *op. cit.*, p. 49.
28. Meldolesi, *op. cit.*, p. 104.
29. Valentini, *op. cit.*, p. 99.
30. *Ibid.*, p. 101.
31. A. Richard Sogliuzzo, 'Dario Fo: Puppets for a Proletarian Revolution', *The Drama Review*, 55, Vol. 16, No. 3, September 1972, p. 73.
32. Ballerini & Risso, *op. cit.*, p. 43.
33. *L'Espresso*, November 23, 1969.

Chapter Three

1. In *Liberation*, 9 January, 1974.
2. Dario Fo, 'Per una nuova gestione degli spazi e degli spettacoli', in Franco Quadri, *Il teatro del regime*, Milano/Mazzotta, 1976, p. 143.
3. Sogliuzzo, *op. cit.*, p. 72.
4. Dario Fo, *Grand Pantomime with Flags and Small and Middle-sized Puppets*, translated by Tony Mitchell, unpublished MS, pp. 19–20.
5. Dario Fo, *The Worker Knows 300 Words, the Boss Knows 1,000 – That's Why He's the Boss*, translated by Tony Mitchell, unpublished MS., p. 30.
6. *Ibid.*, pp. 56–7.

7. Dario Fo, *Fruit of the Loom*, translated by Tony Mitchell, unpublished MS, p. 38.
8. Quadri, *op. cit.*, p. 137.
9. Binni, *Attento Te!*, *op. cit.*, p. 263.
10. In *Playboy* (Italian issue) December 1974.
11. In *Sipario* no. 3000, May 1971.
12. Dario Fo, *Accidental Death of an Anarchist*, translated by Tony Mitchell, unpublished MS., p. 111.
13. *Ibid.*, p. iv.
14. *Ibid.*, p. 102.
15. *Ibid.*, p. 2.
16. *Ibid.*, p. 26.
17. *Ibid.*, p. 34.
18. *Ibid.*, p. 39.
19. *Ibid.*, pp. 63–64.
20. Dario Fo, *Pum, pum! Chi e? La polizia!*, Verona/Bertani, 1974, p. 9.
21. *Accidental Death of an Anarchist*, *op. cit.*, p. 85.
22. *Ibid.*, p. 97.
23. *Ibid.*, p. 101.
24. *Ibid.*, p. 103.
25. Valentini, *op. cit.*, p. 138.
26. *Pum, pum!*, *op. cit.*, pp. 11–12.
27. *Le commedie di Dario Fo*, Vol. 3, *op. cit.*, p. xiv.
28. Binni, *Attente te!*, *op. cit.*, p. 338.
29. Dacia Maraini, *Fare teatro*, Milano/Bompiani, 1974, p. 73.
30. *Pum, pum! op. cit.*, p. 134.
31. Suzanne Cowan, 'The Throwaway Theatre of Dario Fo', *The Drama Review*, Vol. 19, No. 2, June 1975, pp. 112–3.
32. Chiara Valentini, 'Pum, pum! Il questore', *Panorama*, 22 November, 1973.
33. *Ibid.*, p. 57.
34. *Ibid.*, p. 56.

Chapter Four

1. Meldolesi, *op. cit.*, p. 164.
2. Dario Fo, *Non si paga! Non si paga!* Milano/La Commune. 1974., p. 11.
3. *Ibid.*, p. 4.
4. *Ibid.*, p. 18.
5. *Ibid.*, p. 25.
6. *Ibid.*, p. 120.
7. In *La Repubblica*, 19.9.80.
8. In *Panorama*, 12.6.75.
9. Binni, *Attento te!*, *op. cit.*, pp. 389, 395.
10. Valentini, *op. cit.*, p. 163.
11. *Ibid.*, p. 167.
12. Dario Fo, *Mother's Marijuana is the Best*, translated by Tony Mitchell, unpublished MS, p. iii-iv.
13. *Ibid.*, p. 36.
14. *Mother's Marijuana*, p. 93.
15. *Ibid.*, p. 33.
16. Dario Fo & Franca Rame, *Waking Up*, translated by Tony Mitchell, unpublished MS, p. 6.
17. In *Panorama*, 20.12.77.
18. Dario Fo & Franca Rame, *A Woman on her Own*, translated by Tony Mitchell, unpublished MS, p. 1.
19. Dario Fo & Franca Rame, *The Same Old Story*, translated by Tony Mitchell, unpublished MS, p. 1.
20. *The Mother*, p. xiv, in *Dario Fo and Franca Rame Workshops at Riverside Studios, London, April 28, May 5, 12, 13 and 19 1983*, London, Red Notes, 1983.

21. In *Domenica del Corriere*, 26.9.81, p. 60.
22. In *Panorama*, 7.3.78 and 14.3.78.
23. *Ibid.*
24. Dario Fo, *The Tragedy of Aldo Moro*, translated by Tony Mitchell, unpublished MS, p. 22.
25. In *Panorama*, 5.6.79.
26. In *La Repubblica*, 1.9.83.
27. *Ibid.*
28. Dario Fo, *Barps, Blasts and Burps*, translated by Tony Mitchell, unpublished MS, p. 11.
29. *Ibid.*, p. 132.
30. In *Scena*, Vol. VI, No. 1, Feb. 1981, p. 31.
31. In *La Repubblica*, 12.11.81.
32. Dario Fo, *L'opera dello sghignazzo*, Milano/La Comune, 1981, p. 25.
33. In *Plays and Players*, January 1983, p. 41.
34. From a conversation between Fo and the author in November 1983.
35. *Il candelaio*, unpublished MS, 1983, p. 12.
36. *Coppia aperta, anche spalancata* (2nd version), unpublished MS, 1983, p. 44.

Chapter Five

1. *Tribune*, March 14, 1980.
2. *Plays and Players*, August 1983, p. 18.
3. Dario Fo, *We Can't Pay? We Won't Pay!*, Pluto Press, 1978, p. 29.
4. Dario Fo, *Accidental Death of an Anarchist*, adapted by Gavin Richards, Pluto Press, 1980.
5. *Punch*, October 24, 1979, p. 731.
6. *Time Out*, March 16–22, 1979, p. 17.
7. *Accidental Death of an Anarchist, op. cit.*, p. 43.
8. *Theater*, Summer/Fall, 1983, p. 49.
9. *Accidental Death of an Anarchist. op. cit.*, p. iv.
10. *Ibid.*, p. 41.
11. *Tribune*, April 13, 1979.
12. *The Leveller*, April 1980, p. 27.
13. *The Socialist Challenge*, April 12, 1979.
14. *The Observer*, March 2, 1980.
15. *The Leveller*, April 1980, p. 26.
16. *Accidental Death of an Anarchist, op. cit.*, p. 10.
17. *The Observer*, March 9, 1980.
18. *Dario Fo and Franca Rame Theatre Workshops at Riverside Studios, London, April 28, May 5, 12, 13 and 19*, Red Notes, London, 1983, p. 43.
19. *The Leveller*, August 21-September 3, 1981, p. 18.
20. Publicity brochure for the Criterion Theatre's production of *Can't Pay? Won't Pay!*
21. *The Leveller*, August 1981, p. 19.
22. *The Times*, June 27, 1981.
23. BBC transcript of 'Throwaway Theatre', March 15, 1982, p. 10.
24. Dario Fo & Franca Rame, *Female Parts*, Pluto Press, 1981, p. 6.
25. Franca Rame in conversation with the author, May 1982.
26. *The Leveller*, August 21-September 3, 1981, p. 18.
27. *The Guardian*, March 1983.
28. Irving Wardle in *The Times*, January 5, 1984.
29. *City Limits*, January 13–19, 1984.

Chapter Six

1. *The Standard*, 29.2.84, *The Observer*, 26.2.84.
2. *The Times*, 28.2.84.

3. *The Scotsman*, 28.8.84.
4. *La Repubblica*, 18.10.84.
5. Nicola Javarese, ed. *Anatomia del teatro*, Roma Casa Usher, 1983, pp. 36, 142.
6. *La Repubblica*, 24.10.84.
7. In *Il Globo* (Melbourne) 12.11.84.
8. Programme of Washington Arena Stage production of *Accidental Death of an Anarchist*, 1984.
9. *New York Times*, 15.2.84.
10. Dario Fo, 'Cercavo King Kong: Era a farsi una dose', *Oggi*, 5.12.84, p. 47.
11. *Sipario*, September 1983, p. 38.
12. *Ibid.*, p. 37.
13. *The Guardian Weekly*, 25.12.84.
14. Dario Fo, *Trumpets and Raspberries*, Translated and Adapted by R. C. McAvoy and A.-M. Giugni, Pluto Press, 1984, p. 5.
15. *Ibid.*, p. 54.
16. *Ibid.*, p. 36.
17. *Ibid.*, p. 3.
18. Dario Fo, *Clacson, Trombette e Pernacchi*, Milano La Comune, 1981, pp. 36–7.
19. *Trumpets and Raspberries, op. cit.*, pp. 21–2.
20. *The Times*, 17.11.84.
21. In conversation with the author, 20.5.85.
22. *La Repubblica*, 6.12.84.
23. *Oggi*, 9.1.85.
24. *Ridotto*, No. 8–9–10, August–October, 1984, p. 5.
25. *Ibid.*, p. 61.
26. In *La Repubblica*, 20.1.83.
27. *Ridotto, op. cit.*, p. 73.
28. *Ibid.*, p. 83.
29. *Ibid.*, pp. 94–5.
30. In *La Repubblica*, 6.12.84.
31. *Ridotto, op. cit.*, p. 58.
32. *The Guardian*, April 4, 1985.

SELECTED BIBLIOGRAPHY

There are numerous books and articles on Fo in Italian, many of which are cited in the notes. The books I found most useful in preparing this study were *La storia di Dario Fo*, by Chiara Valentini, Feltrinelli, 1977, an admirably researched, journalistic account of Fo's life and work up to *Can't Pay? Won't Pay!; Attento te! . . .* by Lanfranco Binni, Bertani, 1975, a detailed description of Fo's work up to 1975, with documents by La Commune and excerpts from Fo's principal plays; *Dario Fo*, by Marina Cappa and Roberto Nepoli, Gremese, 1982, a lavishly illustrated and detailed survey of each of Fo's plays up to *Il fabulazzo osceno*; and *Su un comico in rivolta*, by Claudio Mendolesi, Bulzoni, 1978, a rather academic approach to Fo's work which includes several previously unpublished articles by Fo. As a reference book on Italian political background, Norman Kogan's *A Political History of Postwar Italy*, Praeger, 1981, was most useful, as was *Italy 1980–81: After Marx, Jail*, London, Red Notes, 1981*. What follows is a bibliography of Fo's work, together with articles and documents about Fo (excluding reviews), which have been published in English.

Plays
We Can't Pay? We Won't Pay! Translated by Lino Pertile, Adapted by Bill Colvill and Robert Walker, Pluto Press, 1978, revised as *Can't Pay? Won't Pay!*, 1982.
Accidental Death of an Anarchist, Translated with an Introduction by Suzanne Cowan, in *Theater*, Vol. 10, No. 2, Spring 1979.
Accidental Death of an Anarchist, Translated by Gillian Hanna, Adapted by Gavin Richards, Pluto Press, 1980.
Ulrike Meinhof and *Tomorrow's News*, Translated by Tony Mitchell, in *Gambit*, Vol. 9, no. 36, 1980.
Female Parts (One Woman Plays), Translated by Margaret Kunzle, Adapted by Olwen Wymark, Pluto Press, 1981.
About Face (*Clacson, Trombette e Pernacchi*), Translated by Dale McAdoo and Charles Mann, in *Theater*, Vol. 14, no. 3, Summer/Fall, 1983.
Trumpets and Raspberries (*Clacson, Trombette e Pernacchi*), Translated and Adapted by R.C. McAvoy and A-M. Giugni, Pluto Press, 1984.

Articles/documents by Fo
Dario Fo and Franca Rame Theatre Workshops at Riverside Studios, London, April 28th, May 5th, 12th, 13th & 19th 1983 (Including texts of *Waking Up, I*

* and the 'Italy: Autonomia' issue of *Semiotext(e)*, 1980.

Don't Move, I Don't Scream, My Voice is Gone and *The Mother*, and an
interview with Dario Fo & Franca Rame), Red Notes, London, 1983.
'Dialogue with an Audience' (Translated by Tony Mitchell), *Theatre Quarterly*,
Vol. ix, No. 35, Autumn 1979, pp. 11–16.
'Popular Culture' (Translated by Tony Mitchell), *Theater*, Vol. 14, No. 3,
Summer/Fall, 1983, pp. 50–4. (Also in *Trumpets and Raspberries, op. cit.*,
pp. 71–5.)
'The Sandstorm Method' (Translated by Peter Caravetta, James Cascaito and
Lawrence Venuti) *Semiotext (e)*, Vol. III, No. 3, 1980, pp. 214–16.
'Aspects of Popular Theatre' (Translated by Tony Mitchell), *New Theatre
Quarterly* Vol. 1. No. 2, May 1985, pp. 131–7.

Interviews with Fo

Luigi Ballerini and Giuseppe Risso, 'Dario Fo Explains' (Translated by Lauren
Hallquist and Fiorenza Weinpple), *The Drama Review*, Vol. 22, No. 1, March
1978, pp. 34–48.
Michael Billington, 'Everybody's Favourite Fo', *The Guardian*, April 26, 1983.
Steve Grant and Tony Mitchell, 'An Interview with Dario Fo and Franca
Rame', *Theater*, Vol. 14, no. 3, Summer/Fall 1983, pp. 43–9.
Catherine Itzin, 'The 'how-to' of political theatre', *Tribune*, March 14, 1980,
p. 9.
Tony Mitchell, 'Plotting to create mirth', *The Glasgow Herald*, May 3, 1983.
David Groves, 'Fo Interviewed', in *Act* (New Zealand) Dario Fo: Special Issue,
Vol. 7, No. 2, April 1982, pp. 18–20.
Tony Mitchell, 'Open House with Dario Fo and Franca Rame', *Theater*, Vol.
15, No. 3. Summer/Fall 1984, pp. 65–8.

Articles and commentaries on Fo

Suzanne Cowan, 'The Throw-away Theatre of Dario Fo', *The Drama Review*,
Vol. 19, No. 2, June 1975, pp. 103–13.
'Dario Fo: Bibliography, Biography, Playography', *Theatre Quarterly*
Checklist No. 17, 1978.
Sandy Craig, 'Accidental Staging of an Anarchist', *The Leveller*, April 1980,
pp. 26–7.
Brian Glanville, 'Master-class from a master clown', *The Sunday Times*, May 1,
1983.
Steve Grant, 'Laughter on the Ramparts', *Time Out*, May 7–13, 1982, pp. 6–11.
Jim Hiley, 'Singing of Dark Times', *The Observer Supplement*, April 24, 1983,
pp. 28–31.
Charles Mann, 'Fo No-Show Doesn't Mean No Fo Show', *The Village Voice*,
December 17–23, 1980.
Sally Banes, 'Dario Fo's Theater of Blasphemy', in *Village Voice*, Vol. XXVIII,
No. 31, August 2, 1983, pp. 1, 33–5.
David Groves, 'Laughter has become a Sghignazzo', in *Act* (New Zealand), Vol.
7, No. 2, April 1982, pp. 16–18.
Tony Mitchell, 'Dario Fo's *Mistero buffo*: Popular Theatre, the Giullari, and the

Grotesque', *Theatre Quarterly*, Vol. IX, No. 35, Autumn 1979, pp. 1–10.

'Dario Fo – the Histrionics of Class Struggle', *Gambit*, Vol. 9, No. 36, 1980, pp. 55–60.

Joel Schechter, 'Dario Fo's Obscene Fables', *Theater*, Vol. 14, No. 1, Winter 1982, pp. 87–90.

'The Un-American Satire of Dario Fo', *Partisan Review*, Vol. LI, No. 1, 1984, pp. 112–19.

A. Richard Sogliuzzo, 'Dario Fo: Puppets for a Proletarian Revolution', *The Drama Review*, Vol. 16, No. 3, September 1972, pp. 72–7.

Caroline Tisdall, 'The Collective Explosion', *The Guardian*, March 1, 1980.

Lloyd Trott, 'So you think that's funny, turning rebellion into money', *The Leveller*, August 21 – September 3, 1981, pp. 18–19.

A METHUEN THEATREFILE

in series with

OTHER SPACES: NEW THEATRE AND THE RSC
by Colin Chambers

THE IMPROVISED PLAY: THE WORK OF MIKE LEIGH
by Paul Clements

THE PLAYS OF EDWARD BOND
by Tony Coult

ALL TOGETHER NOW: AN ALTERNATIVE VIEW OF THEATRE
AND THE COMMUNITY
by Steve Gooch

PEACE PLAYS
(*The Fence* by Common Ground; *The Celebration of Kokura* by Berta
Freistadt; *Clam* by Deborah Levy; *Keeping Body and Soul Together*
by Stephen Lowe; *The Tragedy of King Real* by Adrian Mitchell)
Introduced and edited by Stephen Lowe

HOW THE VOTE WAS WON: AND OTHER SUFFRAGETTE PLAYS
(*How the Vote Was Won* by Cicely Hamilton and Christopher St John; *Votes for
Women* by Elizabeth Robins; *Lady Geraldine's Speech* by Beatrice Harraden; *A
Chat With Mrs Chicky* and *Miss Appleyard's Awakening* by Evelyn Glover; *A
Woman's Influence* by Gertrude Jennings; *The Apple* by Inez Bensusan) Edited
by Dale Spender and Carole Hayman with an Introduction by Dale Spender and
Notes on Performance by Carole Hayman

UNDERSTUDIES: THEATRE AND SEXUAL POLITICS
by Michelene Wandor

PLAYS BY WOMEN: VOLUME ONE
(*Vinegar Tom* by Caryl Churchill; *Dusa, Fish, Stas and Vi* by Pam Gems;
Tissue by Louise Page; *Aurora Leigh* by Michelene Wandor)
Introduced and edited by Michelene Wandor

PLAYS BY WOMEN: VOLUME TWO
(*Rites* by Maureen Duffy; *Letters Home* by Rose Leiman Goldemberg;
Trafford Tanzi by Claire Luckham; *Find Me* by Olwen Wymark)
Introduced and edited by Michelene Wandor

PLAYS BY WOMEN: VOLUME THREE
(*Aunt Mary* by Pam Gems; *Red Devils* by Debbie Horsfield; *Blood Relations*
by Sharon Pollock; *Time Pieces* by Lou Wakefield and
The Women's Theatre Group)
Introduced and edited by Michelene Wandor

PLAYS BY WOMEN: VOLUME FOUR
(*Objections to Sex and Violence* by Caryl Churchill; *Rose's Story* by Grace
Dayley; *Blood and Ice* by Liz Lochhead; *Pinball* by Alison Lyssa)
Introduced and edited by Michelene Wandor

GAY PLAYS: VOLUME ONE
(*Submariners* by Tom McClenaghan; *The Green Bay Tree* by Mordaint Shairp;
Passing By by Martin Sherman; *Accounts* by Michael Wilcox)
Introduced and edited by Michael Wilcox

GAY PLAYS: VOLUME TWO
(*Quaint Honour* by Roger Gellert; *Bearclaw* by Timothy Mason; *Cracks* by
Martin Sherman; *Lies About Vietnam* by C. P. Taylor)
Introduced and edited by Michael Wilcox

If you would like to receive, free of charge, regular information about new plays and theatre books from Methuen, please send your name and address to:

The Marketing Department (Drama)
Methuen London Ltd
North Way
Andover
Hampshire SP10 5BE